Table Of contents– Coaching So

Introduction	2	**INTRODUCTION/HOW TO COACH TA** **COACHING STYLES**
Part 1	11	**COACHING TACTICS**
Part 2	33	**SPACE AND TIME**– The theory behind soccer
Part 3	43	**SPACE**
Part 4	70	**TIME**
Part 5	86	**THE PITCH**
Part 6	89	**THE MIXED PASSING GAME**
Part 7	96	**DEFENSIVE TACTICS** What is the best way to defend?
Part 8	102	**Defensive tactics** - How to zonal mark / Advanced mark
Part 9	110	**Defensive tactics**
Part 10	121	**ATTACKING TACTICS** – The importance of timing
Part 11	164	**FORMATIONS**
Part 12	172	**COMMUNICATION** and the easy ball
Part 13	180	**What makes a good player?**
Part 14	194	**ANALYSING your team**
Part 15	201	**SOME TACTICAL TIPS**
Part 16	205	**MATCH DAY ROUTINE**– Match day routine / Motivating players and the team talk
Part 17	215	**ANALYSING TOP TEAMS** Mourinho's Porto, Ferguson, Wenger, Greece and other top teams
	237	**Glossary**

Published in Great Britain in 2004 by
Phil Wymer
79 Muskoka Drive,
Bents Green
Sheffield S11 7RH   Updated 10th August 2005 pw

Introduction

What you will learn

- The importance of relating tactics to the game
- How to develop and coach your team tactics
- How players learn– general to the specific
- Different learning styles
- How to use questions
- Coaching styles– democratic etc

The aim of this manual is summed up by a recent comment from a customer in the USA

I've been coaching for 12 years, and this is the first book that I've found that actually looks at tactics in real game situations....

So how does a coach get his/her side to play the beautiful game and understand their defensive and attack role. This manual will develop players and a team in 4 ways

1. Develop confidence and enjoyment. Tactics give confidence to a team and its players and help them enjoy the game more as they are clear what they are supposed to do. Tactics get the best out of players as, when attacking, they will regularly get the ball an essential part of enjoying soccer. Understanding tactics will mean a coach will have the confidence to deliver a tactical team talk.
2. Demonstrate to coaches that they need to prioritise development and attacking play over the result. Teams need to play to dominate games, create chances and hopefully score goals and if they do this and lose it does not matter as in the long run as the players will be better and the team will win.
3. Show you how to coach tactics and what to coach. When coaching it is important to move from the general to the specific. To start any coaching session by considering it in the game situation it relates to, this can be on the pitch or a whiteboard etc. Players should always have the chance to ask and answer questions. All the drills that follow can now easily be related to the game. The manual breaks down the movement and passing required to successfully defend and attack. Two attacking tactics all progressive coaches must adopt are firstly play the ball out from the back as often as possible and secondly try to attack and create chances as appose to a safety first approach. Defensivley teams need to play zonally, passing players on and ensuring there is cover.
4. Learn from successful teams and coaches to see the tactics they use.

Football, or soccer as I shall often call it from now on, is far from the simple game that many people claim and in Jose Mourinho's words *football is a game for intelligent people*. As a coach the reason you have bought this manual is that you want you and your team to understand how to be organized and enjoy the beautiful game. You want your players to develop.

Tactics help bring enjoyment. We all enjoy something if we know what we are supposed to do (are confident) and play an active and creative part in the game. Tactics explain what to do when attacking and defending. Tactics can be both creative (attacking) and destructive (when defending).

Tactics release of creativity comes from the attacking movement, timing, choice of pass on offer, technical ability in tight spaces etc. Attacking movement is determined by the attacking side. The team needs to move to create space and let creative players have the ball in places where they can be effective. If for example a player is good ball dribbler with skill the teams tactics will give him/her the ball in the areas where they can be most effective, the movement of the team will help create this space for the individual.

The destructive part of tactics comes from defending which is more about concentration and discipline than technical skill. Defensive movement is determined by the opposition. Defending does not give a player as much chance to demonstrate technical ability or creative skills. The movement and positioning is based of the fact that the ball may arrive in this space as such much defending is based on *'what if'* (the ball arrived) hence the player who has run back and is correctly in position to defend will often not have the ball played to the space they are in. It is therefore important that they do not view their efforts as wasted and they are recognized by the coach and other players. These observations raise 2 key coaching points that all coaches should be aware of.

- Firstly, good coaches should compliment a player whose movement has created space for another player- if not why should they do it? A good expression to get your side to use is *shift him/her.* This can be used when asking a player to move the opposition player in their area away to create space for others. Good coaches, as mentioned above, also need to spot the tireless and disciplined running of defenders to be in correct zonal position and applaud the concentration required to read the game. We all like to be appreciated.
- Secondly, good coaches of all teams aged under 18 should insist that the ball is regularly, if not always, played out from the back. How else can players develop? How to play out from the back is explained later but one useful expression is to help develop this and other attacking aspects is to use the term *passing line.*

> *A passing line is the line between the player with the ball and another player on their team along which the ball can be safely played. The passing line may involve a ball into a players feet or in to space for them to run on to. It is important that players create a passing line that offers support with the correct distance so that when the ball is played and received they have enough time to control or chose a pass, without the opposition players closing them down.*

The hardest thing to do as a coach is to watch a game and decide on what is tactically going wrong. To help you understand the tactical side of the game, for the first time, a theory has been developed called space and time. This theory can be related to all aspects of the game.

As well as developing a theory the manual also looks at what we can learn from successful teams and coaches. Throughout this manual there are quotes from top coaches and top teams are analysed.

Before moving on we need to look at how best to coach tactics as this explains why this manual sets out drills in the way it does. To successfully coach tactics requires a change to current coaching practice as most coaching does not develop a team tactically because it does not relate what is being taught specifically to a game situation. Therefore, coaches need to completely re-think how they organise their sessions and as Jose Mourinho's recently stated-

> **You have to find exercises in football to give you the organisation you need- because football is all about organisation. Tactics form that organisation.**

The biggest change is that to coach tactics players need to start every session by having a look at the match situation it relates to. This means either putting players in the actual match situation and discussing key issues or do the same thing on a whiteboard/using chess pieces etc and allow players to ask questions and discuss issues. This doesn't have to take a long time but the important thing is that players see how the tactic/s they are about to work on relate/s to the game.

In the absence of this type of learning, most players tend to learn through trial and error. They try a position or a pass: if it works they will repeat and learn to be successful. If they make a mistake they try alternative methods. This can take time and it also leads to a more instinctive behavior which is difficult to change. They have no clear understanding of why they perform the way they do. In short, players may do the right thing but they are unaware of the reason they do it. This is typical of most football players at all levels as good players rarely make good coaches. Kevin Mitchell, writing in the Observer (2004), claims of footballers comments on soccer games *what they say is invariably useless.* A good analogy is that we may drive a car and get to where we want to go but we don't understand how it works and what to do if it goes wrong.

An coach needs to create an atmosphere of *guided discovery* (Mourinho). This guided discovery of the often complicated behavior required to develop tactical awareness is to create a level of understanding through explanation and discussion rather than just trial and error. People need to understand in order to change their behavior.

The best way to help them to do this is to set a situation in which they have to think - in this case watch/ take part in a real match situation and analyse it with questions. We all learn better if we go from the general (match situation) to the specific (movement, positioning and passes etc) that make up the match situation. An example of this is made by the following comment

> *A few times Dyer didn't spot Bridge overlapping and they need to work on team play in training so that the Southampton player, who has a super left foot, is given a chance to cross. It might even mean walking through things to build an understanding".* **(Ron Atkinson, Monday March 31st, 2003, The Guardian)**

In short coaches need to start at the end and work back. This means that if you have worked out and explained the end tactic (which are all explained in this manual) and follow the simple guidelines for drills/ small sided games (see later) players will be confident about what to do in a match situation.
All the drills that follow the initial discussion must relate to the technical or tactical requirements ending with the actual match situation on a pitch.

Players with fantastic technique, pace ability with the ball are not effective if they cannot apply this to a game situation. Coaches need to focus on learning as well as knowledge/ technique. Players need to develop skills to learn to reflect, answer questions. This will lead to innovation and creativity. Developing learning means a shift away from coach based learning with a set knowledge base to student centered learning. A Democratic coaching style is the best way to develop learning. The **sharing** approach for a coach would involve (national learning network website) a coach.

> *I will outline the problem, pose questions and invite solutions, I directly involve players in decision making, If a solution is agreed by all of us then it's more likely that it will succeed, I still need to make and justify the final decision.*

Many coaches are uncomfortable with this style of coaching with many ex players in particular not bought up in this environment. Coaches have to ask questions in order to allow players to reflect. The question is a powerful tool if used correctly. Create a situation where players are not afraid of answering a question incorrectly. If a players gives an incorrect answer a coach can guide the player to the correct answer *'do you think this is the best option, can you see any other options?'* The important thing is to develop 'thought' to make people think. Asking one person a question means only one person has to think.

Imagine a situation in a practice game where a player has not made the best decision about the pass he/ she has chosen . The coach correctly stops the game. The ball goes back to the player who made the pass. Now at this point the coach asks the question 'what was the better pass?

If the coach always asks the player who made the mistake (this seems logical) the correct answer then only one player has had to consider/reflect. Maybe some other players involved also followed this reflective process. However a better alternative is to make **all players** feel that they might be asked, **that you may chose anyone to come over and coach the point**. The advantage of this is that every player could get picked to do this therefore every player has to have the answer ready. If you always chose the player who made the pass the other 21 can 'switch off' not think. Use questions well and you will develop learning.

The Key Coaching Points are- has learning taken place? Did all the players have to think? Can they apply this learning to a game situation?

Here is an example of the way the match situation/drills work. In this instance certain players are out of the correct position but it highlights many other factors. In this situation players can discuss issues and tactics answer questions etc. Look at Page 6 and have a go at answering the questions before turning to find the answers on page 7.

Practical Drill – a simple example

Drills – Set up/discuss the position below. Two players are definitely in the wrong position.

Which two? Once you have identified them, describe the key coaching points that highlight what they have done wrong.

You could also ask players what is correct about the positions/shape on the pitch in the coaching points. Explain this, then fill in the boxes below.

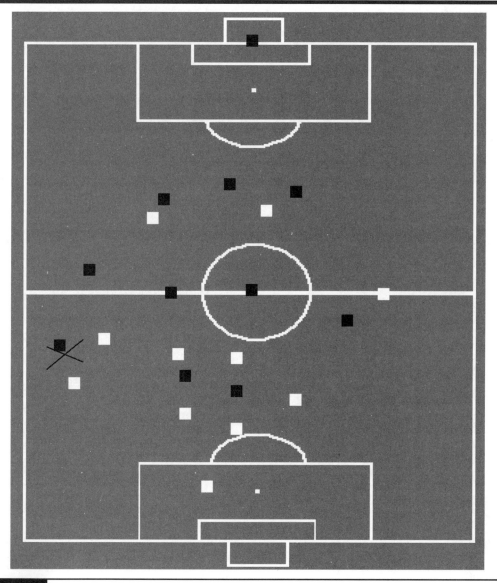

Fill in Key coaching tips	Coaching advice to the players in the wrong position.
	Coaching comments - explain what is correct about other players. **Defending** **Attacking**

5

ANSWER Practical Drills - 'a simple example'. In the example below there are many defensive and attacking tactics at work

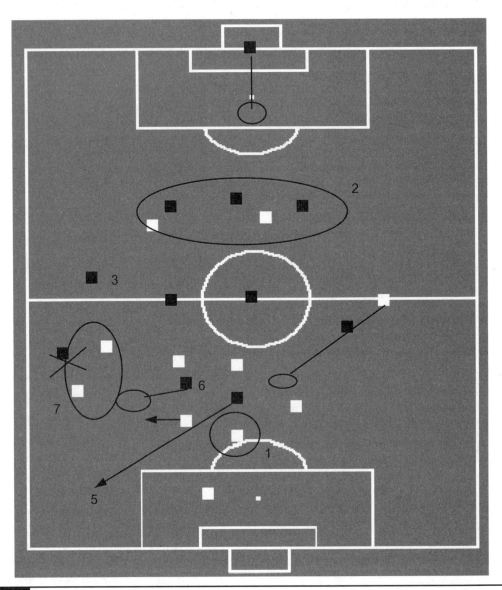

Key coaching tips	Coaching advice to the players in the wrong position – white wide right. Keep compact in midfield. Leave the wide man away from the ball.
	The keeper (shaded) should always act as a sweeper.
	Coaching comments about other players. **Defending** – Both teams are playing zonally. Good cover white centre half (1), mid left has doubled up well-circled (7). They are playing a flat midfield (not diamond). Shaded have gone to back three (2) as they attack this releases (3) shaded right back could overlap. **Attacking** – now one of the shaded forwards (5) needs a run in behind full back from a forward. (6) could help achieve more space by moving to the area circled and creating a passing line (a line along which the ball can be safely passed) this will move the defender to cover and leave more space for the runner (5)

All players may have different learning styles. As has been explained they will all learn better from going from the general to the specific but how you coach also needs to be considered. Do you talk to people/ lecture/give them things to read or diagrams, watch videos, do practical activities? The following may help you chose how you put information across.

Psychologists have identified four different learning styles. While people prefer one style to another to be a really effective learner, they need to try to be flexible enough to move between styles. As a coach/teacher or player you need to be aware of the different styles to help the learning process.

Activists - like to leap up and have a go.
Reflectors - like to think about things before having a go, and to learn by watching others.
Theorists - like to understand the theory and have a clear grasp of the concept before having a go.
Pragmatists - like to have some practical tips and techniques from someone with experience before having a go.

So what can you do to help people learn?On average we remember
- 20% of what we read
- 30% of what we hear
- 40% of what we see
- 50% of what we say
- 60% of what we do
- 90% of what we see, hear, say and do.

This work tries to help learning by incorporating reading, discussion, and practical activities. All coaches should consider a mixed approach. The drills, like the one on the previous page, can be active with time to reflect, they all can be explained by the theory and as a coach you have the experience.

A common theme in this work is the need to use questions to check players understanding of key points. Therefore, to help you check you understand there are a set of questions at the end of each section. These can be used to test your understanding or if you are a teacher as a class based activity.

Some of these activity sheets can be completed as a useful exercise before reading the section, for others it is essential to read the section. In the top right corner of these sheets it will state if you need to read the chapter first.

Throughout the manual you will also find this box on the bottom right of pages. This relates whatever is being discussed to the game in terms of if you are attacking or defending it is a reminder of how players are always doing one or the other and need to look at tactics in the game from both perspectives.

Teaching tactics to players on a pitch is fine on a warm day but players can learn as much and are closer to the tactic being discussed if it is done on a whiteboard or with chess pieces. For example if working with the left back a coach may need to talk to players on the far side, this requires a load voice and it can be difficult to engage in questions and answers. There is even room for home work in developing tactics. Give players a video or ask them to watch a game and note, how many crosses, how deep the defence were etc. You could give handouts of tactics for discussion of for players to solve problems. As has been mentioned before it is important to develop thought and understanding and these are positive and enjoyable ways of promoting this,

Having established the need to move from the general to the specific , prioritise developing players and the need to consider different learning styles in how you coach lets turn out attention to how to incorporate this in to drills to make them realistic to a real game situation.

All players need to know its defensive role

All players need to know their attacking role

Developing by attacking

The best way to develop players and teams is to play an attacking style of play. This means prioritising attacking and creating as many goal-scoring chances as possible. Only by attacking will players develop and ultimately the team be successful. Don't judge success by if you won but by if you created chances and moved the ball successfully up the field. All teams have to be able to defend but this should be balanced against the greater need to play attacking football and create goal-scoring chances. The key question is did you dominate the game and the opposition? In terms of coaching it much easier to coach defending than attacking. Attacking requires more

Movement– which requires the person moving and the person passing the ball to have the correct **timing**. A defenders movement is based around their zone and the need to cover team-mates it is in a smaller area and more prescriptive. A defenders timing is based on interceptions and tackles neither of which are linked to overall success in soccer.

A wider range of decision making as there are more options hence there are **a wider range of attacking tactics.**

A wider range of technique and better technique such as good control, passing, dribbling, shooting, crossing, shielding. A pure defender can get away with poor technique and still function competently in terms of stopping the opposition scoring.

What does attacking play develop that defensive play doesn't? Attacking involves creativity, timing, skill and movement with you deciding when and where the ball is played. This develops technique, body shape, movement and decision-making. Failure to play an attacking game and try to score in a number of ways (there are six ways a team can create a scoring chance) will not develop players as how can defenders and midfielders improve if they don't get the ball? Forwards need to get used to a variety of movement and tactics such as using the space out wide, receiving the ball to feet and in to space, playing in the hole, and looking to exploit the space between keeper and defence (see later).

Defending involves zonal marking with cover and passing players on. To be successful at this is as much about discipline and concentration as technique. What a defender does is to a large extent dictated by the opposition. Arsene Wenger believes that top teams have to be able to attack and that

> *defending is a means to an end. I am a fan of good defending. I want my team to defend well and to express what they have to say when they have the ball. The target is to defend because you want to say something. When I listen to you, I defend; when I speak, I attack.*

Often teams adopt safety-first defensive tactics.

- players are told not to go forward– a tactic favored by Wengers predecessor George Graham

- the number who push up is limited

- the safe often long ball is encouraged

- the ball is not played out from the back

This style of football does not develop players it can lead to limited success. Jack Charlton (when in charge of Ireland) played a long ball safety first game, Sheffield Wednesday recently got promoted playing a long ball safety first game.

However Roy Keane in his autobiography asks of Irelands success, would not the team have done equally as well and probably better playing a different way using the mixed passing game (see later)? Keane's Ireland and Sheffield Wednesday had excellent players who, working on the scraps that the longer ball game provided, were successful. But what could they have achieved playing a more dynamic varied attacking game?

What tactics are required to play the attacking mixed passing game? A team must regularly play out from the back (see later) and through midfield (see later), look for the forward ball (see later), switch play and gain ground (see later). Use a gain line (like Rugby) to measure how well you switch and remember that an attack can be mounted centrally halfway through this process (thread ball see later) as the defence leaves gaps. Try to encourage your players to identify and create *passing lines* (see later) and *bounces* (see later) to move the ball forward.

As we can see attacking successfully requires a range of tactics to help shape the movement of players. The best coaches and teams are the ones where the team has a variety of attacking tactics and in particular can successfully play out from the back. There are 3 key ways to judge how good players are when attacking

- Firstly, their **movement and timing**

- Secondly, **how they bring the ball under control**

- Thirdly, **what they do with the ball once it is under control**

Arsene Wenger talks of his forward Ljungbergs movement –

the knack of arriving in the penalty box a split second before a marker – was a weapon that many sides found impossible to combat.

Lunberg *has the run* (see later) over defenders. Even at top level Wenger claims

now you have to attack because the teams are so good going forward that if you concentrate on defence you will pay the price. You cannot depend on defence because you are under too much pressure and the standard you face is too high.

Brazil won USA 1994 based on their ability to attack not defend the research institute for Olympic sports notes

The strengths of Brasil were in control and passing game and the successful passing play..the greatest weaknesses of Brasil were found in their defensive play. They were 26th in the amount of interceptions and tackles.

Brasil had the highest number of successful attacks built from the back and the highest number of scoring chances.

One thing is for certain these players did not develop these skills playing a long ball, safety first game with defending based around having players stay at the back. They concentrated on developing attacking play.

If players are to develop and play at top or any level they need to develop their attacking abilities when younger. The excellent Alan Irvine (Everton) wont let his keepers kick the ball at under 17 level and plays out from the back through the midfield.

Enjoying the game

- Players have to have plenty of contact with the ball ina game if they are to enjoy it.

Enjoyment- Ask yourself why is it that young players enjoy a game? They enjoy being actively involved throughout the period of time that they play. How can we measure this? By the number of times they touch the ball. Kids may say, if asked about playing for a team or a soccer camp, they enjoyed it. But watch the game, do they say they enjoyed the game because they were involved and clear about what to do, that they received and passed the ball on numerous occasions? Sadly often the enjoyment has only come from their team winning or the fact they are with their friends? Dig deeper and ask if they enjoyed the football? All too often the answer is no. Unfortunately, far too often, coaches let kids play in too larger numbers and don't work on getting everyone passing and involved or building confidence by for example playing out from the back. A coach needs to check everyone is involved, like they would be in a real soccer game.

Coaches often justify large sided 7/8 a side games with no stoppages behind "*well you've got to let them play to enjoy it*" argument. But how often do many players touch the ball in these games? You can often count them on one hand. These kind of games, with youngsters, often turn in to a Roy of the Rovers type game with a few players dominating and having the bulk of possession. This does not develop these players, and it generates bad habits as well as not improving their movement or decision making. When they step up and play against better players or for better teams they are ill equipped.

Often these *Roy of the Rovers* players are bigger and older being at the top end of the school age group and so playing against others who are up to a year younger and who may not be physically developed. A false picture of the ability of both *Roy of the Rovers* and the non Roy of the Rovers develops. Neither benefit.

It is hard for kids to recognise that they are not as good because they are less physically developed. Some research even suggests that up until the age of 11 kinds don't recognise ability but judge everything against effort. So players who make mistakes or who are not involved or confident are seen as not trying.

To make soccer enjoyable and build confidence as well as make it realistic to games coaches need to ensure everyone is clear of their role and involved and has the confidence to try and do the right thing. Therefore, there is one occasion when perhaps a coach should shout! A good example would be to shout at a player, such as a full back, who having received the ball off the keeper has made a mistake and the opposition have scored. The coach should shout to the player that *they must carry on receiving the ball from the keeper and must not hide, that it doesn't matter and they'll get it right next time*. Give them confidence.

With regard to small sided games instead of 7 v 7 split the pitch in 2 and play 4 v 4 and 3 v 3 and rotate players. Stand in the middle and give guidance. In games in general take the emphasis away from winning by awarding a point for a goal but also a point if, for example, 2 defenders being in the correct position to receive the ball from the keeper.
- A point for not turning into a player but laying the ball back.
- A point for offering a good passing option, even if the ball didn't get there.

The score at the end may be 25 to 25 of which 5 were goals. What does this tell us? That 45 good coaching points were adhered to (and you didn't have to keep stopping the game). You could also deduct points for bad movement or lack of movement but be careful to be positive in the way you do it.

Finally, remember that often in kids football a player, often Roy, will make a bad decision and get away with it, it may even lead to a goal BUT, as mentioned above, it develops bad decisions and gives a false picture. COACH kids habits that will stand them in good stead as they improve and the players around them improve, don't encourage bad soccer.

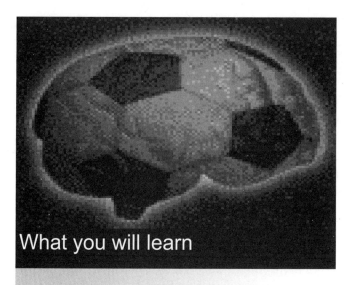

What you will learn

- Different approaches to coaching
- Relating drills to games
- Relating tactics to technique

PART 1 - Coaching tactics

Coaching– Terry Venables

Theory

Later in the manual there is a look at top coaches and teams but we will start here by looking at a few general coaching points from top coaches. One of the best coaches in the UK is Terry Venables. The following points are taken from his autobiography) regarding coaching.

- Venables prefers *to talk to players one to one than lecturing them as a group.*
- Information *is better little bit at a time.*
- With regard to players wanting to win *everybody wants to win, some will do more to achieve this.*
- When coaching the England squad Venables worked with what he termed 'the front six' leaving another coach (Don Howe) with the back five.
- Venables states that team talks only remind players of what is done in training. In other words, don't introduce a new concept at this late stage.
- After the game *avoid talking to the players about the match immediately after the game in the heat of the moment.*
- On training and practice - *practice makes permanent,* Venables claims that coaches who shout all the time to try and motivate or get points across will fail to do so players will ignore it.
- With regard to the often used expression carry *on where we left off* as dangerous unreliable advice to give as the point at the end of the game or half you arrived at a based on what has gone before. You earn it. Therefore you have to go through the process again. His advice *start the way you started week before not the way you ended.*

There are 3 styles of coaching autocratic – I'm the boss do as I say (Peter Reid), laissez faire – do what you think is best (Kevin Keegan) or democratic – a mixture between the two (Eriksson) .All can work but democratic gets the best from both.

- Venables states that the *democratic style lets players blossom but controls excess.*
- Venables sums up *good football not fantasy football common sense in approach and tactics.* Venables believes, as we have seen elsewhere, in organisation and tactics for a team to get the best from all its players.

Will players listen to tactics? Terry Venables points out that

> *Players are quite prepared to listen to someone lecturing them on tactics.*

Will players try to improve technique? Younger players are usually keen to develop and work on their technique as are many older players. However, Terry Venables points out that many players do not want to listen to advice on technique. Venables does not like this attitude as in other sports a great deal of attention is focussed on addressing flaws in technique (golf for example) and in this sport even professional players are more than happy to be coached.

The problem with laissez faire coaching is emphasises by this headline **Furious players demand extra training from Keegan to beat drop (Times April 2004). The article stated**

> *Keegan was astonished by the revolt but he was quick to agree to their proposal of extra training. The players are also understood to have urged Keegan to name his team earlier than normal to allow them to work on set-pieces and on the team shape, which they believe has been undermined by a laissez faire attitude.*

The problem of lack of organization and a laissez faire attitude was highlighted by fellow strugglers Leeds captain (May 2nd Guardian 2004), Dominic Matteo, who observed that one of the key reasons for Leeds relegation was they were less well organised than other clubs.

Autocratic style denies the positive contribution of players and indeed other coaches. It can make players feel undervalued.

Involving the players is a good thing because it means everyone's involved and that's why we've got such a terrific atmosphere in the camp.' Steve McClaren assistant coach of England. Mc Claren credited the England manager for listening to players in a team meeting ahead of a game against Switzerland. There were suggestions the England squad forced Eriksson to abandon his diamond formation in favour of a flat-flour midfield Eriksson listened to the players

> *There's been a big debate about this and it's brought a smile to our faces. Sven picks the team and it's a bad manager who doesn't listen to their players and his staff, is autocratic and says "this is the way to go" Eriksson has the tactical prowess to beat Croatia in Group B tonight. - Metro 21st June 2004.* He was right.

Coaching requires
- The ability to understand and work with all your players. They are all different.
- The ability to look away from the ball and understand time and space.
- The ability to spot 'the little things'.

Roy Keane, in his autobiography, talks about football and the excellent Brian Clough in the following way. *Every football match consists of a thousand little things which, added together, amount to the final score. The manager who can't spot the details in the forensic matter that Clough could is simply bluffing. The game is full of bluffers, banging on about 'rolling your sleeves up', 'having the right attitude' and 'taking some pride in the shirt you're wearing'. A manager or coach who trades in those clichéd generalizations – and there are many of them – is missing the point. Brian Clough dealt in detail, facts, specific incidents, and invariably he got it right. Playing for him was demanding. I love it.*

 Good coaches/managers in soccer are no different from good coaches/managers in other organisations. Football is not so different.

Below I have taken an article by **Richard Scase, (The Observer, 14th October, 2001)** in which he looks at the style of our highly regarded Swedish Manager, Sven Goran Eriksson. This sums up what makes a good coach/manager.

- ➢ Discuss, analyse and then decide. Unlike the ranting of most past managers, the present coach is cool and detached. He sits away from the touchline. The approach is to analyse, discuss problems with colleagues and to arrive at decisions. No place for the dominant, autocratic style of many managers.
- ➢ Keep cool, calm and patient. Under pressure Eriksson doesn't panic, reflecting a management education that gives as much, if not more, emphasis to emotional and social intelligence, as to simple brainpower.
- ➢ Trust and empower. Eriksson can take a back seat at games because he trusts his players. They invest heavily in staff training with little of the employer-employee hostility found in many British companies. Such cultures are not easy to build. Players must know they will be left to achieve what is expected.
- ➢ Build commitment. One of Eriksson's achievements has been to change players' attitudes. Nowadays they play as if they actually enjoy it and it is their priority. They come up with ideas for improvement, making the company innovative and therefore competitive.
- ➢ Eriksson selects players for each match from more or less the same squad. This means they get to understand each other's strengths and weaknesses and the team can develop its overall skills. Erickson gives high priority to continuous improvements by developing staff. By contrast, the strategy for many English football teams is to go for the quick fix: fire, buy-in, continuous change.
- ➢ Teams are the basis for individual success. Eriksson has made England a team rather than a collection of players who get together to play football. For Kevin Keegan, it was built around two or three key players. Teams are the foundation for the development of individual skills. Importance is given to developing shared knowledge.
- ➢ Respect and praise. Eriksson respects his players for their talents and sees his job as bringing out the best in them. His style is facilitative and confidence building – a far cry from the half-time dressings-down that most players get. Respect for individuals leads to greater commitment.

Eriksson's style is very different from the barstool approach of most English managers. He is the product of a cultural environment which has, as its starting point, different assumptions about what motivates people. From these emerge distinctive leadership approaches, organisation structures and ways of doing business. Eriksson consults players yet maintains control. In the 2004 Euro Championships,

Beckham revealed *The diamond formation was mentioned before the game but we all decided that 4-4-2 was the best thing. The most important thing is that they listen to us. He sat us all down and asked us what we felt best doing. He said 'I'm the manager and I'll obviously make the final decision but I'll listen to you as well.'*

Successful teams and players need *the 3 C's* in soccer.

CONFIDENCE- If players know what is expected then this gives them confidence and confidence is an essential characteristic of a successful player and a successful team.
CONCENTRATION– especially when defending is essential. A player slightly out of position can cost a goal and in a game of so few goals, around 3 per game at top level but Chelsea won 16 games 1-0 this season, this can cost the game.
COMMUNICATION– no organisation or team can work well without those with a better view or in a better position letting others know.

We now need to look at the tactics that give players confidence when attacking and the defensive tactics that require concentration.

- Teams should play a mixed passing game (using long and short passes and knowing when to dribble with the ball) and teams should be encouraged to play out from the back. There are two benefits in adopting these tactics, developing players and winning games. The excellent statistician Daniel Finkelstein provides evidence for this

> *If we look at what good sides have in common above all other things it is good passing. There is a direct relationship between overall team success and both the total number of passes and the passing success rate...good teams pass more, and more successfully and also stop their opponents from passing so much. The top teams will only let between 20/25% of passes go astray, bottom clubs around 33%. One form of passing is surprisingly high in terms of overall success – passing by the goalkeeper. Successful distribution from the keeper is a hallmark of a good side. This may suggest that building up from the back is better than launching the ball up field to find one of your own.* (Times, 13th November, 2004)

- Teams should be encouraged to attack and try and win games as a pose to adopting the tactic of 'not losing'. Is there a certain way to attack that good teams adopt? Finkelstein points out about the widely held assumption that good teams cross more

> *good teams do not cross significantly more or, more accurately than bad teams, Manchester United are near the top in terms of number of crosses, Arsenal near the bottom. Crossing the ball is simply a matter of team style.*

Good teams have players who make good decisions. They will have solid well organised defenses that play zonally in open play but may mix this with 'man for man' to defend free kicks/set plays. All successful teams have a couple of players who can score goals and who are capable of beating an opponent. A team needs tactics to get the best out of these and all other players. Successful teams are not bigger or faster (this is proved by Finkelstein*). Neither do successful teams tackle more often or better, with Finkelstein pointing out

> *successful teams do not necessarily tackle better, the number of tackles also appears a matter of style rather than being either positively or negatively linked to success.*

In good teams players understand their role when they are in one of three stages - attacking, defending and the transition. On each theory page the attacking and defensive priorities are identified in the bottom right corner.

Attacking	In Transition	Defending
	When the ball changes hands (which it does on average every 15 seconds) you are in transition between attacking and defending. Teams need to react quickly to deal with an attack or create an attack. Using this time is essential for effective attacking.	

The need to use the transition quickly is emphasized by ex-Wolves manager David Jones regarding the ball –

> we didn't move it quickly enough. We allowed them to get back into shape that was difficult to break down...we were left shooting waywardly from long distance.

Andy Roxburgh (Champions Magazine Dec 2004) sees rapid counter attack

> as *the only effective way ahead ... you need quality of players and passes and you need to prepare it properly in training, you can cause a lot of problems with a groups of players who go straight toward goal with pace and direct fluid combination passing. You could go as far as to say if you can't counter attack you can't succeed. You need this as part of your armoury.*

He points out that In Euro 2004 forty per cent of goals from open play came from counter attack and in the Champions League thirty per cent. It's all about the speed the ball is used in the transition. The transition is often not about tackling it's *about stealing the pass* then moving the ball quickly.

Possession in itself isn't a good indicator of success – Porto (Champions League winners 2004) were twelfth best in the Competition (incidentally they were also one of the smallest sides). Milan finalists in 2005 had 47% possession per match, Liverpool the other finalists 48%. In 2003/4 Deportivo had sixty per cent possession and lost 8-3. However, many teams use possession and a slower build up to adopt the tactic of the Brazilians, what Roxburgh calls a *Rattlesnake eye*, to wait for the opportunity/space to attack quickly. Building with many passes has two effects.

1. Firstly, your opponents have time to take up their formation and close down space.

2. Secondly, like the Brazilian *Rattlesnake eye*, it allows a team to probe and switch looking for a defender slightly out of position.

Teams need to work on tactical movements to keep possession and create space if they are to keep the ball.

When defending it is important not to be demoralised if you don't have the ball. In Euro 2004 only Latvia had a lower average possession of ball than winners Greece. They used the ball well when they got it. Be patient!

It is important to realise that tactics do not stay the same throughout a game. They change according to the score, to reflect the opposition, playing conditions and the availability of players. Therefore, a successful team needs a range of tactics: they need to be adaptable and flexible. To have flexibility in the tactics adopted requires flexibility in the type of pass used.

Finally a word about the term bravery. In football bravery is as much about players wanting and offering themselves for the ball when their team are losing or under pressure as it is the big crowd pleasing tackle. It is important to remember this and drive it home to your players as often the big tackler will look down on this other kind of *bravery* and criticize players who do not get *blood on their boots/do big tackles.*

The problem is usually that the big tacklers, and often the crowd , criticise other players who do not follow their example run hard and tackle. The Real Madrid assistant manager Mello comments

> of football *positioning is everything. That is why I like to emphasis the tactical part of the game. If a player runs too much during a game it is because he has lost his position.*

With regard to tackling, successful talking and a teams success are not linked as shown earlier. The bigest problem teams face is that players are not tactically organised and able to, especially when behind, create chances. Player that criticise are often the ones who 'hide' and don't offer for the ball. Players need confidence and 'bottle'. Rafael Bentiez critisised his players, after qualifying for the Champions League semi final, for not keeping the ball well enough– not having the 'bottle' to pass it and were 'belting it long'.. Jamie Carragher claimed

> *everyone was delighted and he (Benitez) was saying we bottled it.*

The same argument about bravery also applies to coaches many of whom are too scared and sadly often too ignorant, to play anything other than a safety first game aimed at not losing the game as a pose to winning a game. In the words of Johan Cryuff

> I *see defenders booting the ball away shamelessly. We could never play like that..*

The current Real Madrid coach (Vanderali Luxemburgo) claims

> *if you don't risk anything you don't win.*

How do players and coaches work together? The PSV coach Hiddink notes of coaching

> *it is important to have one or two players on the pitch with whom I can share my tactical thoughts, so they can implement them.*

Coaches try to develop players and a team. Some enormously technically gifted players lack tactical awareness and it is down to the coach to develop this. Players who have this *football intelligence* a term used by Jan Molby (former Liverpool player) to describe Liverpool's Xabi Alonso or to describe Andriy Shevchenko European footballer of the years 2004 *improved tactical awareness* being credited to coach Ancelotti. Joe Cole has credited Mourinho with developing his game and Steven Gerard is beginning to look like a more complete player thanks to Rafael Bentiez.

At the top level of football, what are a teams objectives? To win is always the most important. The best way to achieve this is

> *In defence the key principles are pressuring the ball, covering space and players and closing down. In attack, I like to stress the importance of playing the ball forward where possible, whilst also understanding when a backward pass is more appropriate. Understanding the type of forward pass is also vital: when to play short through midfield and when to release the long ball and when and how to change the nature of attack. Technically, players have to be better, more skilful, all over the pitch as they have less time on the ball. A centre back will need to control the ball and contribute to attacking play.* **Tord Grip (the England managers assistant) Insight, Winter 2003.**

David James, recently interviewed, (June 2004 in the Observer) noted that when he committed a number of errors on crosses the coaching staff did not make a specific effort to improve this. It was the case that it was assumed players have the necessary technique.

Understand that winning is important but developing your players and team is more important.

As a coach you need to recognise that players and teams should not simply be judged against whether they won or not. Why? Well If winning is success then to lose is to fail. All good managers / coaches know that

- You can lose games you deserve to win (luck is a factor more so in football than other sports) also consider the pitch / the referee etc.
- It may be that 9 or 10 of your players played well but the keeper let in a goal. A centre half slipped.

Winning is always important but not always an accurate measurement of how well a team played. It is better to ask key questions about your team. Did they create chances? Did they have a good team shape defensively and cover the dangerous spaces? Did players make good decisions when in possession? Did you play a mixed passing game? Did you control the tempo of the game.

If you get these thing right then you will win more games than you lose. Alan Irvine Everton's excellent Assistant coach states

I do want to win games but it has to be by controlling games.

If you control a game it means your team can use a variety of tactics and dictate play. Irvine feels it is more important to be winning at the end of a season than the beginning as this shows the team and players have developed.

Use video analysis.

Dario Gradi (Insight Winter 2004) talks of the importance of Video analysis (sometimes called Performance Analysis)
- Grady claims the intention is to be *inspirational as well as educational.*
- It allows the coach and player to be clear about the facts and the coaching point *finding out who was right.*
- Gradi is very cautious about what he says after a game because *quite often the video will prove me wrong.*
- Before you start putting things right you *have to get the diagnosis correct.* For example if a player is *not passing the ball quickly enough or you don't see things.*
- *As much as it is important to exercise the players legs and bodies it is important to exercise their minds.– video analysis is the best way to do this.*
- Gradi tries to nurture an atmosphere where the players are inquisitive and want to see the video. He wants *player participation* with ideally him *not doing any of the analysis instead the players would come to me with their edited highlights and say 'what do you think of this?*
- *At academy level the boys all get a copy of the match video with commentary.*
- He warns of creating computer like responses from players talking of *players working within what he wants. Sometimes we play teams who look programmed. The ball goes in to a certain area and they knock it in to a certain channel. I do not want my players to be programmed when they play.*
- *The biggest problem is some players at all ages do not like being criticised.* Without diagnosing the problem you wont get the solution. *If you practice badly you get better at playing badly*

To be successful teams and players need to be tactically flexible and adaptable. Tactics win games. Successful teams develop players who are able to adapt their game and collectively the teams tactics throughout a game to meet the circumstances, being behind, in front, to deal with the oppositions danger players.

We need to play more with our heads. Foreign players have helped develop tactical knowledge we *see them playing in the hole sitting in front of the back 4* (Irvine). Tactics change during a game teams need to adapt.

Give a team and players time to develop. Try to have a settled side. The team will improve more as players get used to each other and their roles. Keeping a settled side may be at odds with giving all players time on the pitch, and it is always a balance in this area, but the more settled a side the better. If players are used to each other and their role then they will be more successful when going forward as they have good timing. The ball is played to players in space as they arrive. Developing a working relationship with each other is especially important in defence

> *At any team I have ever had ,the goalkeeper and defenders have not changed much.* Paul Sturrock (Sheffield Wednesday Manager)-

Getting the defensive 'line right' depends on teamwork. With regard to a team in Spain who consistently bought new players each year SKY TV commentator talked of the need for team to have

> *consistency to develop personality and allow the squad to develop*

Play a mixed passing game and try to win. Teams should adopt a positive approach and try to win as opposed to a more cautious 'not to lose' mentality. The mixed passing game includes

> *The back 4 must be confident on the ball (Irvine).*

Good teams can therefore play out from the back and through teams as well as over them. Irvine insists

> *At under 17 level I wont let the goalkeepers kick the ball* and *If I'm asking players to play out from the back I've got to accept they will lose goals...if I bawl they might not do it again.*

With regard to the midfield Irvine claims-

> *I wont go back to front–* the team and players *must be able to create space for themselves and to be comfortable receiving the ball.*

Having watched his academy side play I saw excellent movement, variety of passes, and dribbling/ taking players on when appropriate. Good coaches encourage players who can beat players to do so and don't critise when they fail. Some forwards and some midfielders in any team need to be able to dribble beat players

> *Success is only achieved not only by ...good organisation, but by having exciting players who could beat defenders and score goals. In tight and difficulty situations these players invariably put defenders on the back foot and force defenders deeper to stop the threat of players attacking the space behind them. Patience then becomes critical in trying to prise an opening from which to attack. Good dribblers are essential in any team– remember the best teams possess quite a few. Attackers need the skill to beat a player in a 1v1 situation instead of going backwards .* John Peacock National Coach (Insight Autumn Winter 2004)

Both Peacock and Irvine are clear about the need for players must not being afraid of failing. Fear of failing can lead to players not taking on opposition players, **'hiding'**- they do their defensive duty but avoid offering themselves when attacking, not playing through teams but choosing a 'safe' ball long and forward instead of a harder and riskier ball that could be more effective (a threaded pass).

We have now looked at numerous coaching quotes and ideas. The final stage of this section is to look at the summary of all the tactics that are to follow. The tactical team talk.

The 3 team talks

Theory

If we are to learn we need to move from the general to the specific– to the start at the end. This is why the first thing to look at is the tactical team talk– the end product that all coaches wish to master. The need to relate to the game, which current coaching does not, means all the drills in this manual take place on a football pitch with a ball and if we use drills we work back from this. On a side issue if we do fitness work we always use a ball and do it on the pitch– our place of work. The team talk is a summary of the work on the training ground (where we always use a pitch) and all the tactics a team and the opposition employ. So it is here we will start.

Effectively there are 3 team talks.

1. One ,the tactical team talk with specific points to players as to how they fit in to the overall team plan. This, in an ideal situation, takes place sometime (a few days) before a game, and involves a whiteboard and or chess pieces. In reality as often teams only meet on match days it may have to happen then. If this is the case it should be around and hour before kick off.

2. The second team talk (Motivation and general) is 10 minutes or so before kick off need to stick to a few simple general points and motivating players (motivation does not mean shouting all players are different and so individualise the talk). It is worth remembering that players need confidence to do well. **The best way of giving anyone confidence is by making them clear as to what is expected, their specific role. The first team talk therefore does most of the work for the second.**

3. The third talk (half time) which needs top be a short combination of all 3. Specific to individuals, general about for example not giving away free kicks, Motivational to get players re-focused.

The tactical team talk is the most important way a coaches can impact on the game. As mentioned above, it is the ultimate aim of any coach is to be able to deliver a tactical team talk.

It is the end result of all the drills and coaching relating them to a match situation. It describes and explains how the team is organised and will play.

On the next page is an example of a tactical team talk. In this the coach outlines how the opposition play, their tactics and how to respond defensively and when attacking- how they attack may determine how you attack- the opposition full back gets forward you can exploit the space this leaves when you re-gain possession.

This talk will also go over the general tactics that happen in every game, As the season progresses this will become less detailed, the team just need a gentle reminder not detail but initially or in pre –season or with new players the whole thing needs going over.

The 3 key aspects of the talk are defensively, attacking and in the transition (the time when the ball changes hands and a team is most vulnerable defensively).

The following talk that assumes an opposition with a fast forward who like to play long and sometimes in to feet as well as trying to cross etc. They have a couple of skillful wide players and a forward who likes to hold the ball up and 1 midfielder who goes beyond the forwards.

The talk below covers many areas of this manual so any terminology etc you are not clear about is covered later on.

Example of a tactical Team Talk– approx 15 minutes

Theory

A tactical team talk can only build on what has been learnt in training it is perhaps one of the few occasions where the coach will do all of the talking…..so here goes!

Lets start with the fundamentals. We play to win not 'not to lose'. **Remember** Its all about creating or denying space and time **and following 2 basic principles**. When we defend we are compact when we attack spread out.

Defensively we are compact and organised by playing zonally and making sure we always have cover as well as always *doubling up* on wide players when they are level with our 18 yard box or further forward. Brains will sort out the correct offside line. Remember the three C's we concentrate when defending, we are confident when attacking– want the ball (don't hide) and know what is expected of you in terms of movement– And the final C which applies to both attacking and defending COMMUNICATE. The player passing, the player receiving anyone with a good view talk to each other—pass players on defensively, time the runs when attacking , back means give it back quick don't delay, turn when you get the call and look up when you have time, we switch constantly and quickly and pass to make it easy for the player receiving the ball, not too fast or too slow and in front of them or on the correct foot.. Defenders you should all know the favored foot of the players they use to attack and be shouting show him left or right to drive them in to defending players or make sure they shoot or cross with their weaker foot. How we attack is often determined by how they attack– the right back pushes on so use this space when we win the ball on the transition. We do these things every week I will remind you every week.

Our formation, we know, is constantly changing as for example full backs push up, midfielders go beyond forwards. Defensively we will try to get to a 4 4 2.

They sometimes play or will be (if a full back pushes up) 3 5 2 and if they do we won't match up but the midfield 4 will play a diamond and really compact and we will play the ball wide often to stretch their defence. With our pace up front they will probably change but if they stay 3 5 2 and start dominating midfield we'll pull a forward back, Holdy as he is slower and hit them on the break. We will play out from the back as often as we can and push a full back into midfield to create a numbers up/level if they play 5 situation BUT at this point remember we play 3 5 2, which if we lose the ball we try as quickly as possible to get back to 4 4 2. So try and delay them and work hard at getting our defensive shape back.

If we are 3 5 2 the central Midfielder, Claud, needs to stay deep and offer cover.

If they play 4 4 2 the shape of the midfield will be flat to use width and help deal with the oppositions wide players who are good, we always double up on them with the full back near our area. A Flat midfield, when attacking, also creates space for Holdy, our forward, who likes to drop in to the hole and have the ball to feet.

The oppositions wide players both like to push up so this may leave space for us to exploit. Speedy may drop in to this space to receive the ball on the transition.

We will commit at least 5 forward and sometimes 6 to try and break them down. Our defence is good enough to cope and they are not the best team at fast breaking, remember to slow them down on the transition. If you foul- foul early or not at all. We want to win so we will attack with the 2 wide players, 2 forwards and one of the central midfielders along with maybe even a full back to make 6.

Defence- you all know you must concentrate for the whole 90 minutes 1 mistake could lead to a goal. Its about being in the right place every time a few yards out could cost us a goal. I'll spot if you weren't where you should be and even if the ball doesn't arrive there this time it may do next time and one goal could and often in soccer does win the game. Don't go to ground/slide and don't give away free kicks leave 50 50's alone you've got a 50% chance of giving away a free kick or being beaten. As the game goes on and your tired don't get lazy and start diving in/slide tackling which seems easier than standing off.

Chelsea have had 16 1-0 wins this season and not conceded a penalty kick. The message- whatever happens in the penalty area don't give any cause for the ref to give a penalty. There is always a chance the keeper will save it or they will miss and if you look at the majority of penalties that are conceded you find that they are in areas where the player with the ball was unlikely to score or even create a scoring chance.

They have pace and a midfielder who likes to time his run and go beyond the forwards so we need to prioritise, as we always do, that our defensive line does not allow an easy ball over the top in to the gap between defence and keeper (the danger zone). Be too deep rather not too far forward. Make them have to work harder to create chances.

They have a player with a long throw so do everything you can to avoid giving them a long throw in the area around the scoring zone. The other thing they will do if they get set plays is spend a great deal of time getting their centre halves up, this will cause us problems as they work on this and also breaks up the flow of the game and slows the tempo down which on the hole suites them not us. Remember, up to 60% of goals come from set plays.

Brains you sort the offside line out make sure 3 things.
    1)   **That we target only the player who is going to receive the ball**. Don't march forward catching a player offside who will be moving back/not interfering and not receive the ball and so not be given offside. It goes for all of you- don't be distracted by this player and get caught by a player who times his run well. If there is an obvious ball for them get the player offside if you can but make sure that you are close enough to react if the linesman misses it not 5 yards away with your arm in the air. Remember when the ball is played you all should be dropping off.

    2)   **In open play get them out of the penalty area as fast as you can**- give the keeper room to work in and make it harder for them to score if they win a header or shot BUT drop back in as an organised zonal unit as the ball is played. The exception to this is something we've worked on in training. If they have a free kick from out wide and can deliver in to the area between defence and keeper many teams, like this one, have a player who can deliver a pinpoint ball here. So we are going deeper than we would in open play and zonal as this gives us two advantages. Firstly, we are running towards the ball and so are less likely to be beaten in the air– we are not back tracking, secondly, we can guarantee a good defensive shape in the area where they want to deliver and where there danger players will be. We are swapping Holdy (the centre forward) with out left back here as he is better in the air.

    3) You all know the importance of **making sure we have cover.** Full backs tuck in and support the centre halves and Brains drop off whenever you can to provide sweeping cover, remember if they don't see you drop off and no opposition player moves into the space you are fine, if they do use offside to get them out then sneak again, *it's a game, they aren't clever enough to see it most of the time.*

Claud, you're the guy in central mid who is sitting in front of defence and patrolling the hole. The opposition player who likes to run from midfield needs to be tracked as he comes through your area and make sure that the defence have seen him before passing him on and returning to your space. Their forward who drops in to the hole either you pick up or one of the centre halves but if it is the centre half then the remaining back 3 need to close up and become a back three as soon as possible.

They will switch the ball so the whole team needs to shift across and if the ball is played via the middle be careful you don't allow them a ball into feet for the forwards (the kind of ball Arsenal are always looking for). If they play this ball from central or wide they will try to thread the ball through the thread zone so the keeper must be ready to react and come off his line to any threads. The defence be compact and central to deny this. BUT DON'T FOUL.

Attacking- We need and have a variety of tactics to attack. We will score.

The first thing the keeper or any player should do is quickly look if the ball into the danger zone is on.

If not is there another ball forward that you can 90% deliver to feet or space? If this option is not on and they begin to re-organise we play out from the back .

Attacking wise we try to use all 6 attacking tactics

1) **Set plays**- you all know what to do off corners, free kicks and throw ins, Tricky try and commit defenders and win free kicks. Set plays remember off corners we have identified the player who we are aiming for and the run. The rest of you have to do your bit to confuse the opposition and create space for him. Look convincing and accept this role.

2) **Into the space between their back 4 and keeper over the top or on the ground**- if it is on do it for Speedy

3) **Crosses**- switch the ball and use *inside out and overlaps* to get wide and to the byline and cross. Play the 'Shearer' ball if its on. Midfield and forwards try and create an *inside out* situation where the player with the ball (or even just running inside to take a player with you) deliberately goes inside taking the player marking him, this creates space out wide for a full back if it is a midfielder doing it or midfielder if it is a forward- which the ball is played to by another player or the player with the ball.

4) **The Thread ball**- we know how to use this, create the space and use it.

5) **Long shot**- Try and have as many shots as we can we've worked on using *'overs'* where a player stands in front of another from the same team, so being difficult to mark, the ball is played to him he lets it go its T' d up for a shot

6) **Skill**- Tricky will try and get their defence out of shape and create space as well as earning set plays.

The ways we can launch these attacks are

· **From the keepers hands** long in to danger zone or flicked on or second ball. From a goal kick or throw- build from back- we have worked on this.

Fast break- quickly attack on the transition- a couple of you run well with the ball so if the space is there and they are backing off *take the space* and draw defenders towards you. Off their corners if the keeper gets it in his hands then the three players we've identified charge forward in a line and the ball is played long and central. They have there centre halves up for the corner and even if they win the ball the fact we have 3 players bearing down on them may mean we get the second ball and can attack whilst they are re-organising.

· **Suck them in** by going back and deep then attack at pace as they push up to try and win the ball.

· **Switch** in all areas to find space. We needs to switch all the time quickly to find space and move forward, As the ball goes across the middle always look in to the thread zone we can play one touch in here to get a runner in or create a shooting opportunity.

· **Ball to feet** of Holdy our forward who likes playing in the hole and as their defender comes to meet this try and play back and first time into this space before their defence reacts and becomes a back 3.

· **Ball to space** If they are a back 3 then we need to look wide as this is where the space will be. Our 2 forwards against a defensive 3 or tight 4 may stay central and ask for the ball to be played out wide into space down the line for them to run on to. Don't do this ball to Holdy as they will outpace him.

If they push players on to try and win the ball this will create space in midfield, remember if they push a player on from midfield we've got 25% more space to work with in this area which we can find.

If during the game we regain possession in midfield always look for a forward ball but if nothing is on go back to keep possession. The defence may have to drop right back to receive the ball as the opposition like to press on. Go right back give yourselves space and time, they will get tired and as they push further forwards after the ball and will leave gaps which we can exploit. Look to switch all the time.

In midfield we are playing flat so as to leave the space for Holdy, the forward to drop into the hole

If we play a diamond in midfield the player at the top of the diamond Pointy will use the hole. If Holdy is substituted then we will go to a diamond shape in midfield if behind. The 2 forwards will keep pushed on to their centre halves and leave the space for Pointy to play in the hole.

We needs players to make the runs to create space for others I recognize this and the hard work and intelligence it involves the rest of you need to. Last week we scored a goal because Brian made a run and took the defender slightly out of position so we could thread the ball through, he didn't touch the ball but made the goal.

Time your runs and ask yourself the question- *is there a line between the person with the ball and me that it can be played along*? If not make one or put yourself in a position where you can receive the ball from a *bounce*.

How are you *plugged in* to the attack.

Finally, use your brains football is a game for intelligent people and be patient. The team with the most possession has little if any more chance of winning. Its what we do with the ball not how long we have it for. Lets finish on one of Mourinho's philosophy that applies to this group of players– *we have to defend well with fewer people (forwards are their to score) - dominate more and be dominated less. We have to counter attack less and attack more and score more goals...we have intelligent and skillful players*

When to put tactics in to the match day routine

Theory

Thanks to Shane Kent (MSC) who helped write this section

You will need at least seventy minutes before a game if you are to prepare properly.

Minutes to go	Activity
70	Individual chats to team (explain why playing or not) and name team
60	10 -15 Go through tactics formation, set play. Anything about opposition (e.g. they have pace up front so don't push up too far)
45	Get changed (give people ten minutes and expect them all to be out for warm up)
35	Collective warm up fifteen minutes (try to include as much ball work as possible)
20	5 minutes for individuals to do their 'own thing'
15	Back in (ten minutes) last minute information and motivational chat, beware this does not go on too long as players can get cold and at this point it should be simple)
5	Players go out ready with five minutes to go - let them chat amongst themselves or do their own stretches, routines with ball. Keep it simple. Remember a team talk involves working with different individuals who have different needs and need different coaching approaches and tips

Terry Venables likes to talk to players all together not 1 to 1 True/False

Practice makes…………………………….

Name the 3 coaching styles and give examples of each

What does the best coaches look away from the ball mean?

All players should be treated the same True/False

Name 2 old rules for football . What is the problem with them.

Coaching tactics is best done on a small pitch. True/False

Walking through situations is the best way for players to understand. True/False

How much time do you need before a game to prepare. Fill in the box.

Minutes to go	Activity
70	
60	
45	
35	
20	
15	
5	

Coaching – *relating drills to games*

We have discussed the need to ensure that all practice is as close to a game situation as possible. The following outlines how to make drills / small sided games as game like as we can.

Use offside when it applies in the game situation you are working on and in ALL small sided games-it makes it realistic to the game.

Play zonally, in defence and midfield. This is the best way to defend and gives structure to attacks. Zonal defence is something players need to constantly work on, defensively working together and providing cover, and when attacking how to time runs and try and cause problems for the defence.

Give the drills direction In a game a team is always trying to move the ball in a certain direction. So in drills make sure as often as possible that the way to success/win is to move the ball in a certain direction. For example, when working on playing out from the back, the intention is to play from the keeper and a player to put their foot on the ball at the end of a large half pitch sized grid, showing that the ground has been gained and the ball is under control. There is nothing wrong with going back to go forwards but in a game situation a team is always trying to move the ball in a certain direction- towards the oppositions goal

Always look for the forward ball, this doesn't mean going long or not going across the pitch and switching but the point is if a forward ball is available it should be taken.

Use a realistic space ideally the same width as your home pitch, the length may vary depending on the tactic being worked on e.g. up to half way to develop playing out from the back. *Make the numbers realistic* (and hence *the time available to players*) to the game e.g. a keeper 4 v 2/3 if playing out from the back 4 v 4/5 if playing through midfield. It is obviously better to use players who play at the back or midfield in these drill but it develops everyone understanding of the tactical side of the game to make all players do it.

Use realistic technical drills that relate to game situations. For example playing out from the back may require a full back on one side to play the ball direct to the full back on the other side. This needs to be done in a way that allows the receiving full back to move forward (give them a direction) and is best done by having a third player closing down from the middle as this is realistic to the game. Simply driving the ball to each other is not realistic to a game. Other situations may require a full back to deliver a range of ball driven, floated etc in to forwards feet or in to space.

Players need to choose the best passing option is an essential tactical point to develop. Often players will chose the wrong option but will have maintained possession. In this situation the game/drill should be stopped and the player shown the better option with the game re-starting with the better pass being made .If you do not do this, how can players learn? Video analysis is an alternative to this. This rule also applies when coaching technique. A good example would be stopping a 6-a-side game and getting a player who had avoided using their weaker foot to use it. This is a better way of learning than simply pointing it out after the event, they have not actually done it or seen why it is better to choose a different option.

All players and forwards need to practice 1 touch soccer as this is the best way of improving there decision making, awareness, delivery and first touch. Again give this direction, Brazilian beach football involves a small sided game with small (1 meter/3 ft) goals and a lot of one touch soccer. The game has direction.

EXAMPLE of starting a coaching session in the context of a game situation

A good starting point is to think of a key question that players and coach have to consider. A general problem such as how are goals scored? Then consider the facts.

- The most successful teams need 16-30 attacks and 7-10 shots to score one goal.
- The attacks which produce a goal take less than 25 seconds
- There are between two and six players taking part in these attacks
- The number of passes is between one and six passes to score a goal.
- In 2004/5 Manchester United were more attacking than anyone else in the Premiership, had the best passing and more shots yet the conversion rate was the 2nd worst in the League and they scored 29 less than Arsenal. Goal scorers are important. Liverpool won the Champions League with a midfielder Gerard as their top scorer for the season on 13 so it doesn't have to be a traditional centre forward but this is unusual and something Liverpool are trying to put right.

If we look at how goals are scored we can identify 6 ways of scoring. Knowing the 6 ways is a very useful tool for you to use as ideally your team has tactics to use all 6 and it gets your players and team thinking about a variety of tactics. The 6 ways are

1. **Set play**
2. **Ball into danger zone over the top in to gap between defence and keeper**
3. **Cross byline, Cross Deep (around 30% goals in open play from crosses)**
4. **Thread zone– threaded in to the area (see PAGE 29 for more detail on this)**
5. **Skill**
6. **Long Shot– outside the area**

The ball can be moved to the oppositions goal in a number of ways. Played out from the back, won during open play, a kick or throw from the keeper. We need to use all these tactics to get the ball to the oppositions goal. Once there in open play it can be crossed or threaded.

Having set the general overall picture you can look at the specifics.

Today we are going to look at the Thread Zone **(see Later PAGE 34 for more detail on this)** Talk about how attack thread zone. Get the players in to a match situation on page 34 and discuss key issues
- Discussion about how to thread the ball.
- Set up defence and forwards.
- Talk of the need to switch and how Arsenal use the switch to create space in the middle and thread the ball..

Players now all now know that the session is about attacking the thread zone.

Specific tactics– In grids 30 by 30 with a halfway line 3 v 3 or 4 v 4 cant cross halfway till ball played. AIM is to put foot on the ball on the end line. If you do this get 1 point if you do it in centre 3 points.
Relate to game-Then back to game situation (above) using goal and keeper. Set up thread zone with cones– 4 v 4 with 3 attacking players outside thread zone (spread across its width) switching ball looking for a thread and one player passively chasing ball so forcing a decision.

Defenders must stay in zone attackers can move in and out.

HOMEWORK= *watch a game and note down which category goals fall in to.*

Relating tactics to technique/ fitness/ small sided games and decision making

Technique– if we want to improve technique we need to have as many balls and as many touches as possible including a lot of work on your weaker foot– don't be scared of making a mistake. **KEY QUESTION– should many coaching sessions involve players having a ball each? Answer YES-** *You have got balls use them, don't let them get dusty*

The warm up
Always use a ball/balls *e.g. run* round pitch ball various tasks to perform with a ball. Then some technique work.

Fitness work
Always use balls and do it on the pitch. This means players are working on Technique as well as fitness. Mourinho shocked his employers when he first started by not doing runs in the forest etc but all ball work.

Small sided games
Coaches often play games of 8 v 8 (often with youngsters) when if they halved the pitch and split in to 4 teams of four the players would touch the ball twice as often and, in a round robin competition, enjoy the game more as it is competitive. Remember 4 players may also find it easier to organise themselves tactically– their shape/positions and the need to do this to succeed highlights the importance of tactics.

Drills to develop decision making– one of the best ways to develop this is by using 1 touch. It also reflects the game and moves the ball quickly– do a drill then chat.
At top level game 900-1000 actions will be executed of which,
* 350 passes with one touch,
* 150 with 2 touches
* The rest with more touches and after dribbling etc

If we look at Brazil in the 1994 World Cup fifty per cent of their passing prior to a goal was one touch. One touch moves the ball quickly, so exploiting space. One touch football is also a fantastic way of developing players and perhaps the best means to judge how good they are. It is the best judge of decision making as players into a one touch situation they have to do the following
* Get good body position– body Shape
* Good movement- Positional sense- have you found space and time are you available for an easy pass,Having passed the ball, find space.
* Have a good first touch
* Be aware of what is happening (where the space is) have a Picture in your mind
* Deliver a well weighted and directed ball to their own player which gives him/her the chance of making a good pass
* Need to be 2 footed and think left

Is there a case for in most sessions to do some 1 touch? It would seem YES. Far too often teams play too much two touch (2 touch is still a good drill) but the extra touch changes everything (the picture) and time is a lost as is the opportunity to use space and catch the defence out. If you use two touches instead of one it will take at least twice the time to get there.

Tactics are linked to technique. It you have a forward who holds the ball up well you devise tactics to deliver this ball. Conversely if you have players who for example do not drive the ball well you would not expect them to play direct switch so don't ask they to.

Set plays and problems with the modern game

The modern game has some fundamental flaws that will need addressing if it is to remain beautiful.
1. Set plays and defensive strategies are too dominant
2. Coaching needs improving and FA courses changing.
3. The size of the goals in youth football needs increasing to encourage more developmental attacking play.

SET PLAYS

An Interesting Article (Times) by Crystal Palace midfielder Aki Riihilahti demonstrates the negative side of the modern game. *Often you play 90 minutes of football but still one set piece is the difference between many sides. We lost to Middlesborough because of one corner kick. Apart from that there was nothing in the game. This is Modern football.*

This Saturday 7 out of 17 goals in the Premiership came from Corners, Free Kicks or Penalties. About 40% of all goals over the season. It is becoming very hard to score in open play. Too many things just have to go perfectly. Teams are well organised. Teams like Bolton and Everton build their game on set plays. Teams are bringing the big men up from longer range – this also breaks the flow of the game and brings it to their strengths. Complicated Free kicks are likely to go wrong. Crystal Palace have scored 18 out of 33 goals from set plays. You can score from a free kick by doing one of three things
1) Outsmart
2) Outmuscle- although you'd need 4 or 5 beasts to do this as most teams have enough strength by using forwards to defend set plays.
3) Concentration- if a team plays a mixture of zonal and man for man then it is more specific for some who their player is, failure to concentrate like the Juventus player did against Hyypia and it is a goal.

In open play there are many explanations as to who marks who but off set plays sometimes there is not. Set pieces are so important that we seek them. It encourages cheating to get them.

COACHING

Whilst coaching has developed in terms of how to improve a players technique it has not when it comes to applying this to the game tactically to get the best out of a team and its players. Soccer coaching is in need of a radical overhaul. The FA courses fail to address this as they do not give coaches an overall understanding of the game. The courses divide the game along simple but irrelevant lines, 6 a side up to 8 a side and then 11 a side.

They are knowledge based and do not promote genuine learning and understanding of how to apply what is taught to the 11 a side game. The courses make little if any attempt by teams to develop tactical awareness of players and to develop tactics themselves.

There is no theory, no drills that help explain the basics. It is assumed that players learn through 'doing' drills and there is no real attempt to develop understanding. From the outside it appears that the FA uses its courses to promote from within the game and to control knowledge and recently by imposing more rigid 'standards' to maintain their hold over the game.

There are some excellent coaches involved in soccer but many, many coaches do not have the necessary teaching skills to promote genuine learning. The FA needs to change its coaching course structure and genuinely try to develop understanding of the game not use its power to exclude and perpetuate its domination. Its an old boy network of the worst variety.

MAKE THE GOALS BIGGER

The small goals of youth football reward defensive play. In under 11 small sided games (and arguably at adult level) too often teams get away with prioritising negativity and defense. The goals are too small. The game needs to be changed to have goals that are bigger and will reward attacking sides with flair, creativity and technical ability.

What do we mean by tactics?

What does Michael Rosen mean?

Why is the best way to learn to move from the general to the specific?

What is meant by instinctive behaviour?

What does bravery mean in football?

What is the biggest difference between British teams and those abroad according to Alex Ferguson?

In a game what are the 3 things that can be happening to a team?

Why do you think people often blame lack of fitness for a team losing?

Do the teams with the best players always win? Give examples of this

Does coaching matter? Many in the professional game still think not but the top team's and coaches disprove this. Bobby Robson *I asked him (Bryan Robson) if he was going on any coaching courses, and he said he didn't need to because there was enough money at Middlesbrough to buy talented players (observer Dec 04)*
What are the problems with this attitude?

Test yourself/ Activity Sheet
Key Questions

Chalkboard/Classroom
You need to read the theory section before answering these questions

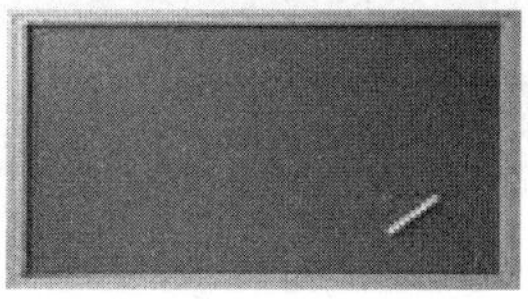

What are the four learning styles?
1
2
3
4

Which one are you?

What are the advantages of being able to learn from more than one style?

Fill in the % below

On average we remember
of what we read
of what we hear
of what we see
of what we say
of what we do
of what we see, hear, say and do

How could you try to ensure learning takes place?

What is meant by '*People need to understand in order to change their behaviour?*

At what age do you think children should start to learn the tactical side of the game? Explain this.

What is meant by 'people often learn by trial and error' and how does this make changing behaviour difficult?

Eriksson, Wenger, Mourinho– top managers who never played at the top level. Why is it that good players don't always make good coaches/managers? Relate this to the above.

New 'rules' for coaches and players

What you will learn

- The passing game needs to be played with confidence and without fear of failure

To play the passing game requires that coaches adopt a new set of coaching rules that are different from those of the past. The aim is to develop players individually and collectively. Outline these 'rules' to anyone associated with your soccer club. You might like to guess what the new rule is by covering the right hand column.

Traditional rule	New rule	The reason why
'If in doubt kick it out'- Safety first kick it out	Never kick the ball out	Around 50% of goals are scored from set plays - why give one away? At top level players don't simply kick the ball out. Remember, if you are under pressure, and they have 'numbers up', if you can get the ball forward then you will have numbers up. The very least you should do is try to win a throw in by kicking it against them.
'Never play across your own area'	Play across your own area when it is safe to do so	You have plenty of players at the back and the keeper as insurance. You can play across the area all season and not give the ball away.
'Don't do a short corner'	Short corners work if taken quickly	Statistics show quick short corners are very effective. An interesting coaching point is that, if you have 2 players who look as if they are going to take a short corner, the opposition will send a second man out. This means fewer defenders in the area so may be worth doing anyway.

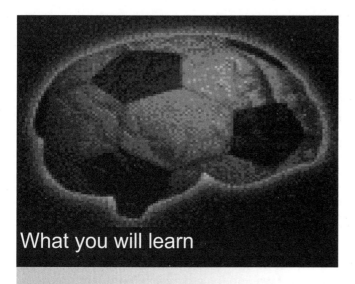

What you will learn

To understand how a team is tactically organised requires players and coaches to be aware of:
- key **spaces** and how to defend and attack them
- how to use ball travel time

Soccer is fast moving - space that was there last time you looked, could have gone. Other space may have been created elsewhere. It is about using space quickly when it is there, creating space by moving players out of it, or timing a run so that you are in space when the ball arrives and the defence can't close you down.

PART 2 - Space and Time The theory behind soccer

Space and Time

Theory

What you will learn

- Soccer can be viewed as a battle between two teams trying to use time and space to maximum effect. To understand these concepts, and how they affect all other factors in the game, is to understand football
- 'Having the run'
- 'Timing'

Coaches and players need to be aware of both the defensive and attacking use of time and space and timing if they are to really understand the tactical side of the game. If you look at every situation in soccer in terms of time and space you will be able to explain it. Defending is about denying time and space in critical areas. Attacking is about creating space and finding space, about moving the ball quickly, probing the oppositions defensive position, testing their concentration and waiting for a player to be out of position to pounce.

> If a ball can be moved quickly from end to end, and side to side, it makes life more difficult. (John Peacock, Insight, winter 2004).

A football game between two sides who are well organised, and whose players have reasonable technique and tactical awareness, will follow a similar pattern. The attacking team will spread out. The defending team will compress the area around the ball and avoid leaving an 'easy ball' for the opposition in to the space between the back four and keeper. This will leave space out wide away from the ball.

The object of the game is for the attacking team to get the ball into this space and move forward. This is often done by switching from one side of the pitch to the other and moving forward gradually as the 'easy ball' over the top is not available. The defending team will try to stop this. If the attacking side moves the ball quickly, players support each other, and have reasonable technique, they will get the ball to the opposition's 18 yard line.

They will then try to deliver the ball into the penalty area. Three things can then happen.
1. They lose possession as they run out of space, are tackled, or the ball is intercepted.
2. They are forced to go back as there is no realistic forward ball available and they wish to maintain possession.
3. They may score if the ball is delivered into the penalty area and a player arrives in a space at the same time as the ball and, usually, with one touch, shoots/heads at goal. This **timing** is critical. If the timing is right there is nothing the defence can do about it, no matter how good they are as individuals or well positioned they are in anticipation. This, if you like, is a **good goal**. You cannot blame the defence. It is important to be aware of the concept of a **good goal** in these circumstances as too often players are blamed for not being tight enough, or not concentrating - when in fact there was nothing they could have done.

Timing is the link between time and space. It determines when a player arrives in a space. There are two elements we need to understand about timing.
1. 'Having the run'.
2. It's a two way process between the person with the ball and the person making the run. Far too often players with the ball won't see the run or a player won't make the run or make it at the wrong time.

Lets firstly look at 'having the run'.

All players need to know its defensive role

All players need to know their attacking role

34

Having the run'

Imagine a players is running whilst another is static. As the player who is running draws level with the static player a ball is played a short distance in front of both of them. The static player has to react, which takes time, and get up to speed, which also takes time. In this instance the player running will get to a ball first no matter if he/she is slower overall.

A similar logic is followed when considering a player who is static with a ball traveling through the air on to their head. A player behind/to the side who 'has the run' can run and jump. His/Her momentum means he/she can jump slightly ahead of the other player and gain more height.

A player 'having the run' has the advantage even if they are not as good in the air as the static player.

The timing of the run/'having the run' into the space can lead to
*   a 'good goal'
*   winning a header
*   being in a position to cross
*   receive the ball in the 'hole'
*   simply gain possession
*   intercepting a pass.

Success in soccer is often measured in feet and inches. A foot in soccer is enough space to play a ball for a pass or score a goal! An inch in front of an opponent means winning the ball or a chance to pass or shoot. There are as many goals scored from defences not being in the correct position, often by feet and inches, than brilliance on behalf of the opposition.

Test out 'having the run' and make sure your players are aware of it. The drill on the next page highlights this. Ask players to be static and only react as the running player comes level. Note the distance before they are caught. This will vary according to the speed and reaction time of players. Ensure players are aware of how important feet and inches are.

One touch soccer best uses time and space and creates 'good goals'. Try to include one touch in all sessions. The drill on the next page highlights this.

To be successful when defending you need to slow the opposition down and make play predictable, or speed things up to make them make mistakes

A ball played in to space for a forward who is already moving will suc-

SPACE Practical Drill – 'Having the run' and 'one touch soccer'

'Having the run'- the players at edge of area are defending, the shaded players attacking. The drill emphasises that the attacking team can thread a ball through (a diagonal ball to straight run or straight ball to diagonal run THIS IS EXPLAINED LATER)

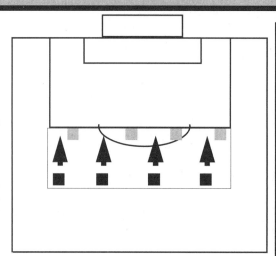

The 'thread zone' is just outside the area. A ball played into the area as a running forward arrives will lead to a chance on goal. The space is limited here with lots of defenders so the chances are it will be a one touch pass which defenders cannot stop.

DRILL The shaded players (attacking) run. When they get level with the white players they are allowed to run. Note how, even if slower, the player moving will have a few yards advantage. Ask if , with a ball played through, this could be an advantage.

Explain the term 'having the run'. This explains why pace is overestimated as an attribute and highlights the importance of timing.

Do the Drill above in 3's with a 1 player standing and a ball thrown to land on their head by another. The third player has a run up to head the ball. Who is successful ? 'Having the run' is an advantage.

Play one touch in half a pitch the object being to put a foot on the ball at the end. Then get the players with the ball to play as much one touch as possible. Ask the defenders which one they feel makes it harder for them.

One touch soccer is harder to defend against.

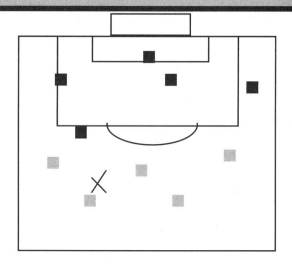

Timing - 'Working together'

The second part of timing is the need for both the person making the run and the person passing the ball to work together. For players to have good timing is, to a large extent, out of their hands. The player with the ball dictates when, or if, it is delivered into a space. Hence, players can have excellent timing, they are in the correct position and the ball should be passed to that space, but the player with the ball delays or chooses another option. To the un-educated eye the player's excellent run will not be seen. It is impossible to measure timing unlike size or speed, as most people only see the situation as the ball arrives. They do not note the timing of the run.

Another problem is that a player with the ball may not see or choose the ball to a player who has timed a run in to an effective space, for example in the 'hole' (space between midfield and attack), but plays a ball to someone in the same team. To many this ball was a good choice (it was not given away). However, it was not the best decision. A coach needs to stop a game and point out to players that they have missed a better option or they will not appreciate the movement of players. Good players may not get the ball in position where they can be effective. Good players without the ball can be seen as ineffective or 'drift out of the game'.

Good players make good decisions, they see the best pass. This can be greatly helped by developing the teams tactical awareness. Good players seem to have a knack of being in the right place at the right time. However, how many good players, particularly forwards who rely heavily on the service of their team, have 'under performed' at clubs simply due to their teammates lack of timing of passes or developing the teams tactics to ensure this player gets the ball? This is where tactics can help by encouraging players in possession to look for certain runs or space. Thierry Henry observes *I always know where my team mates are before I receive the ball. If you can win time on the pitch - have a look before you receive the ball, see things before* everyone else - that's the difference between an average player and a player who will illuminate the game. Roy Keane in his autobiography observes. A midfielders role often is about doing the right things and waiting for something to happen *We desperately needed a break.* **If you keep doing the right things**, *you'll get your break in every game.* It is also about **timing** *You need luck when timing a run into the box, but you do need to make the run. I did. Beck's cross was perfectly flighted. I just glanced it into the back of the net.*

Many good players (often smaller players) at all levels are wasted. **As a coach, timing and tactical awareness/decision making (again not easily tested) are reliable judges of good players alongside technique and concentration.** Players also need good concentration as soccer, unlike Basketball, Hockey, Rugby or American Football, is a game of few goals. Tactical or technical mistakes/one lapse in concentration can cost a game.

Assets such as size and speed are bottom of the list and not even of the same value. There is no evidence to support 'bigger is better ', in fact, in terms of passing/dribbling (passing makes up four out of five actions players do with the ball once they receive it) being smaller is an advantage (statistical analysis by Daniel Finkelstein) as well as the fact that, believe it or not, it takes longer for instructions from the brain to reach the feet of taller players (scientifically true).

A team needs a range of defensive and attacking tactics. In the absence of this, defensively teams are vulnerable and when attacking teams/coaches resort to playing long ball forward and choosing players based on speed and size. As we shall see the long ball game does not work if used as the only tactic.

No matter where you play it is important to work with players who are likely to regularly deliver the ball to you and to discuss movement and timing with them. As a general principle this is the basis for successful attacking play.

Having looked at space and timing we need now to be aware of two important times. Firstly, the **transition**. The ball changes hands approximately every fifteen seconds. The transition is when the team with the ball loses it to the opposition. It is important to use this time because a team is vulnerable. For the brief time that the attacking team is spread out the opposition can exploit the space this leaves.

Secondly, **ball travelling time**. The ball takes time to move between two points and be controlled. This time allows defenders to mark key spaces or double up on a wide player and move to the player receiving the ball as it is travelling.

These factors are also dependent on the pitch (a bad pitch may result in more mistakes or cause a team to lose possession: a small pitch means less space, so teams lose possession more often). A players technique will also effect how often they lose the ball. If they have poor control or passing technique, play will break down. The better a player's technique, the more likely he/she can operate successfully in less space as they need less time and space to control a ball, they will also be able to move the ball faster between spaces, for example, driving the ball from one side of the pitch to another denying the defending team as much 'ball travelling time'.

The next stage is to look at the key spaces and the time it takes to move a ball between spaces. This can be summarised as a team need to do things quickly and switch the ball quickly to find space before the opposition react.

There are four exceptions to this

1.   If you make a tactical decision to pass the ball around (usually at the back) with the intention of encouraging the opposition to push forward. This leaves space further forward which you will then exploit quickly. This tactic is called 'sucking a team in'.
2.   A team may also go backwards as there is no space to exploit further forward. They want to keep possession and move the ball around to find space.
3.   A team may wish to slow the tempo of the game down and tire out the opposition. By playing the ball around at the back they can do this. Another benefit is that to be compact when defending requires the whole team to be compact and, as a unit, move across from one side of the pitch to the other. The attacking side can remain spread out using the ball to move the opposition around. The opposition will get tired chasing the ball, they may commit too many players forward or not respond to a switch defensively and leave space to be exploited.
4.   If playing a team who are very good on the break (the transition) you may decide to be more measured/slower when attacking so as to keep a more defensive shape when the ball is lost.

Bearing the 4 points above in mind it is however true to say that a team is defensively more vulnerable art the time they lose the ball. It is usually important to use this time quickly.

Glen Hoddle, when England manager, tried to get his team to have a shot on the opposition's goal within 10 seconds of regaining possession. This is consistent with the quote from Eriksson below.

This, however, should not be used to justify a long ball game. It is the speed that the ball moves at that is most important, one touch soccer, intelligent passing, often short ,and movement, those are the components that matter, not resorting to a long ball.

The need for speed is also highlighted by Eriksson

By the time you have made four passes there are eight or nine men back behind the ball every time. Against Sweden, if you want 15 seconds to play the ball anywhere you have to beat eight players. The Guardian, 12th November, 2001.

As has been mentioned earlier, teams have different ways of attacking/different strengths. This is reflected in how they defend.

 Attacking sides with players who run with the ball well like an open game with plenty of space. This point is highlighted in a game played between Man City and Bolton (October 18th, 2003) . Sam Allardyce (The Bolton Manager) is quoted (Observer):

We have a difficult problem understanding what's needed in the premiership when we go a goal behind. What's needed is a more solid defensive unit to make sure you don't concede another goal. Not for the first time our players decided they would go and chase and play open attractive football which meant City, whose strength is in attacking, found more space. Hence you get that result (Bolton lost 6-2).

To be successful when defending: you need to slow the opposition down and make play predictable or speed things up to make them make mistakes. You can also be very difficult to beat if you don't commit players forward and allow the opposition to exploit space on the transition. Tottenham early in 2004 adopted this tactic. (Jaques Santini as manager).

Successful teams nearly always have the best defences without always scoring the most goals. The reason: in soccer, going a goal down is very hard to come back from. The tactics of the two teams change. Allardyce (above) is pointing out that his team were not able tactically to push forward. They needed to be patient ... Mourinho (Champions League, winning coach of Porto) claims that a team needs to go through its tactical response to a number of things including going a goal down. The failure to discuss this before the game meant Allardyce's team did not adopt the correct tactics. They chose the wrong tactics and it cost them the game.

 There is another key issue pointed out by Alex Fergusson, that is, perhaps, the most common fault of defences in football. Giving too much space between the back four and the keeper (danger zone). This provides the opposition with the easy attacking tactic of playing the ball into this space.

The pace of Andreir Kancheski and Ryan Giggs on the wings were a threat to anybody playing around the halfway line. The result was that the opposition started to drop back to the edge of their box so they wouldn't get caught by the speed of our wingers .

As we shall see, this area, the Danger Zone, needs to be guarded carefully. When the opposition start to defend deeper to deny this space Ferguson had to adapt his tactics and the players he used.

That was why I decided to buy Andy Cole. We needed razor sharpness in the box.

Soccer is a tactical battle between two teams trying to best use time, space, and timing.

We are now aware of time, space and timing. Now we need to look in more detail at Space and Time.

We will start with looking at how important the correct position is, then we will look at how important timing is.

Finally, before going on to look at three key spaces, we will look at how teams try to control the 'tempo' of a game – the speed it is played at.

What you will learn

Theory

- When talking about a players position, it is often a case that a yard in the wrong direction can lead to a goal

The space players occupy is critical. As we shall see, players need to be in a particular position and the team needs a certain shape to react to the position of the ball. Whilst sometimes players only need to be approximately in a certain space often and, in particular, when defending in your own half and near the penalty area players need to be in exactly the right position. It comes down to yards and inches. Why? Well, if the opposition can thread a ball through, a defence is determined by a player near to the ball stopping the pass and a player at the back being able to block it. A yard to either side and a goal can result. In addition, players need to be near enough to team mates to cover them if they are beaten by a dribble, lose a challenge or header. The fraction of a second it takes to make up this space is enough for the opposition player to thread a ball to a player to score or shoot themselves. To be in the right position in a game which is determined by the odd goal requires great concentration for the whole game. Teams will probe the opposition switching the ball; someone who switches off will leave sometimes a tiny gap. This can lead to losing a goal.

A teams tactics determine its shape. The players need to know this. As teams are always changing, when players are injured/suspended/lose form, it is essential to ensure that those playing tweak their position. A coach/manager can do this during a game. Individual players will make slight errors in where they are positioned. A coach may point out to two players in the same position that one is two yards too far forward, another two yards too wide. Know your players. Let them know where they should be and at half time why.

When players are tired they either do not have the fitness to be in the correct position or they lose concentration. This is when goals are conceded. Many teams lose games in the last few minutes. Often the team defending will give the ball away as the opposition becomes more desperate.

Defending is more tiring than attacking. Why? When a team is defending they need to be compact (when attacking they are spread out) as the ball may be switched from one side of the pitch to another. The whole of the defending team therefore has to move over. Wider players move further. The attacking team increases the pressure and switches constantly, the defending team players are constantly moving. The result - they get tired. They are not in the correct space.

As defenders get tired, instead of standing up and keeping their position they will slide in. Celtic lost a goal in the ninetieth minute away to Milan (Champions League 2004) as a result of a lot of pressure led ultimately to a player sliding in. Milan passed round him, moved forward unchallenged into the space he should have occupied and a goal was scored. The blame often is apportioned to the defender nearest to the player that scored. This is not where a good coach would look on this occasion (see timing and the concept of a good goal).

Defenders need to concentrate for over 90 minutes. often they need to be in exactly the right position down to feet and inches

Attackers probe teams and switch the ball. They are looking for space. The more attacking a team does the more running the opposition so the more chance they will tire and make a mistake

Controlling the tempo of a game

What do we mean controlling by tempo? Controlling the speed the ball is moved around at and choosing the timing of an attack. A team may be forced to retreat but they still have control of the ball and therefore can regain control of the tempo. To control the tempo a team must be able to keep the ball when they have it and slow the game down. How does a team do this? A team can only keep possession, and have the option of slowing the tempo, if they are able to play the ball around at the back. This is where the space is.

Whilst teams can maintain possession further forward, it is more likely to break down because of the increased pressure on the player with the ball. They may have the ball but they do not fully control the tempo. They need to go back when under pressure to maintain control.

Without this ability a team may be able to raise the tempo, use one touch passing when they have the ball or pressure the opposition when they don't. But they will not be able to slow the game down (lower the tempo) as they do not control the ball. As mentioned above, you have more influence over tempo when you have the ball.

The tactic of playing the ball around at the back to 'suck' the opposition in and create space further forward, or switching the ball at the back to find space is discussed elsewhere. Both of these tactics may form part of a team controlling the tempo as they keep possession. However, playing the ball around at the back also needs to be viewed as a means of slowing a game down. The team controls time, it allows the players with the ball to look for free players. They can play with their head up so seeing space and runs; it tires the opposition (teams work harder when they are defending).

Manchester United have not lost a Premiership game having scored first since November 2001 (this section was written in September 2004). Part of this success, and their success in Europe, is down to their ability to keep possession and hence control tempo.

The Euro Championship winning team Greece were excellent at keeping the ball. They maintained possession and slowed the tempo down by winning free kicks, throw-ins, etc. as well as playing around at the back. If a team controls the tempo they can slow the game down and wait for a chance to exploit space quickly.

Teams need to practice keeping possession at the back. The keeper needs to be used alongside often a centre midfield player who drops back to bounce the ball (see section on bouncing the ball) and link play.

A good passing and moving side will prefer a high tempo game. Lesser teams often rely heavily on set plays and breaking up the momentum, slowing the tempo of a game.

The defence need to be able to play the ball around

Controlling the speed and space attacked often relies on the ball going back

Describe the pattern of a game between 2 good sides. In terms of time and space. Areas to consider

♦   What the defending team try to do (in terms of space and time),

♦   What the attacking team try to do (in terms of space and time)

♦   When and where space runs out

♦   How teams find space

♦   How teams deny space

As a general attacking rule do you do things quickly or slowly? Explain this.

There is an exception to the above. What is it, and Why?

What is it called when a team regains possession?

How many players do you think a team who prioritise defence (such as Sweden) get behind the ball after 15 seconds?

How soon after re-gaining possession did Glen Hoddle (former England Coach) try to get a shot on goal? Why is this?

What danger does trying to push players forward when you are a goal down hold (especially with plenty of time left)?

What is meant by a 'good goal'?

What is the link between Time and Space?

What is meant by 'having the run'?

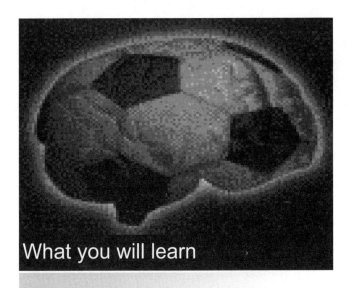

What you will learn

The key space. *The scoring zone*

A key space. *The danger zone*

A key space. *The thread zone*

Space - three key spaces

1. **Scoring zone**
2. **Thread zone**
3. **Danger zone**

What you will learn

◆   Players need to be aware of the two spaces. This affects where they position themselves throughout the game

Theory

Soccer is similar to basketball in the way that the area where a team can score is small . The key defensive point is to prioritise this space (the scoring zone) and space that allows a free run to this space (the danger zone) or a ball to be threaded in to this space (the thread zone) or a cross in to this space (players with the ball in wide areas in dangerous crossing positions need to be marked by 2 players). You can defensively prioritise these spaces because you can use the time it takes the ball to travel between players to re-position. Coaches and players must be aware of the 3 key spaces and ball travelling time if they are to understand the game.

*   The scoring zone

The scoring zone is the area within the penalty area where an attacker who has a free shot is likely to score, which is roughly the width of the six yard box to the edge of the area (see drill 2). To score a goal a team has a number of options

1. release a player centrally in the danger zone (see below) with a free run – a simple tactic that good defences don't allow by defending deep enough to deny this ball,
2. go wide and get a cross in - Manchester United use this tactic extensively (also see section on where crossing and the Shearer tactic).
3. A team may thread the ball through to a player running on- Arsenal use this tactic extensively (see below).
4. A set play allows a free delivery in to the scoring zone and as a team can work on 'timing' and 'having the run' they have an increased chance of scoring don't give them away defensively and work on them offensively.

As stated earlier, good teams can attack in a number of ways, it is not essential to adopt all tactics but clearly it helps to have a variety.

Shots that are scored from %

Inside the 6 yard box	35%
Inside the 18 yard box	13%
Outside the box	4%

*   The danger zone

The danger zone is the ever-changing space between the back 4 and the penalty area. In soccer the wide areas are less important.

*   The thread zone

If we imagine a 5/10 yard extension to the penalty area that runs its length, we have a space in which good teams try to get a player, usually facing forwards, to be in a position to thread a ball through to a member of their team or shoot. If we watch top level games, we find teams try to play one touch soccer in this area (due to the lack of space) and create a 'threading opportunity'. Obviously if a shot is on then this should be taken but, often it is not so a pass is the option taken. The defence are trying to avoid dropping back into the scoring zone in order to protect the space and keeper but have dropped back to this space to avoid the easy ball in to the danger zone. This point is where the defence makes   its stand.
The attackers in this area have the advantage of 'having the run' (see later). The other advantage of playing the ball around in this area is that you may get a free Kick which is very likely to lead to a goal. Playing through the middle using the thread zone can be frustrating as you may lose possession and be vulnerable on the break. A defending team uses ball travelling time to keep as many players in the key spaces as possible. A team leaves players in wide positions and is compact and central. Ball travelling time is emphasised and linked to the key spaces in later drills. Ball travelling time can be used by a player (usually a midfielder) to both attack and defend throughout a game.

Attacking – Use the space out wide to move the ball forward then into the scoring zone

Defensive - priority should be given to central areas. It is the same principle as the basketball key - teams fall back and defend the centre

A team also needs to be aware of the danger of crosses into the scoring zone (thirty per cent of goals come from crosses).

It is important to stop crosses from the by-line area here into the scoring zone as a cross from here has the effect of freeing up a lot of space for attackers (they are onside). This is especially true if the opposition has strong players in the air. *Brian Clough used to say that if you stop the cross you stop the goal* (**Ron Atkinson, Monday October 20th, 2003, The Guardian**). Two players should always defend wide players in this area-the full back and wide midfielder. This point is emphasised later.

Whilst all this may seem obvious, if a team is not clear about them, and their importance, it will not react in the correct way to different situations. Players will be in less important spaces or concentrate on players who can do little harm at the expense of those in dangerous positions. How often in a game do you hear coaches or players shouting 'get close to your man'? Often this man is in a wide area and harmless as the player can use ball travelling time to close them down if they receive the ball. A good response is 'I am guarding the scoring zone and have ball travelling time to close this player down'. I have never heard this response used. YET!

Another common fault I often hear is 'it was your man that scored/had a free run'. Defenders do not have 'a man', they have whichever player is in their space.

Marking key space is the basis of zonal defence (advanced marking), which we will look at later.

It is essential your team is aware of key spaces. **Use the simple drills on the next pages to highlight these spaces.**

Key Coaching Points

THERE ARE THREE KEY SPACES – THE SCORING ZONE, DANGER ZONE AND THREAD ZONE, AS WELL AS AN AREA WHERE TEAMS NEED TO STOP CROSSES INTO THE SCORING ZONE. TEAMS SHOULD 'DOUBLE UP' ON PLAYERS HERE

BALL TRAVELLING TIME IS USED TO ALLOW PROTECTION OF THESE KEY AREAS. WIDE PLAYERS ON THE SIDE FURTHEST AWAY FROM THE BALL COME CENTRAL TO PROVIDE COVER

DEFENSIVE SIDES TRY TO KEEP ATTACKERS OUT OF THE SCORING ZONE (BY USING OFFSIDE)TO PROTECT THE SPACE FOR THE KEEPER AND MAKE SCORING OFF A HEADER OR SHOT HARDER. AS THE DEFENCE HOLDS ITS LINE AT THE EDGE OF THE AREA– THEY MUST DROP BACK AS A UNIT AS THE BALL IS PLAYED

SPACE Practical Drill – the danger zone and scoring zone

Drill– How many goals (out of 20) will players shooting from position 1 score?

How many goals will a player shooting from position 2 score? TRY this as a team

How many times will a player score running from position 3 and position 4. If given, say, 5 seconds? Position 5 defenders and 3/4 attackers in the zone below on the edge of the area. Discuss the type of ball that will lead to a goal. Perhaps the best description is to 'thread' the ball through (this is explained on the next page). What can we learn from this? Devise a name for the 3 zones highlighted x (the scoring zone) and y The (thread zone) and z (danger zone)

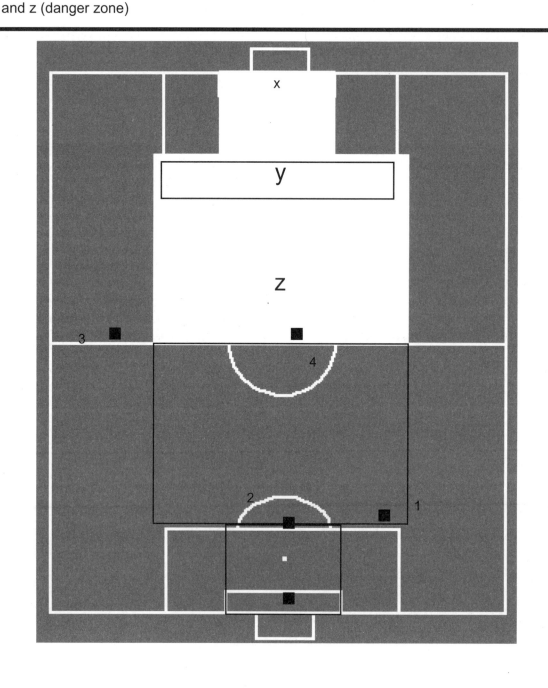

SPACE Practical Drill – Attacking using the thread zone

DRILL Play the ball between the three players outside the thread zone.

They look to play a pass into the thread zone and the player in there tries to thread the ball through or set up a shot in the scoring zone.

Offside is always played. Try to score. Discuss how players feel and the movement to best exploit this space. The passing in the thread zone will be usually be one touch it can be lofted over defenders. A defender harrying the 3 players outside the zone can be introduced and the attacking players in the thread zone can move in and out of the area the defenders cannot.

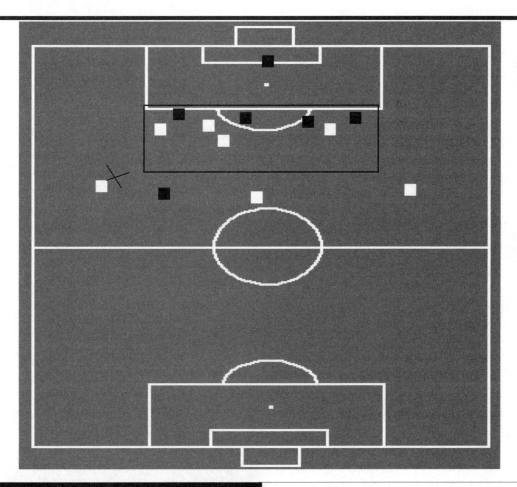

Key coaching tips– there is little space and time, one touch having 'the run' and timing are all critical as is the angle the ball is 'threaded at' SEE various runs in attacking section

The 'thread zone' is just outside the area. A ball played in to the area as a running forward arrives will lead to a chance on goal. The space is limited here with lots of defenders so the chances are it will be a one touch pass which defenders cannot stop. Often the ball will be played back out of the thread zone.

TIME Practical Drill - ball travelling time related to the 3 key spaces

DRILL– Set up the situation below. Ask players to count in their head **how long it takes the ball to get from one side to the other** and be brought under control. **The answer is between 3 and 4 seconds. This will obviously vary with pitches and the technique of the player receiving the ball.**

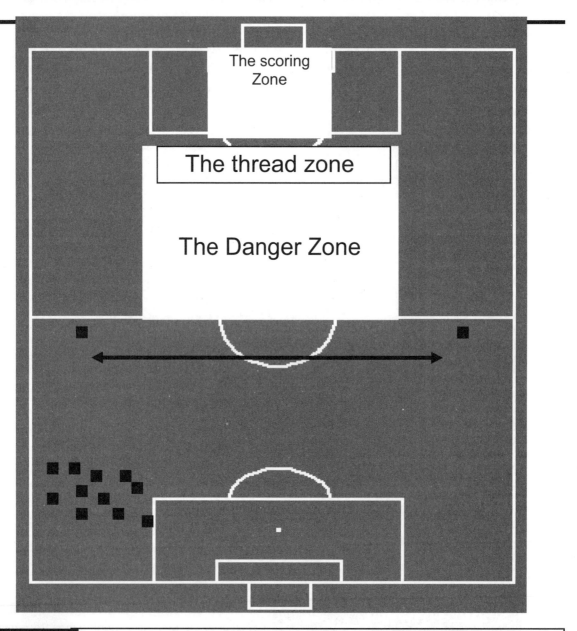

The scoring Zone

The thread zone

The Danger Zone

Key coaching tips	Use the ball travelling time to concentrate on key spaces and cover other players. How well the opposition uses ball travelling time depends on size of pitch, area the ball has to travel, how many players are involved in moving the ball, how many touches they have, wind, ball trajectory, first touch of the player receiving it, pace of the player receiving it, pace of the defender.

Defending around the scoring zone/penalty area

Theory

Offside is used to deny the opposition space and to move them out of spaces such as the scoring zone. This is best emphasised by the drill on the next page. The theory underlining defending around the scoring zone is based on 2 basic assumptions.

If defenders and attackers are directly around the keeper s/he will have many players in between them and the ball.

In the top example below we see the defence defending on the 6 yard box. Set this up and ask 2 questions:
1) How does the keeper feel?
Answer: restricted in going for the ball by own players and the opposition.

2) If an attacker wins the ball has s/he got a good chance of scoring?
Answer: yes.

In the bottom example we see the defence defending on the 18 yard box. Set this up and ask the same 2 questions:
1) How does the keeper feel?
Answer: S/he has space to get to the ball unhindered.

2) If an attacker wins the ball has he/she a good chance of scoring?
Answer: no.

It is well worth doing the second drill and pointing out that, as soon as the ball is played, the defending team <u>all</u> have to fill the space (drop back a few yards so that they can challenge for the ball). Too often players don't do this.

The top example gives the attackers (white) more of a chance to score.

The clear message is if you are in your own penalty area, get to the 18 yard box as soon as possible but be ready to drop back as a unit as the ball is played.

The change in the offside law means defenders now have to be extra vigilant for deep lying players who time their run, often relying on a team mate who is clearly offside as a distraction.

Liverpool's use of offside in the 2005 Champions League was of a trap. The tactic was very targeted only used when it was obvious who the ball was going to and the nearest defending player would be close enough to track back if the linesman missed it.

Offside should be focussed and defensive players ready to cover.

Get the attackers away from the goal. Fill the space if the ball is played in between you and the keeper

Attackers like defenders who can be drawn into the penalty area. It opens up space near the goal and increases chances of scoring

SPACE Practical Drill– Protecting the scoring zone

SET UP THE POSITION AT THE TOP OF THE PITCH IN THE TOP EXAMPLE BELOW
we see the defence defending on the 6 yard box. The ball is in the position shown.
Ask 2 questions:
1.   How does the keeper feel?
Answer: restricted in going for the ball by own players and opposition.
1.   If an attacker wins the ball has s/he a good chance of scoring?
Answer: yes.
SET UP THE POSITION AT THE TOP OF THE PITCH IN THE BOTTOM EXAMPLE
BELOW Here we see the defence defending on the 18 yard box. Ask the same 2
questions:
1) How does the keeper feel?
 Answer: S/he has space to get to the ball unhindered
2)   If an attacker wins the ball has she/he a good chance of scoring?
Answer: no.

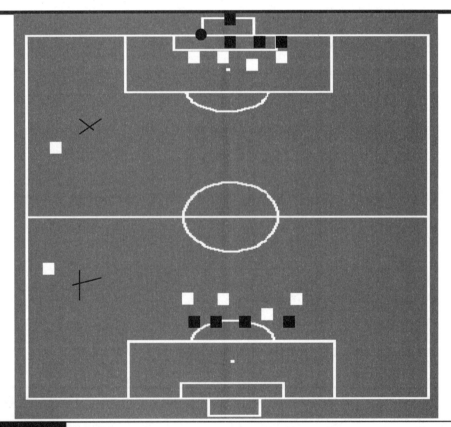

Key coaching tips use ball travelling time to create space for the keeper	Coaching advice to players **Defending-** Get the opposition out of the scoring zone as soon as you can. Whilst the movement from the edge of the area out may be a walk, the movement to the edge of **their** area must be quick. If the ball is delivered back into the space between keeper and defence, then the defence must react and fill this space in advance of the attack.
	The top example gives the attackers (white) more of a chance to score.

Practical Drill – protecting the scoring zone –
going deep and central, pushing up, dropping back to fill the space

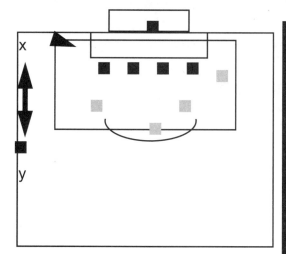

DRILL 1: a ball played from (y) to (x) who crosses. The defence has left the players and **zonaly defends deep and central**. They react using ball travelling time if the ball arrives at a shaded player from the cross.

DRILL 2: even with a free shot, because the defence is covering the goal, it is very difficult to score. TRY THIS.

DRILL 3: play the ball from (x) to (y) the defence pushes out as a unit to 18 yard line. GOOD PRACTICE.

DRILL 4: (y) is about to cross the ball. The defence drops back as one. This is worth practice as often defending teams do not drop back as a unit to **'fill the space'** but drop back when the ball is played, or concentrate too much on players and not the key space.

The flat midfield shape dictates protection around the scoring zone.

A flat midfield shape like this with two players trying to stop the cross.

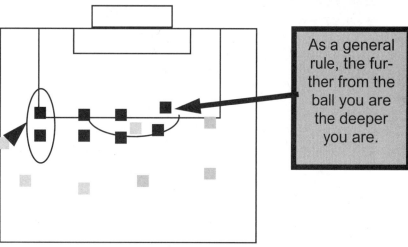

As a general rule, the further from the ball you are the deeper you are.

The 'roaming diamond' in midfield compresses the space around the ball better, but is more vulnerable to a switch – although better equipped to stop the switch as two players are still trying to stop the cross.

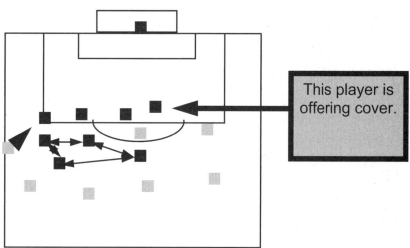

This player is offering cover.

SPACE Practical Drill – Defending the scoring zone 'mark space not players'

SET UP THE POSITION BELOW Get the player with the ball to run from the edge of the area and the defence to drop back in this shape and defend it. Try with man for man. The most effective defensive shape/space to cover is the one below. Get players to observe the chances of the circled player of scoring Try this with the 4 or even 3 defenders reacting as the ball is crossed. See how many goals are scored. There will not be many.

If a **defence is compact, level, deep and central they are hard to beat.**

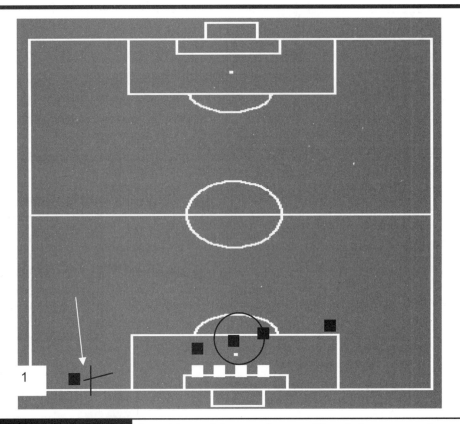

Key coaching Tip– mark the key space it makes it very hard to score. Use the ball travelling time to close down players and deny them space

Coaching advice to players. The defence now faces a ball delivered in from a good wide crossing position. The defence has reacted in a similar way to the previous drill they have dropped back and formed a unit centrally in front of the goal. They have adopted a position that the attackers would want in advance of them. They are advance marking. As the ball is played across they can move out to challenge. If you watch games on TV you will see the defensive players are compact, deep level and central. Many times in a game the opposition may cross into the area but they will find it very hard to score.

The Offside line
protects the danger zone

What you will learn

- The offside line is critical in determining how much time and space is available. Who calls offside?
- The place you cannot afford a mistake is centrally - in the danger and scoring zone.
- One of the centre halves should determine the offside line.
- To look at a game and decide if a team is playing an intelligent offside line.
- That playing a high line is too risky.

Both time and space are affected by the use of offside and the tactical decision of how high up the pitch to begin defending - hence how much space is available.

Offside has been used as a highly organised trap to catch players off time and time again (the Arsenal back 4 of Adams, Bould, Winterburn, Dixon in the 1990s). With changes in the rules (level is onside, players coming back are onside) teams now use it as a way of moving the opposition away from their goal when they push forward. This is if you like an honest game, not relying on trapping players as an end in itself. The biggest single concern about offside is that if you play a line too far forward, and leave space in the danger zone and get it wrong, the opposition may score.

A goal in football is hard to get back. Therefore many factors have to be considered when deciding how far forward the offside line is.

- Are you leaving an easy ball for the opposition into the danger zone? If you are, you are too far up.
- The Pitch size, which is linked to the point above
- Conditions (wind etc),
- If the opposition has pace up front and so would like space in the danger zone to exploit,
- How good your opposition are (see later). The better they are the deeper you defend.
- How good/fast your keeper is as a sweeper.
- If your covering player is being consistently seen and the space used by the opposition. The forwards are clever.

It is essential that the whole team reacts as the ball is played as effectively the opposition become onside. The team needs to drop off and cover team mates and space. If one of the defending team is sweeping/covering, and the opposition move in to the space, s/he simply steps up to catch them offside, dropping again when they are not looking.

If the opposition is successful in delivering balls in behind our defence to forwards, the line is too far up. It is better to be too far back than too far forward. It is also very dangerous to play offside if the opposition player with the ball has lots of time to wait and pick a pass. So if the ball is cleared into a wide position, or up to the opposition's back four, be careful how far you push up. In central areas where you can pressure the ball more easily and deny time, you can push up in more safely. When your own team has a corner the defence will be at the half way line. This leaves a lot of space in between them and the keeper (danger zone) . If the opposition's keeper can deliver a ball into this space then you could concede. The key point is **be aware of the danger and drop back to deal with it**. On the next practical drill you will see a drill that will emphasize the danger of defending too high up the pitch.

Where the defence draws the offside line is one of the hardest tactical decisions to make

Attackers with pace (most teams have one) love playing teams who push up too far and leave space for them to run into. They may get caught offside sometimes, but when they beat the trap they will score.

Practical Drill - offside used to protect the danger zone

If we look at the offside line being held by the defence we can see that they are not covering the danger zone. The player with the ball has a straight forward ball into this area for the two forwards to run onto. If the opposition can play a ball easily into the danger zone behind the defence, the defence is too far up.

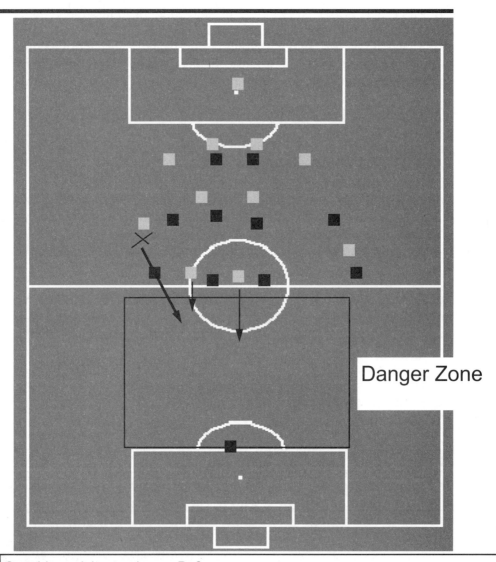

Danger Zone

Coaching advice to players **Defence -**
Protect the danger zone. Do not give the opposition a free run into it. This is especially true if they have pace. The keeper above is in a good sweeping position but there is still plenty of space for the opposition to play the ball into. Houllier noted of the Middlesboro defence against Liverpool with pacey Michael Owen (Observer 23rd Nov 2003) *'Middlesboro are difficult to beat. They retreat quickly'.* In other words, they drop back so denying space behind them for players like Owen to run onto.

Attack – if they drop deep, switch and be patient.

The bowl of the shape of the back 4 -offside

The bowl shape that defenders tend to adopt is explained by the shaded back 4 below. It took me some time to work out why defences like this shape. There are 2 reasons

1)   It allows deep cover centrally.

2)   It allows the centre halves to make the offside decision and trap the opposition forwards. They simply step up in line with the full backs– see arrows. This tactic relies on 2 not 4 players moving so is easier and safer to employ.

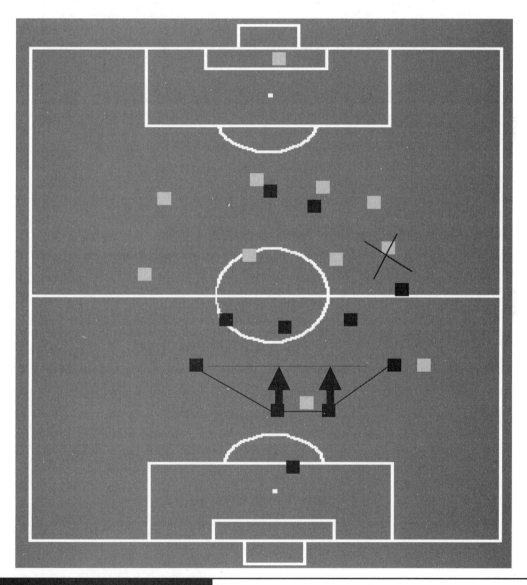

The bowl shape become flatter nearer the scoring zone but when this far up the field it is an effective tactic.

Test your knowledge

Theory

On the next 8 pages are a set of defensive problems. Try and work them out then check how you did on the next page.

SPACE Practical Drill – protecting the danger zone using a back 3

SET UP THE POSITION BELOW a drop ball up the centre from the
Keeper to the centre forward.
 As the ball arrives draw/predict the position of the shaded back 3

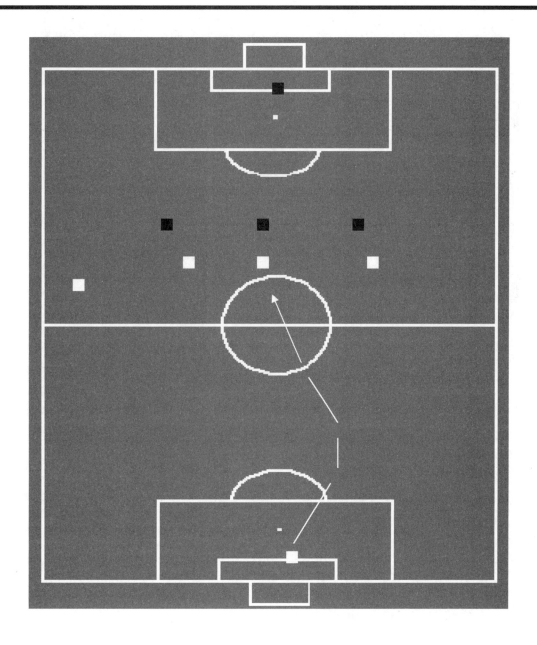

ANSWER Practical Drill – protecting the danger zone– providing cover

This is the correct position. It provides cover and marks the key space.

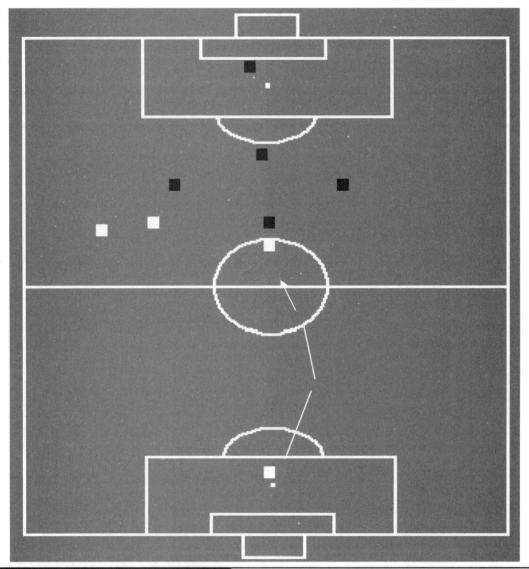

Key coaching tips– its about space not players, if the ball is played to the wide players the defence can adapt the attacking team will not get a good goal scoring opportunity as the space is marked

Coaching advice to players **Defending-** It's about spaces, not players. This will be further explained later. The concept is to be in the space in advance of the forwards .and offer support to each other whilst covering the danger zone. The defence is happy to deal with this ball because it is predictable. They would much rather deal with this than have the point of attack constantly switched. This requires a great deal more concentration and teamwork.

SPACE Practical Drill 20 – protecting the danger zone using a back 3

SET UP THE POSITION BELOW a drop ball up the centre from the Keeper to the centre forward.

As the ball arrives draw/predict the position of the shaded back 3

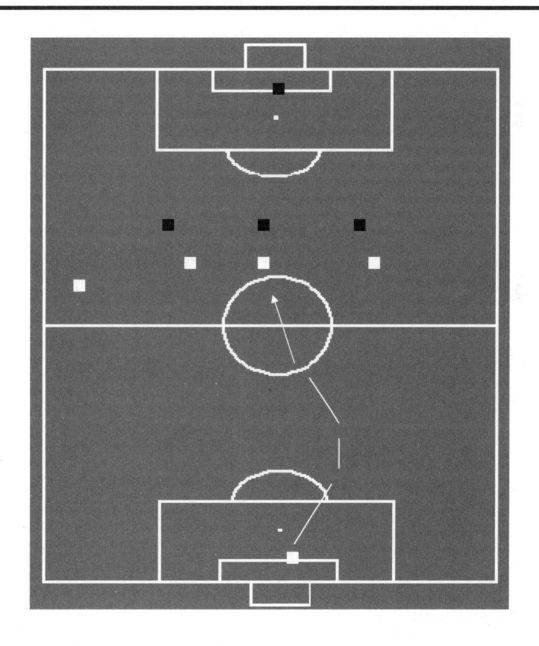

ANSWER Practical Drill 20 —protecting the danger zone using a back 3

This is the correct shape

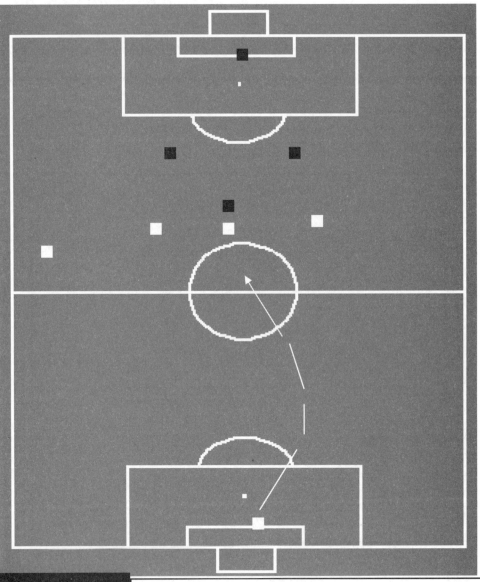

Key coaching Tips– the 3 players have moved in to a position to cover the space

Coaching advice to players–

Defending- The priority is the scoring zone. Keep central and provide cover. It is necessary to buy time for the rest of your team to re-group. The reason there are 3 at the back is a full back may have pushed up. He/she will return and a back 4 diamond shape be formed.

SPACE Practical Drill - protecting the danger zone around the area

SET UP THE POSITION BELOW a drop ball that is going to land on the wide players head or at their feet

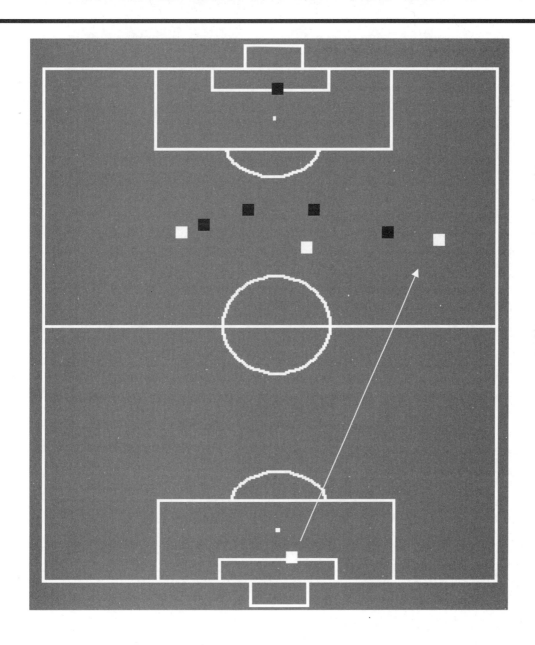

ANSWER Practical Drill —protecting the danger zone around the area

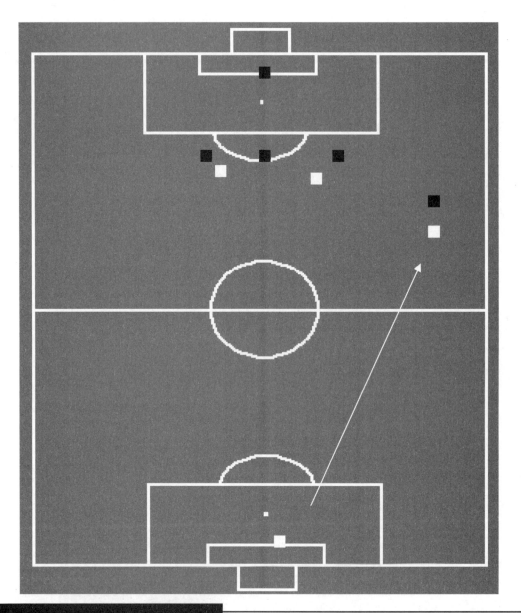

Key coaching tips– the defence has moved to a position that denies any space between back 3/4 and scoring zone for a player to exploit

Coaching advice to players–

Defensive- protecting the central area is the priority. One player has gone to challenge, all the other three have moved into position to deal with a ball played on centrally if the opposition player wins it. The wide defender wants help from the midfielder on that side.

SPACE Practical Drill —protecting the danger zone around the area

SET UP THE POSITION BELOW a ball played to a forward who has dropped off the defence into space often called the hole.

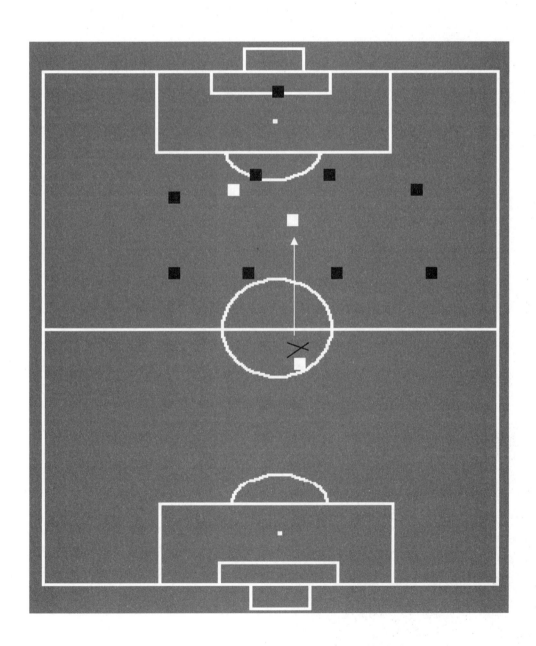

ANSWER - Practical Drill - protecting the danger zone when a player moves into the hole

DRILL a ball played to a forward who has dropped off the defence in to space often called the hole.

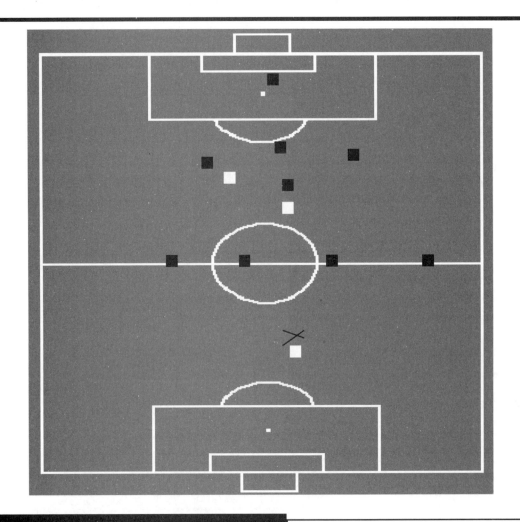

Key coaching tips– the defence cant allow a player to turn with the ball and pick a pass in to the scoring zone, shoot or dribble. Reluctantly a player moves forward and the other 3 close ranks

Coaching advice to players–

Defensive– A forward has dropped off the defence in to what is known as the 'hole' between defence and midfield. It is in a dangerous central position with an easy ball to play to the player. The defence needs to adapt. One of the centre halves goes to the player the rest of the back four become a compact three.

How the ball being crossed affects the two key zones/spaces

Theory

We have discussed so far the need to prioritise central areas when defending. It is certainly true that a ball crossed centrally from the danger zone should not cause defensive problems. However, a cross from the 18 yard box into the scoring zone can lead to a goal.

Firstly, lets look at the facts about crossing.

- **Around one third of all goals come from crosses.**

- The wider the area the ball is crossed from the less the chance of scoring. Between the 6 yard box and just outside the penalty area is the most effective place to cross from.

- The game is changing as technically better players at top level are attacking more centrally where there is less space.

Crosses to the middle, as opposed to far post, are the most effective (the near post is the least effective) and attacking players need to make contact with the ball first.

If we apply the above in terms of time and space we can conclude that, if the ball is crossed from the by-line, then everyone is onside and there is plenty of space. The ball, unlike a cross from further back, is not going towards the keeper. The extra space in the scoring zone means that players can get ahead of defenders, or the cross can be pulled back.

If an opposition player has the ball level with the penalty area/scoring zone two players, the full back and wide midfielder, should stop them crossing or taking on one player.

Do not leave full backs isolated (1 v 1) when the ball is in this area.

Defenders need to decide if the area the ball is in merits leaving the centre

Simply delivering the ball into the centre will not work as a tactic

Practical Drill - the impact of crossing

DRILL 1 – cross the ball with a couple of attackers trying to score from the three positions 1, 2 and 3. Players run in and finish the crosses

What conclusions can you draw?

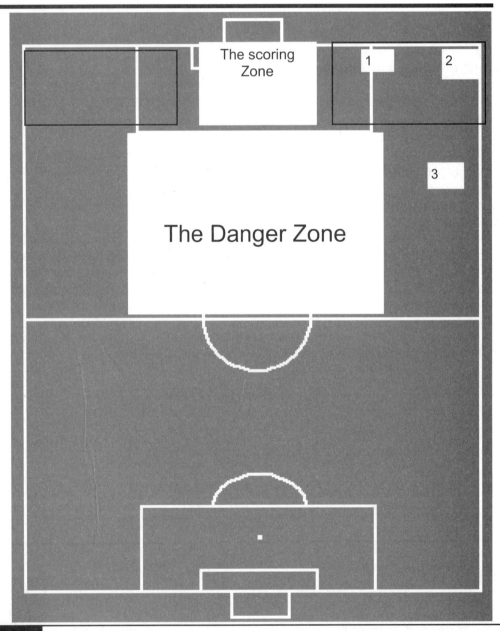

Key coaching tips Stop crosses from 1, 2 here as they are very dangerous. In the boxed area 2 defending players should always mark wide players to prevent crossing. The is called 2 up (see later). Statistics show that 1 is the most effective place to cross from. Crosses from around 3 are not likely to lead to a goal. However, they can form the basis for another tactic (see next page), Players in this area should be marked by two defenders using ball travelling time to close other opposition players in the area.

SPACE Practical Drill *attacking the Scoring zone The Shearer way*

Drill– Alan Shearer uses his ability in the air to exploit a deep cross from position 1 or 2 he then heads the ball back into the scoring zone or tries to score. The further forward the ball is delivered and the wider the better for the forward as it is easier to direct towards the scoring zone or goal. Try crosses from this position and work on staying onside, delivery, how to exploit the knockdown.

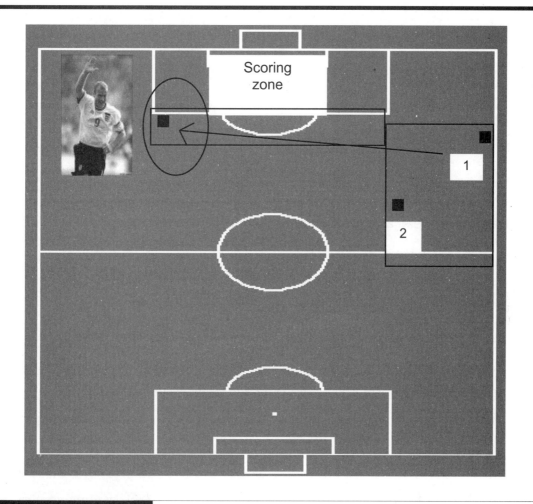

Key coaching tips– the delivery of the cross need to be practiced as does having players ready to exploit the header in to the scoring zone.

Shearer has 2 advantages by utilising this ball. Firstly he 'has the run' on the defender who may be stationary holding an offside line. Secondly, the player he is likely to be against will be a full back who as a general rule are not as good in the air as a centre half. In an ideal situation the ball is delivered into the space between defence and keeper. This is, however, very hard to do. The chances of scoring direct are not good unless the ball is delivered here and even then the angle makes it easier for a keeper to save.

Name the 3 key zones and explain why they have their name.

Explain how players and teams use ball travelling time.

Why do defenders defend tonally, deep and central in the scoring zone?

Explain the difference between a flat midfield and diamond defensively.

The offside line is used to protect the keeper. How and Why?

The offside line between the edge of the penalty area and halfway line is based on what?

Where are the most effective places to cross from and too?

What is the defensive response to this?

Explain the 'Shearer' tactic

Explain how the offside line determines the time and space available.

What is meant by an honest offside game?

What is meant by a high line?

If you play a 'high line' what attributes do some of your defenders have to have?

If you play a 'high line' what do the midfield and forwards have to do?

What is the fundamental mistake many teams make who play a high line

If a team plays a high line well, they are successfully pressing the ball. What tactics would you tell your side to adopt? There are 2 responses. One forces them back, the other gives you more time to pick a pass and switch the ball.

What rule changes have made offside even more risky?

In football if you get offside wrong it is critical. Justify this statement in regard to rugby, or a mistake in basketball.

What can happen if a team push up and catch forwards offside? Who can exploit the space beyond the defence?

Watch a video, (one with plenty of goals works well), and concentrate on the 'offside line' the team play. Comment on this.

Put together a team talk on how to beat the opposition who play a 'high line' and rely on catching some-one offside: they are well organised, and will all appeal to the ref.

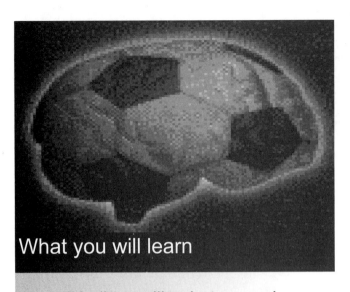

What you will learn

- A ball travelling between players takes time. This time has to be used to allow you to prioritise defending in dangerous spaces.
- Sometimes the ball needs to be played quickly, at other times slowly, to draw the opposition in and create space elsewhere to exploit
- Players need to work on arriving into a particular space at the same time as the ball

Ball travelling time

Theory

Ball travelling time is used to describe the time it takes for a ball to travel between two points. For example, from one side of the pitch to the other, between players, etc.

The key points that your team should be aware of are:

Ball travelling time, as far as **defending** is concerned, should be used to stay in the danger zone and the scoring zone.

When **attacking** the ball needs to be switched quickly, or the chance to exploit space will be gone.

The size of a pitch will obviously have an impact on ball travelling time, as will:

- How the ball is passed-driven, lifted along the ground, in addition to how hard it is struck.
- How many players are involved - the more players that touch the ball, the longer it takes.

Ball travelling time is a defender's friend. It gives them more time. Therefore, attackers should practise moving the ball quickly and reducing this. The faster the ball moves, the more space is gained.

The practical drill on the next page will help all your players understand the concept of ball travelling time.

All players in a team must understand the concept and how to use it. Fitter players can use it to push up and support attacks knowing they can get back. Judging ball travelling time well means a player will be in the correct space at the correct time.

Too often players who do not understand the concept are asking others to 'get tight' in areas where this is not necessary.

Ball travelling time, as far as defending is concerned, should be used to stay in the danger zone and the scoring zone

When attacking, the ball needs to be switched quickly or the chance to exploit space will be gone

TIME Practical Drill – ball travelling time

Drill– Set up the situation below. The team starts in position 1. As the ball is played from O1 to O2 they close the receiver (O2) down. 'Easy'. They then move to position 2, 3 and 4. Notice the starting point (1) is outside the danger zone. Defenders should try to stay in the danger zone but have to weigh this up against allowing a wide player too much time. The key point is to realise how much time you have to close people down by using ball travelling time.

Ask them which position is the best in terms of defending the danger zone/scoring zone/ thread zone.

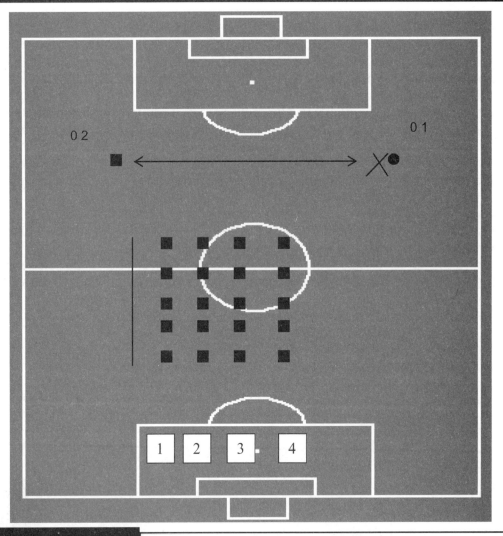

Key coaching tips– leave wide players	The time it takes to move the ball should be used defensively to close space down where the ball is and leave wide players on the opposite side. Attacking wise the ball needs to be moved to this space as quickly as possible.

How to use our understanding of ball travelling time– 'doubling up'

What you will learn

* Once you understand the concept of ball travelling time you can use it to your advantage. This applies to both attacking and defensive tactics, and over long and short distances

Theory

Now players are aware of how long it takes to pass a ball from one side of the pitch to the other, they need to see how this affects attackers and defenders.

There are 3 basic defending tactics
1. **Stay in the danger zone and scoring zone** and use ball travelling time to close players down.
2. **Double up (**have 2 players marking) on wide players who are in a dangerous crossing area. **Ron Atkinson, March 17th, 2003, The Guardian**

> *To my mind Arsenal left him to face one-against-one scenarios too often … they have to make sure the midfielders cover any weaknesses. Gillespie would knock the ball down the line past him, knowing he could beat him for pace time and again a negative square pass*

1. A midfield can **compress** the area around the ball and try to win it. See example on page 78

If we consider moving the ball when attacking a useful lesson is emphasised by the drill on the next page. Ask the back four to pass the ball as quickly as they can from one full back to the other, using firstly all four players. The team times this. Then three, then two as before. Ask the team what this tells them. If this is done slowly (with the exception of the example above) you will be closed down and cannot exploit space. It is the same in midfield.

The way the ball is passed obviously impacts on ball travelling time. Players need to practice moving a ball as fast as they can between 2 spaces.

Ball travelling time allows players to both attack and defend. You can cover the ground quickly between the two penalty areas. The midfield (at least three of them) should do this to create chances then defend if possession is lost A player in midfield (Roy Keane is a good example) can easily both attack and defend box to box. Roy Keane, in is his autobiography, comments

> *I worked box to box, unceasingly defending as well as I attacked.*

The key point is, however, to remember that if you commit players forward then you have to be able to switch to defensive positions quickly. During the transition it is the job of the players near the ball to slow play down and allow the team to get its defensive shape. The danger during the transition is highlighted by Houllier who says

> *This is why the switch from attack to defending has got to be a bit better and we are working on that* (Observer, 2nd November, 2003).

Players often don't realise how easily this is done, as a midfielder can soon cover the ground between the opposition's and his own penalty area. A sprinter would do this in between 6 and 7 seconds. An average player would do this in around 8 seconds.

A wide midfielder or full back can be in position 4 when the ball is on the opposite side of the pitch and still cover the wide player by using ball travelling time

The basic point is to see how far away this player can be to use ball travelling time to close the receiver down

The key then, is to buy time in the transition. Often players waste time tutting or putting their hands on hips or shouting their disappointment. This one second can be costly. Centre halves can also be used to attack, especially if a wide player has the ball and will cross. They can use this time to get to the opposition's box and back. The team should have players in their position until they arrive back.

Practical Drill - when switching the ball, moving it between the least amount of players, you can reduces ball travelling time and help create space.

DRILL - set up the positions below. Ask which one moves/ switches the ball fastest. Do it one touch, then two touch, and time it. Try a direct pass and one via the keeper - time them. Exactly the same principles apply in the midfield. Time it and discuss your conclusions.

A

B

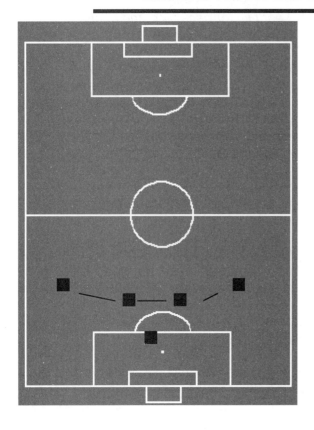

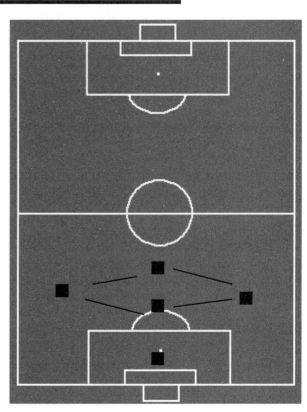

Key coaching tips

Defenders use ball travelling time to close players down and help cover players in their own team.

When attacking, it is usually important to use ball travelling time to move the ball quickly. The more touches or players involved the longer the ball travelling time. One touch passing, and well struck passes, move the ball quickly.

Switching the ball from one side of the pitch to the other quickly exploits time and space (this is dealt with in a later section).

TIME Practical Drill - box to box

Drill – Set up the situation below.

Get the whole team on the edge of the opposition's penalty area facing forward towards the opposition's goal.

They then have to run, on your command, back to their own area, Time it takes? (8 seconds ish depending on size of pitch and speed of player).

Then set it up so that the ball is played to a full back down the line and then to a centre forward. They race against this.

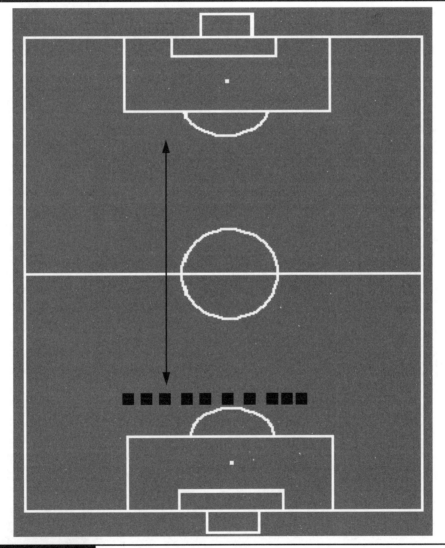

Key coaching tips– you have time to attack and defend	It is possible to get forward and back if you are fit enough. Players underestimate this. Roy Keane points out that. *I worked box to box, unceasingly defending as well as I attacked.* Keane also points out that *…run that produced this chance requires timing and luck. You might make the same run fifty times and never receive the ball. Or receive the ball and miss.*

SPACE Practical Drill - compressing play

SET UP THE POSITION BELOW TASK position the white team to compress play and avoid the ball being switched to the space on the opposite side to the ball.

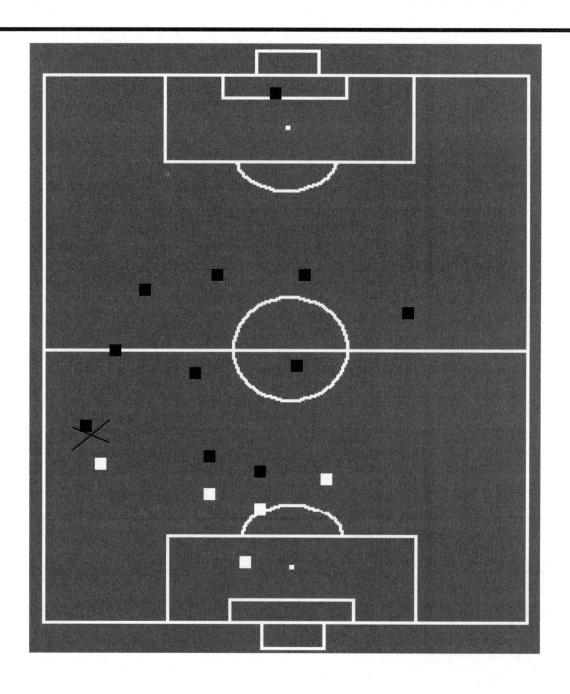

ANSWER Practical Drill - compressing play

To pressure the ball the players would adopt position such as this.

Put your team in this position.

Allow the shaded team to switch the ball to / see if the midfield and defence can adapt to this switch.

A good way to describe the role of the midfield in this is 'a roaming diamond'.

The 4 players move across the pitch to pressure the ball.

They must work together and be clear that they must stop the ball being switched over to the space on the other side.

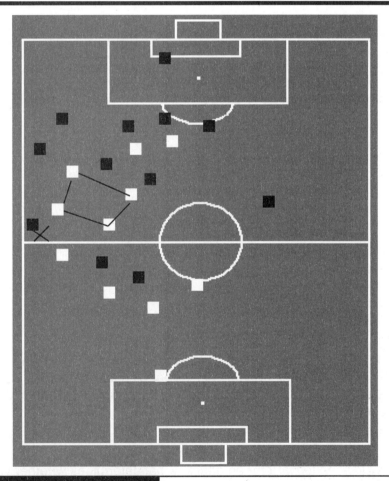

Key coaching tips– the defence works as a unit to cover space, the midfield can do this also

Teams such as Man United will try to put pressure on the ball. They will rely on the fact that they can stop the opposition switching the ball. If the opposition do switch the ball they have to be fit enough to move across using ball travelling time.

If this technique is called the 'roaming diamond' it may help players visualise it..

Comment on the time taken for the ball to travel between players if the ball is in the following.

* The ball is in the air, lofted or driven

* The ball is along the ground

* A good first touch by receiver/a bad first touch

* If the third player plays the ball 1 touch or 2 touch

* A poor pitch

* Wind

Watch a game: -

Look at the positioning of the full back and the wide midfielder on the defending side away from the ball. You will find they are very central. As a rule (useful for 11 year olds for example) if you drew a line from the centre of one goal to the centre of the other a full back and wide midfielder should be around this area when the ball is wide on the opposite side of the pitch.

You are a midfielder who has gone forward for an attack. What determines whether you rush back to defend?

Comment on the following 2 statements.

Roy Keane in his autobiography comments *'I worked box to box, unceasingly defending as well as I attacked.'*

Houllier – *This is why the switch from attack to defending has got to be a bit better and we are working on that'* (Observer 2 Nov 2003)

Time and Space applied to a range of soccer situations

Time and space applied to a range of soccer situations, – questions 1

Fill in the gaps and then check them on the next page.

You should now understand the key concepts of time and space. From now on, when looking at issues such as 'what you see' or 'playing out from the back', ask how this could be done faster and how this affects space and you will understand the game.

Here are some examples – fill in the gaps and check your answer on the next page– do the same for the next 3 pages.

Issue	Time	Space
A player's first touch in any situation		
What makes a good player?		
What makes a good coach?		

Answers 1-Time and space applied to a range of soccer situations

Issue	Time	Space
A player's first touch in any situation	If it takes a long time to control a ball	The space will disappear
What makes a good player?	A good first touch to bring the ball under control so that a decision on the next move can be made. Awareness of what is around them. An ability to play one touch soccer.	Finding space when they haven't got the ball and arriving at the right time in that space Playing the ball in to opposition spaces when it will hurt them. Good decisions about which space to use.
What makes a good coach?	Awareness of how time affects the game and being able to apply this knowledge of time to a given situation. Explaining how offside should only be applied when the opposition is denied time.	Awareness of how time affects space and how to exploit space and create space by movement. Explaining how offside changes the space available

Time and space applied to a range of soccer situations - questions 2

Fill in the gaps and then check them on the next page.

Issue	Time	Space
Playing the ball out from the back effectively		
What you see		
How important is pace?		
Switching play		

ANSWERS 2 Time and space applied to a range of soccer situations

Issue	Time	Space
Playing the ball out from the back effectively	Look at how quickly the keeper releases the ball Look at the body position of the full backs and their first touch They need to open out Look which foot players use Are players informed of options? Are players passing the ball firmly enough? Is it taking too long to get to where it is intended?	There will be more space the quicker he does it They need to open out into the space and have an open body position that allows them to see all the options. Too often, especially with non-confident players or young players, they will take their first touch back towards the keeper
What you see	Does a player with his back to goal take an unnecessary touch when he has an easy pass on to someone who can see better options? If he does, then the whole picture and opportunity will change	Taking longer allows defences to react and fill the space
How important is pace?	Not as important as how fast you think, or your first touch, but an ability to do things quicker can be an advantage	Means that if the opposition aren't aware, or don't take measures to deal with your pace, then space will be exploited
Switching play	If the defence is slow passes are not hit with pace or directed behind players	The opportunity to find the space on the opposite side if the ball is lost

Time and space applied to a range of soccer situations– questions 3

Fill in the gaps and then check them on the next page.

Issue	Time	Space
Pushing up to the edge of the area to help the keeper and reduce the chance of them scoring from a header		
Offside		
Playing zonal defence		
'Sucking a team in' or quick, quick slow.		

84

ANSWERS 3 Time and space applied to a range of soccer situations

What you will learn

Always try to get the opposition out of your penalty area (scoring zone)
- Offside determines the amount of space available.

Issue	Time	Space
Pushing up to the edge of the area to help the keeper and reduce the chance of them scoring from a header	Delay means they can deliver into an area in which they are more likely to score	The space allows the keeper to operate unhindered and makes it harder for them to score off a header or shot
Offside	You will only succeed if you do it quickly to catch players out	Beware of leaving too much space in the danger zone. An intelligent line is essential, as is effective cover play and how to use offside as a trap.
Playing zonal defence	As the opposition move the ball are your defence reacting quickly to cover the space?	Where the space is will change. Players need to advance mark where the opposition wishes to go- the scoring zone. Key Spaces.
'Sucking a team in' or slow,slow,quick.	Sometimes players, often in defence, will play the ball slowly in an attempt to 'suck' the opposition in to a particular area. The ball will then be played quickly.	Sucking the opposition in to a particular space leaves space further forward which can be exploited

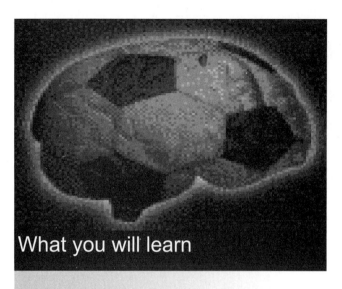

What you will learn

- Size is important as also is the surface
- To play the passing game requires a reasonable surface
- Time and space are influenced by the size of the pitch

Dario Grady, Observer, Sunday 7th March, 2004

This is a difficult place to come because Wigan are a cracking side - and the pitch doesn't help our passing game

PART 5 – The Pitch

The pitch

Theory

What you will learn

♦ The objective of this section is to highlight the differences that exist between the size of different team's pitches and the advantages it may bring. The size and condition of a pitch clearly will influence how much <u>space</u> players have and hence how much <u>time</u> players have on the ball, as well as <u>how long it takes them to control it</u> (bobbley pitch)

A good surface affects the way you play. Before deciding on the tactics you are going to adopt look at the pitch, its condition, its size.

Playing the passing game on a muddy or uneven surface can be difficult for a number of reasons
- It slows the game down.
- Players need to adapt to suit conditions.
- Passes may need to be played more in the air to avoid the surface. If this is the case then players need to re-consider the normal passes they will make (is it too risky?)
- Spaces, where the surface is better, need to be used.

If you want to play the 'passing game' you will need a flat pitch of a reasonable size with a good surface. Not to have this means changing the style played. Roy Keane observes in his autobiography

> *This was frequently the case. Jack Charlton never seemed particularly upset by the state of the playing surface at Landsdowne Road. On the contrary, he seemed to believe that it would upset the opposition more than us.*

Does size matter? Although at first sight it seems reasonable to argue that it is the same for both sides, a team learns to exploit the special characteristics of its own pitch.

For example, a wide pitch is more suitable for developing wing play than a narrow one, and the latter better for 'Route 1' (direct football). Graham Sounness was even reputed to have his pitch re-marked to stop two very good opposition wingers from having the space they crave.

Similarly, a pitch with a pronounced slope, even though the teams change round at half-time, will favour the team more used to it.

If you have choice of ends it is advisable to play against the advantage in the first half. There are various reasons for this.
- More goals are scored late on so give yourself an advantage
- The second half is longer - more added time
- The game will open up as players get physically tired, so exaggerating any advantage
- Concentration will be more likely to falter as players get tired.

Any tactic regarding an advantage kicking a particular way needs to be discussed in the team talk before the game. If we kick uphill we play 4-4-2 with the emphasis on playing out from the back and slowing the game down. If we kick downhill with the wind we will play 3-5-2 and play longer.

Defenders like to keep play compressed so prefer a small pitch

Attackers prefer large pitches with plenty of space

Write a team talk that deals with the way you would play on the following
Muddy pitch
Wide pitch
Large pitch

Does size matter? How does it affect the way you play.

How does a pitch with a pronounced slope, even though the teams change round at half-time, favour the home team.

If you have choice of ends it is advisable to play against the advantage in the first half. There are various reasons for this. What are they?

Any tactic regarding an advantage kicking a particular way needs to be discussed in the team talk before the game. Explain why.

What you will learn

- Why the mixed passing game works
- How to play the mixed passing game
- The limitations of the long ball game

'What about that straight pass you gave ... Pass the ball to help your man make progress or do damage, not put him in trouble or stop him dead.'

Alex Ferguson - Managing My Life.

What do we mean by the mixed passing game?

Theory

What you will learn

What is required if we are to develop the passing game
♦   A good pitch
♦   Reasonable technique
♦   A willingness to learn
♦   Tactical awareness – movement and positioning to help the person with the ball

You should now be familiar with two key issues. Space, and how to use Time to find space. The next stage is to look at the way the ball is moved between spaces. This is usually by a pass. Football is essentially a simple game based on giving and receiving of passes. On average, four out of five times when a player has the ball he will pass it. These passes can be long, short, lofted, etc. Playing the ball long at every opportunity was a tactic used by Ireland under Jack Charlton as well as teams such as Sheffield United and Wimbledon. As we shall see, this tactic was limited. However, many teams in rejecting it fell into the trap of over playing using too many short passes. Successful teams use a mixture of long and short passes to exploit time and space.

> *It is not a question of believing in short passing as opposed to long passing, it is a question of combining the best of both. Terry Venables.*

The mixed passing game also reflects a desire to pass and move and create space. The long ball game has often resulted in a more gladiatorial (physical) soccer as teams constantly battled for the fifty/fifty ball this tactic generates. A description of this type of game follows (football in the 1990s).

If you look at the build up to goals or general team play you will find that passing makes up the vast majority of the game. Other skills, such as running with the ball and skill on the ball are important, but none so important as passing. Terry Venables points out that *brains and good passing are as effective as trying to go past defenders*

Passes can be long or short. It is the choosing the correct pass that determines if a team is successful. Tord Grip believes that a team needs to know *when to play short through midfield and when to release the long ball and when and how to change the nature of attack.*

These passes can be played quickly to exploit available space, or slowly to attract the opposition to the ball and create space elsewhere. The best way to draw players in will probably be a short pass, the best way to exploit space on the transition may be a long ball.

The easiest attacking tactic is to pass the ball in the space between the opposition's back four and their keeper for a forward to run onto. If this option is available in any game it should be taken. Therefore, using a long ball option is fine (on a bad pitch it may be the best tactic). However, as we shall see, using the long ball game as the dominant tactic throughout a game is limited: good defences don't allow you to deliver balls into this space.

Passing is a two way process. Without tactics to determine player movement and good communication a player will not have the full range of passing options.

Defenders need good technique to play the ball out from defence

The whole team attacks and defends

The mixed passing game is a tactic in which the ball is played long and short and regularly out from the back. It relies on a team/players being aware of a number of tactics - how to switch the ball, bounce the ball, and the angles of passes and runs. They need to be aware of the movement that is required to offer options. It relies on players being confident and not afraid to fail. All successful teams, at all levels, play the mixed passing game.

How to play the mixed passing game

What you will learn

- Developing players and the passing game.
- Setting out what you are trying to do

Once you have decided to play the mixed passing game, the next step is to decide if all eleven players have the necessary technique, or if your priority is to develop that technique.

One thing is for sure, if your team adopts a 'safety first, kick it out' when defending, get it forward, don't fanny around, then you will not develop the players in your team. They will not develop the technique to operate in tight space; they will not develop the decision-making or be aware of the movement required. Any youth team or academy that fails to develop their team in a way that incorporates a range of tactics, and passing long and short, is failing that team and its players. Even if an academy has a first team that adopts a long ball type game, their youth teams should not follow this blindly. It is a disservice to the players and will not develop them. One final point: as you will see later in this section, only teams that play the mixed passing game are successful. This is true in nearly all cases at all levels.

To play the mixed passing game and the ball out from the back, which is an integral part of it, does not require eleven fantastic 'ball players' but that a certain minimum is evident throughout the team (basic control, passing and a willingness to learn). Having decided the way you are going to play, the next stage is to explain to all players, coaches and other interested parties (supporters, parents) what the team, coach, etc. are trying to do. Not to do so will mean players may argue and parents or supporters will complain (people may disagree but at least they will know what the intention is).

The more people are informed the more they are likely to support coaches and the more involved they will feel with the club. The bottom line is that if you fail/get the sack at least it is based on the full picture. You can, of course, try to play the mixed passing game whilst accepting that some players do not have the necessary technique. If you do this, you will have to accept it will break down more often. If dealing with a young side you may take the decision that you will try to play the 'mixed passing game' whilst accepting that, with the players you have, there will be mistakes and you will lose goals. Results may suffer at this stage, as the priority is how you play and the development of players.

Three final points.
1. It is easier to defend than attack. Players with poor technique, but tactical awareness, can be competent defenders. However, they are limited in what they can contribute to the mixed passing game and the effect on the team may be to adopt a long ball tactic.
2. Be aware that playing the mixed passing game is a lot easier on a good surface. You will need a good home pitch and the ability to change the way you play to suit conditions.
3. A comment from the Observer from West Hams coach Peter Grant also shows a disadvantage of over reliance on height. *Talking of Sunderland...benefiting from the absence of their towering centre forward...no disrespect to him..but I think Sunderland have been forced to pass it more with him out the side. Sometimes , when a team have a big target man and are struggling to create chances , they are inclined to go direct too early. They tend to want to take the easy way out.*

In conclusion, playing the mixed passing game is the best way to develop players and fully exploit time and space. One technique that needs developing is driving the ball as this moves the ball quickly between two points to find space.

A really positive development is the changes in the rules of the game that benefit the mixed passing game. We will then look in a bit more detail at what is required for the mixed passing game and the limitations of the long ball game.

The limitations of the long ball game and the need to play 'the mixed passing game'

Theory

Roy Keane

Jack Charlton

To win in football means being able to score goals.

The easiest attacking tactic is to put the ball in the space between the opposition's back four and their keeper for a forward to run on to (the danger zone).

If this option is available in any game it should be taken.

However, good defences don't allow you to deliver balls into this space. It is only available if you move the ball quickly having regained possession.

Using a long ball option is fine (on a bad pitch it may be the best tactic) . But to use the long ball game as the tactic throughout a game is limited. There are 2 reasons why.

Firstly, it is easy to defend against: the defence drops deeper and stays compact and central. Defenders know what is coming so it is easy to maintain concentration (a key factor in good defence). This means the attacking side needs other options. This is where the passing game comes in.

The passing game involves probing the defence by, for example, switching the ball. This means defenders have to concentrate even more. If they have to deal constantly with movement and different angles, they will lose concentration, 'switch off'. If they leave a space for a fraction of a second this can be exploited.

Secondly, teams such as Ireland added to the long ball game the fact that no risks should be taken in defence or midfield. Players were all intent on getting the ball forward. How can players develop if this is all a team does? Does this make the best of the players available?

As we shall see, Roy Keane shows the limitations of the game.

It would be fair to say that for a team with very little technical ability and little tactical awareness (and who wish to develop neither) the long ball game offers a simple tactical plan. This is especially true if the pitch has a bad surface. Does this description fit most teams or should it be applied when players are developing? The answer has to be no.

We shall now look at the long ball game the Republic of Ireland played under Jack Charlton. We are given an amazing insight by Roy Keanes excellent autobiography.

Defensively the long ball game is easy to deal with

If you have no pace up front it is even harder to play the long ball game

92

Roy Keane on the long ball game

Theory

One of the most controversial tactics adopted in English and Irish football is the 'long ball game'. The two most famous teams for using this were Ireland under Jack Charlton and Wimbledon.

Roy Keane, in his autobiography, gives us an insight into these simple team tactics. These tactics, as we shall see, if adopted in the way Ireland adopted them, are directly at odds with the 'passing mixed game'. Keane states:

Charlton's approach to football was profoundly at odds with the game played at Forest. Passing the ball was not a priority. What he demanded was a kind of football by numbers, the emphasis being on inconveniencing the opposition rather than being creative ourselves. The idea was to fire long balls in behind the opposing defence, then hunt them down, with the intention of trapping them in their own half of the field, where we hoped we'd force them to make mistakes.

In terms of playing the ball out from the back *Jack's football conviction was 'make no mistakes, don't fanny around in your own half of the field'*

Keane observes that there was NOT *more to Charlton's magic formula than there appeared to be on first acquaintance.*

Keane was clearly upset by these tactics:

My Forest background was where we played a passing game. Ireland had some very good footballers – Dennis Irwin, David O'Leary, Paul McGrath, Andy Townsend, Ray Houghton and Kevin Sheedy among them. Yet playing football in any systematic way, in the pass-and-move style we adopted at Forest, for example, or Dennis Irwin was accustomed to at Man. United, was frowned upon by Charlton.
Charlton's game plan was simple
(a) to win the long balls knocked up to them
(b) to try and get in behind their markers for long balls played into space behind defenders.
In situation (a) myself and Andy Townsend were to push forward to try and win balls knocked down or flicked on by Cas or Niall.
In situation (b) the whole side pushed forward with the intention of trapping our opponents in their own territory. Situation (b) didn't really suit Cas and Niall, neither of whom was very mobile. John Aldridge was better suited to making runs in behind defenders. 'Knock it into space down the gulleys' Charlton urged.

Charlton's game had some success, as Keane earlier observes, due to the fact that Ireland had some talented players. What would they have achieved if they had played the passing game? Keane reflects on the use of the tactic at this time: *this was football Wimbledon/Watford style, and it had proved very effective in the international arena of that era.* Charlton did indeed have success using this. However, as teams developed technically, they simply passed around the onslaught and dropped deeper to deny space between the defence and keeper. As was mentioned earlier, defenders find this tactic easy to concentrate against as it is predictable.

Keane also makes an interesting observation about the state of the pitch .

> *Charlton never seemed particularly upset by the state of the playing surface at Landsdowne Road. On the contrary, he seemed to believe that it would upset the opposition more ,*

The rule change of not allowing the defence to pass back to the keeper, who then launches it forward, has also made it less effective.

It would be wrong to deny that there is a role for the long ball but as the entire basis of a team's tactics it is limited and can be dealt with. No team using entirely these tactics has won a major international tournament and, with the exception of Wimbledon in the FA cup, domestic success has also been very limited.

The limitations are also emphasisied by Ron Atkinson (Monday May 19, 2003 The Guardian)who highlighted how Southampton sold themselves short by sticking to the long-ball game.

> *Southampton didn't often look like scoring and I think there were a couple of main reasons. In the first half they tried to play too long ...Initially Saints launched too many early balls towards James Beattie without having mid fielders up in support to pick up the scraps. Arsenal knew Beattie would be the target, so Gilberto Silva often positioned himself down the line of the ball to stop Lundekvam being able to play an easy pass and make him have to put it up high. That made it a fighting ball and Arsenal's central defenders often won it. Then Gilberto or Ray Parlour would collect the loose ball before any Southampton midfielders got up field. I thought Southampton improved after the interval because they played through the midfield. That meant they weren't surrendering possession so easily or allowing Arsenal to break so quickly. Gilberto and Parlour were drawn forward to engage Southampton's midfielders, so it became easier for Gordon Strachan's side to get better-quality passes into Beattie or Brett Ormerod. But they didn't get into the final third much in wide areas and Arsenal deserve credit for that. Their full-backs were very disciplined. Ashley Cole and Lauren knew that if they were lured forward Southampton could hit the space behind them and either get crosses in or enable Beattie to sprint in there, turn his marker and run at people.*

Southampton's and Ireland's limited game was easily dealt with. They needed to vary the tactics they adopted.

The mixed passing game, on a decent pitch, is the only way to succeed today at all levels and a youth level it develops players.

Don't play the ball out from the back in this game

The tactic was simple:chase down and try and get beyond the defence

When a player receives a ball how many times out of 5 will he/she pass?

In terms of judging how good a player is how important is passing?

What is meant by a mixed passing game? Is dribbling/beating a player part of this?

Why does this style benefit players at academy or who need to develop technique?

Sometimes passes need to be played quickly at others slowly. Can you explain why.

Why is passing a two way process? Explain this.

How does the pitch size and surface affect passing?

Why is it easier to defend than attack?

Why is important to have clear team objectives?

List the changes in the game that benefit a mixed passing game? Do you agree with the changes?

Summarise Keanes views of the long ball game.

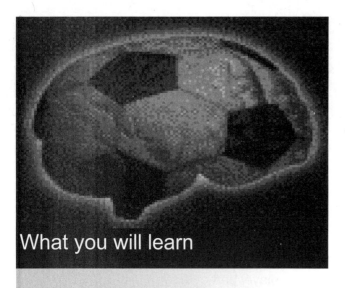

What you will learn

♦ The best ways to defend

Gary Neville states *Eriksson's defence like to be prepared for every eventuality. Eriksson (the England Manager)went through the oppositions movements to make play predictable.*

Patrick Vieira (Champions Magazine April May 2004)

The thing that stands out about our first ever victory in Spain is that we have finally learned how to defend as a team.

We work hard as a unit. This is the type of game we might have lost two or three seasons ago.

Viera was also quoted regarding England *'England have a good chance in Euro 2004 as they know how to defend a 1-0 lead'* This may not have proved the case, but England's defence was as good as any. It was England's failure to keep the ball and hence the amount of pressure that eventually cost them success.

England's failure was lack in attacking (keeping the ball) not defending.

Is the best way to defend man for man or zonal (advanced marking)?

Theory

The first step is to look at the two basic ways teams can defend - 'man for man' or zonal. The conclusion of this will be that only a zonal system is effective in soccer.

Why? Because only the attacking player, who may be slower than the defender knows where he is going. It takes time for the marker to adjust (he can't mind read) the attacker 'has the run' (see earlier). In short, no matter how fast you are, the person you are marking will always find space.

Get your players in pairs. Emphasise that the two players will be of differing pace. You can put them anywhere on the pitch; the penalty area (scoring zone) is probably best. When you say 'go' players have to find space. After a couple of seconds stay stop. Ask if the player was in space. The answer will usually be yes. If not, (at that particular point they may have been caught up with) ask if the player could find space. The answer is yes. Move the situation to a free kick.

Go man for man. Have a separate word with those trying to lose their marker and point out that they can run their marking player into another marking player (encourage them to do this).The outcome is obvious.

The example on the next page is intended to make it clear why zonal marking is called advanced marking

♦ 'Man for man' marking is less effective. It is better if players mark spaces in advance of the opposition moving into them. The Italians call this 'advanced marking'.

♦ Zonal marking is about identifying where the danger areas are at any given time and ensuring a player is in that space 'in advance' waiting for the opposition.

♦ Zonal marking allows players to crowd the area around the ball and re-gain possession. This concept can only be understood if you understand time (ball travelling time).

We can relate zonal marking to the professional game. In an article in Champions Magazine (December, 2004) Andy Roxburgh made some interesting comments

Fifteen out of sixteen teams at Euro 2004 played a flat back four with zonal marking.

Clearly at professional level zonal marking is the preferred tactic. Lets now look at some specific examples of why zonal marking is the best defensive system.

Man for man marking is less effective than zonal. Defenders know where attackers want to go (the scoring zone). It is better to cover the space and wait. (advanced marking)

Players play zonaly even if they have never been formally taught, because they have learnt through trial and error (see how we learn)

SPACE Practical Drill – problems with man for man marking

SET UP THE POSITION BELOW Ask the following question. Do we know where they want to go? What is an easy way for the attackers to cause us to bump into each other? What if they are faster than us? **The simple fact that attackers can bump the man who is marking them into another defender makes the system flawed. We can predict where the attackers want to before they arrive and wait in this space (advance mark) this is much more effective. We may guess where they want to be but the other factor is when they arrive there, timing. We may be bigger, stronger faster but 1 player can lose another player simply because of the time it takes the marking player to react to movement (reaction time).**

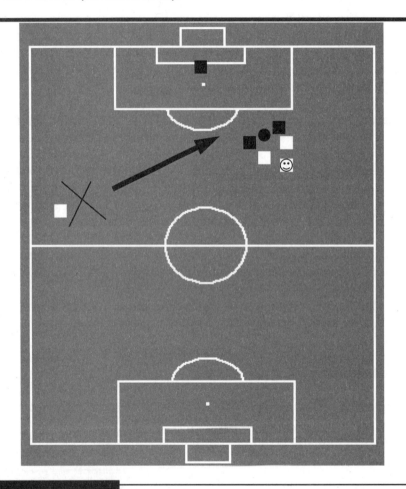

Key coaching tips– the defenders know the space they wish to protect. Only by working together and filling the space in advance of the opposition can they de defensively sound

The shaded players cannot be next to their man. They don't know when they will move. They know the area the forwards (white players) will be aiming for (scoring Zone). In their present position they are not going to score. When the forwards run, if they follow them, they could bump into each other. An attacker with pace (like Henry) would love to get a defender out wide and then use the space to beat him, and move in to the scoring zone.

Off a set play corner free kick we may decide to go zone and team up man for man players who can compete with opposition players who are good in the air.

SPACE Practical Drill – explaining advanced marking (a useful term to help us understand zonal defence)

SET UP THE POSITION BELOW Ask the players what is wrong with the position of \. There are 3 things wrong.

Firstly, s/he is not offering support in the danger zone.

Secondly, the player with the ball x will play the ball into the space that \ has left. The attacker may well be faster than x and beat him to it, or another player may utilse the space that x is not covering and be free to shoot. So to mark in advance the space where the attacker would like to be \ should stay in the position at the end of the arrow..

If the wide player o received the ball, then the defender could use ball travelling time to close him down (he is not in the danger zone at the moment).

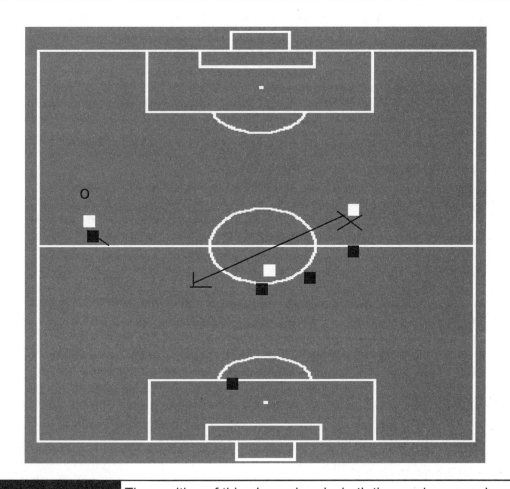

Key coaching tips– mark space not players	The position of this player breaks both time and space rules. S/he has left the key space (danger zone) and has not allowed for ball travelling time to close down the player. In addition, the player is not offering cover for the central players.

Conclusion

Theory

No matter who is faster, an attacking player will always have a couple of yards on a defender. The reason is simple: s/he will know where s/he are going. S/he can stop running – or pretend to go one way, then not.

So why man for man when

♦   We know where they want to go (the scoring zone)?

♦   We know that if we follow them they will always be in a space before we are? No matter how much faster and better than them we are (we may run into our own defenders as we follow them - they may cause this deliberately).

Is it not better to advance mark (go to where they want to be) and wait for them?

With other defenders we could divide up the scoring zone. This will stop us running into each other. Cover the space and wait.

In conclusion, Man for Man doesn't work. Zonal advanced marking is the only system that can offer adequate defensive cover.

Offside is another tool in the defence's armoury because, as the ball is played, or the position of the forwards changes, they can drop off and cover our team mates.

If the opposition move into the space, we simply catch them offside. It is much easier to play offside when you have a zonal system with players aware of their position in relation to the ball. Imagine trying to have an organised offside system, when players are charging all over the place marking mobile attackers. It would be impossible..

Occasionally a player is so exceptional that sides will man mark them putting a player on with the role of specifically marking one player. Alex Fergusson was sufficiently worried about Ronaldo to have a player man to mark him. However, this was done within a zonal defence system and is very rare.

One final important factor. Around the scoring zone teams play zonally. This relies on a defending player spotting an offensive player in their zone. If we take an example of a midfielder tracking a forward through their zone who is heading for a defenders zone. The zonal system dictates that this player is passed on left. However, the defending midfielder in this example needs to be sure that his/her team mate has seen the oncoming player from the opposition enter their zone. Once this is clear the 'tracking ' midfielder can leave the player and return to their zone.

Communication is an essential part of defending.

So having established that zonal marking is the best way to defend we now need to look at how to teach your team zonal defending (see page 57 for the correct bowl shape).

All teams play zonaly. They may not be aware of this as it may be instinctive and not understood (see section on how we learn)

Regardless of the physical and technical difference, the defender is not a mind reader. The attacker always has a few yards

Ask the following

- If you are slow, can you lose a fast marker on a football pitch? (yes)
- If you man for man what is the danger? (defenders not marking key spaces)
- In the example of a free kick, or any situation near the penalty area, can we predict where the player we are marking wants to be (general area)? (yes)
- How could we best deal with this? (Zones pass players on).

If in a zonal situation we saw a situation where our fellow defender may be exposed for pace (set up 4 v 2) how could we help? (drop off to cover). What if an attacker then utilises this space? (Step up and catch them offside).

List 5 situations (specific to players) eg

- The centre forwards run horizontally past each other,
- A midfielder with the ball runs past another of his/her own players.
- That players could create space by running a player from the opposition into another player from the opposition.

Devise you own drill to show players how man for man does not work.

Watch a game of football and look at how teams let players come into their zones and use ball travelling time to close them down. You can see this even in the penalty area.

Why is the term advanced marking an accurate one?

Watch a game and see how teams use zones and how they operate on free kicks and corners.

What would you say to someone if they said– 'it was your man that scored'. What would this depend on?

Explain why it is that teams don't just identify a player for you to mark and you mark them all game?

Have there been occasions when teams have given the job of marking a particular player all game?

How would you explain this role in terms of how it affects the rest of the team formation etc (use a central midfield player as an example)?

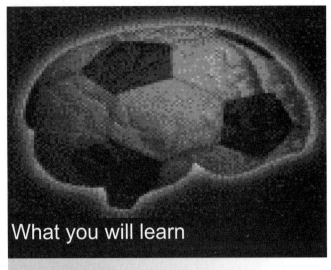

What you will learn

◆ The way that all successful teams organise their defence

To be successful a team must
Move the opposition to the 18 yard line as soon as they can– *protect the scoring zone and keeper*
Drop back as a unit as the ball is played forward by the opposition– *mark space not players*
Defend zonally passing players on, centrally and with cover– *use ball travelling time and offside to maintain cover*
Not give the opposition the chance to play pass into the space between the defence and keeper– *the danger zone*
Deny space to players immediately outside the area– *the thread zone*
Try and stop crosses from the wide area level with the 18 yard to the by-line– *'double up' in this area*
Stay on their feet and not give away free kicks—*up to 60% goals come from set plays*
Be able to stop 'the supply' *e.g. the opposition plays out well from the back. By changing formation to a 4 3 3 a side can stop the supply line*

I didn't ask any of my players to mark an opponent out of the game, not once. I would give them the instruction 'you look after your own patch no matter who comes into it.

'You couldn't get to him on the near post because he's quicker than you. So you stand in your patch and if he comes into your patch you deal with it … if he goes hold your position … The ball will come across at some stage and if you're nor around it will be the one they put in the net

Brian Clough, Walking on Water

How to mark zonally/ advanced marking

Theory

The four defenders or midfielders take it in turns to mark a player as he moves across the pitch and enters their zone. It is exactly the same in midfield.

If two players from the opposition are in a defender's area, there is nothing different. In other words, two defenders would not move over. Stay in your zone.

If players do not have the ball, the defender whose zone the centre forward is in will be close enough to challenge as the ball arrives. They judge this distance according to the ball travelling time. In other words, the closer the ball to the player the closer the defender to the player - as they have less ball travelling time.

It does not matter if the players have the ball or not.

The difference is that, if a player is moving across a defender's zone without the ball, the defender will use ball travelling time to determine how close he goes. If the player has the ball the defender will be challenging him as he moves across the pitch into another player's zone: the other player will take over and the defender will go back to his zone.

In the examples on the next page it does not matter if the players have the ball or not. The difference is that, if a player is moving across a defenders zone without the ball, the defender will use ball travelling time to determine how close he goes. If the player has the ball the defender will be challenging him as he moves across the pitch into another player's zone. The other player will then take over and the defender will go back to his zone.

The four defenders take it in turns to mark a player as he moves across the pitch and enters their zone.

It is exactly the same in midfield. If two players from the opposition are in a defender's area, there is nothing different. Defenders mark space and do not follow players or more specifically, defenders mark players in their space even if there are two.

Zonal marking always allows for cover the defenders are on a zonal vertical line but not necessarily a horizontal line.

Players from the opposition move between zones. Defenders stay in zones

When attacking, try to exploit the spaces between zones where there is space or confusion over whose zone you are in

SPACE Practical Drill – identifying your zone

SET UP THE POSITION BELOW The 2 shaded players move across the pitch.

Defenders are told that their concern is with their zone. Anyone in your zone you are responsible for. Get a player to run across the zones. As he moves across s/he becomes the responsibility of different players. If the player has the ball it is the same principle . As s/he moves across the zones the player in that zone challenges. As the ball is central the whole shape is central. We have to look at a couple of issues
1)   What happens if there are 2 players in your zone? NOTHING
2)   How does shape change according to where the ball is? EVERYONE MOVES OVER (See next page)
3)   Leaving the wide player USE BALL TRAVELLING TIME TO CLOSE THEM DOWN

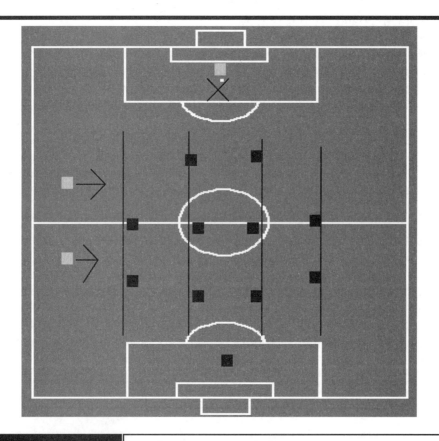

Key coaching tips– zonal marking effectively mark space	It's about spaces not players Your man is the one in your zone It matters not if you have 2 men in your zone Leave the wide areas and players if the ball is on the opposite side. Stay central only closing wide players down as they receive the ball Zonal play applies all over the pitch. The only exception may be specific marking of key players off corners or free kicks

SPACE Practical Drill – identifying your zone

SET UP THE POSITION BELOW

1) How does shape change according to where the ball is?
2) Ball on Left team adapts as below.
3) The wide shaded player is left as s/he can be marked using ball travelling time. The player with 2 shaded players in his/her zone is not concerned. Remember only one of them can have the ball at any one time!

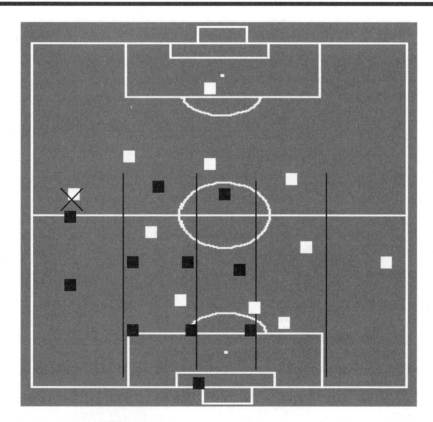

The team has dropped back to the 18 yard line. The keeper may become the covering player here.

The defending team can drop before the ball is played so they can mark the space in advance– drop back as a unit

Key coaching tips- zonal marking effectively marks space	The team moves as a unit in response to where the ball is. The team always tries to stay in the danger zone and keep the opposition outside of the scoring zone. Its about spaces not players Your man is the one in your zone It matters not if you have 2 men in your zone Leave the wide areas and players if the ball is on the opposite side. Stay central, closing wide players down only as they receive the ball. Zonal play applies all over the pitch. The only exception may be specific marking of key players off corners or free kicks

SPACE Practical Drill – identifying your zone– *making sure there is a covering player*

SET UP THE POSITION BELOW

How does shape change according to where the ball is? Essentially everyone moves over one . Play the ball across the pitch to players in position 2 and 3. Get the team to react. Ensure 1 player is aware of the need to provide cover (the circled player on this occasion) and link this in with how to use offside, see drill 12

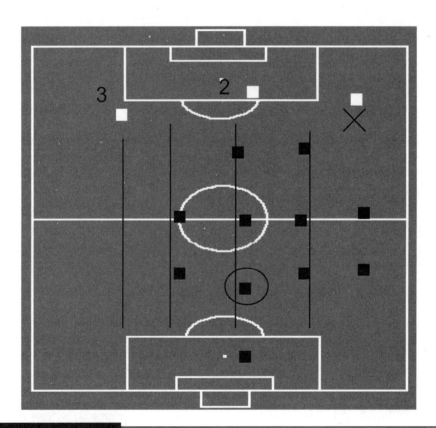

Key coaching tips **zonal marking effectively marks key spaces**	The team moves as a unit in response to where the ball is. The team always tries to stay in the danger zone and keep the opposition outside of the scoring zone. It's about spaces not players Your man is the one in your zone It matters not if you have 2 men in your zone Leave the wide areas and players if the ball is on the opposite side. Stay central only closing wide players down as they receive the ball

SPACE Practical Drill – mark space not players

SET UP THE POSITION BELOW This is an example where the shaded side have attacked lost the ball and are trying to get back. 2 players are next to the right back shaded (1).

This makes no difference- the rest of the team stay in position.

In other words 2 defenders would not move over. Stay in your zone.

As the defence is at the edge of the area they are aware that a ball over the top from that distance and angle will be dealt with by the keeper.

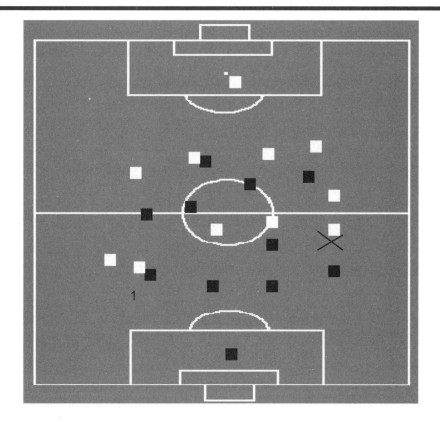

Key coaching tips-

Ball travelling time can be used to cover players. the closer the ball to the player the closer the defender to the player.

If players do not have the ball the defender whose zone the centre forward is in will be close enough to challenge as the ball arrives. They judge this distance according to the ball travelling time.

In other words the closer the ball to the player the closer the defender to the player, as there is less ball travelling time.

'Cheating'

Theory

What do we mean by cheating?

In this sense it is not about foul play or gamesmanship. Cheating is a term used to describe players who do not follow the usual tactical pattern when defending. In any team a player is either attacking, defending or in transition.

Cheating is when a player ignores his/her defensive role and tries to exploit space left by the opposition attacking. The player will occupy the space left by the opposition attacking and wait for play to break down to exploit this.

Cheating can occur all over the pitch. It is where players do not play their defensive zonal role. (If your team has the ball then the opposition should move back and defend the correct space zone). Sometimes players don't do this.

Why do players cheat? There are various reasons:

- it may be because the player is unfit
- a player may be tactically unaware
- it could be seen as a deliberate way of exploiting space. If the "cheaters" team adapt to cover and release this player, it can be effective.

How should you treat a cheat?

Firstly, decide which category they fall into. As a general rule ignore a cheat - a player should still go forward.

However, this depends on how effective the player is who is cheating. If a player is, for example, out wide, not in the danger zone, s/he can be relatively safely left. However, if the player is a good dribbler, and uses the space to get into the danger zone or scoring zone effectively, then a tactical change needs to be made.

It is a good idea to point out that a player is cheating to others. This allows the team to adapt, and means they accept that your role is to go forward. Factors, such as the score at the time, and, as mentioned above, how good the 'cheater' is, will need to be considered.

It is important to identify when an opposition player is cheating. A strategy to deal with them can be implemented

Cheating can be used as an effective tactic. It can be used to find space

The defence always plays zonally. The midfield also do BUT if they are fit enough and have good decision making skills and work as a unit they can take a more proactive role and try to win the ball back. Man United are superb at this. (see later)

How do you think you could describe in a team talk the how the midfield plays zonaly.

If a team is behind with not long left will its players be inclined to cheat? Explain why.

How should this be dealt with by the defending team who are in the lead?

Can 'cheating' be used as an effective tactic? Explain how it could be used to release one of your players.

Write a team talk that describes in simple terms how your team could suck the opposition in and then exploit this space. Watch top level games to see how a team will not attempt to get the ball back too far forward or will limit the players it commits to try and re-gain possession.

Look at the situation on the next page and outline if the nearest forward should go for the ball or wait.

Watch a game to see how and when the forwards try to win the ball back. Devise a simple team talk that emphasises when to win the ball back.

Write a team talk that outlines your teams tactics when defending a corner. Imagine they have 3 players, one in particular, who is good in the air.
Watch how top teams defend corners on TV.

- Write a team talk that outlines the tactics you should adopt against
- A team you are better than
- Are better than you

What is the effect on space of playing deep. How might this benefit you, how could this be used as a tactic?

Watch a game and see how many times players go to ground (slide). Predict how many there will be. Check out match stats for number of tackles. You will find there are fewer than you think.

Explain the statement: -

After scoring the first goal a team need not commit players forward and therefore are less vulnerable on the transition.. They can sit back and hit the team chasing the game on the break.

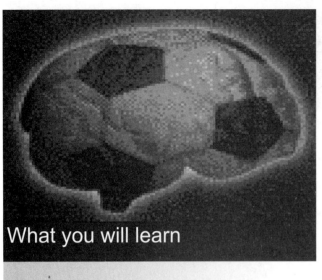

What you will learn

- How to avoid getting sucked in, offside tactics, defending free kicks

Paul Bracewell (Observer, 2004) highlights the importance of defending.
'we had a game plan, we stuck to it and it almost paid off. I've pointed out to the players that the difference between winning and losing is <u>not making mistakes</u>'

A defence needs to <u>concentrate</u> for over 90 minutes on where they are , how they support each other and how they deal with a constantly changing attack (in other words, it's not all long ball down the middle which requires a basic level of concentration). Concentrating for 90 minutes on anything is hard. A mistake – the wrong defensive line, a free kick given away or bad positional play, can cost a goal, and in a game of relatively few goals, the game. Mistakes are usually positional.
<u>This section contains</u>
- Factors to consider (particularly for forwards) when trying to win the ball back
- How far up the pitch should you pressure the ball?
- What do we mean by 'too deep' or 'too flat'?
- 'Going to ground' – wastes time and frees up space for the opposition

Don't concede the first goal!

Defending set plays – corners, free kicks, etc

Theory

What you will learn

- In simple terms, it is about defending the key spaces. Leave the keeper with enough room to operate in.
  As the ball is played, fill the space with defenders

Whilst a team will always play zonal in open play, there is good reason to adopt a mixed approach at a set play. When we consider that so many goals are scored from set plays, often with the head, it is understandable that teams may choose to pick players who can deal with this threat. Alex Fergusson picked Sheringham (a tall forward) in one game specifically to help out when defending set plays against a taller team. It is often the case that taller forwards are often asked to come back and defend set plays and often they are replaced with a smaller player up front. The most important thing for the players to realise when defending a corner or free kick, is how important it is to actually challenge for the ball. Even if the player does not succeed in winning the ball, s/he make it difficult for the opposition who, with a free header, may score.

A mixed approach (zonal and man for man) is desirable for the following two reasons:
- It is predictable, you know where the opposition players will be going.
- The opposition may have players who are particularly good in the air. These players need to be matched with your own players who can compete.

Defending a corner (the principles are the same for a free kick or long throw).
- The best system is a combination of zonal and man for man, because it not only delegates specific areas of responsibilities to defenders and the keeper, it also provides the opportunity to cover the opposition's most dangerous players.
- Make sure you consider where goals are scored from. Defend these dangerous spaces - near post, central area, far post, edge of box and defending a ball that the keeper punches or a player heads (the second ball). Make sure you are organised and consider the roles of individual players. Height, determination and aggression are important. Ensure defending players have good body shape They can see the ball and men/the space they are marking. Players must not lose concentration and just watch the ball. Ensure that players are on the front foot and ready to attack the space in front of them.
- How far should they be from each other? The simple answer is can the opposition move into the space unchallenged. How far out should zonal markers be from the goal and each other? It is better to be too close to the goal and danger areas than too far away.
- Don't forget corners are an ideal chance for a counter attack.
- If you happen to have a keeper who is very good at catching the ball off a corner you could leave three players up front and the keeper quickly delivers. However, there is a reason not to leave three players up from every corner with what seems like the positive effect the opposition have leaving three or four defenders at the back. The more players you have in the scoring zone the less space there is and so the less chance of the opposition having the time and space to create a chance. It is harder for anyone to score with twenty players in the penalty area than it is with ten.

Defending free kicks, Edwin Van Der Sar pointed out (Champions Magazine April 2004)

> *Seven years ago we tried building a wall with 5 men and I'd place myself in the middle of the goal. Then at the moment the free kick taker took his run up, the wall would separate slightly, 3 players one way 2 the other, creating a meter gap so I had a clear view of the ball. It worked until scouts picked it up and opponents started putting a player in the wall to block my view.*

This tactic seem worth a try.

Defenders need to be clear about what their team does to defend corners and free kicks. The first consideration is don't give the opposition corners or free kicks

Look at how the defence marks the space. Are there any gaps to be exploited. Defenders like time to get organised. Do things quickly when they are not ready

Factors to consider (particularly for forwards) when trying to win the ball back

Theory

What you will learn

Factors include:
- The score
- Fitness
- How good the opposition is
- Is there a good chance of regaining possession? Can the opposition pass round the players trying to win the ball?

The decision of a forward, or a team, as to whether to try to win the ball back to press play, is determined by a number of factors. The most important factor to consider is that it is very risky for few players in a team pressing the opposition and not the whole team. The result of only a few players pressing is pockets of space in dangerous areas which the opposition can pass to and exploit. Other factors include

- The score at the time. A few minutes to go, a goal down, it is worth chasing everything.

If the score is level, then the first consideration (which is explained later) is:
- How high up the field you would try to win the ball back against a team you are better than.

- How high up the field you would try to win the ball back against a team you are equal too

- How high up the field would you try to win the ball back against a team who are better than you

How fit you are?

- If a centre forward chases the ball, does s/he have the energy to do the attacking role?

The player nearest the ball has to make a decision as to if it is a realistic chance of winning the ball. This is dependent on:

- How technically good the player is with the ball. Poor technique then is worth closing the player down as s/he may make a mistake (bad control or over hit the ball).
- How many passing options the player with the ball has.
- If s/he has plenty of space and, hence, time it is not worth trying to win the ball back as s/he will simply pass round you.
- It is better to wait until s/he are in an area where you can go for the ball with support from other players in your team.

A defender's instinct is to demand that attackers close the ball down. Defenders need to be aware of the points raised in this section

An attacker should consider if he/she is fit enough to chase the ball deep in the oppositions half and still make forward runs

SPACE Practical Drill – when to press play

SET UP THE POSITION BELOW Is it a good idea for the centre forward nearest the ball to close it down?

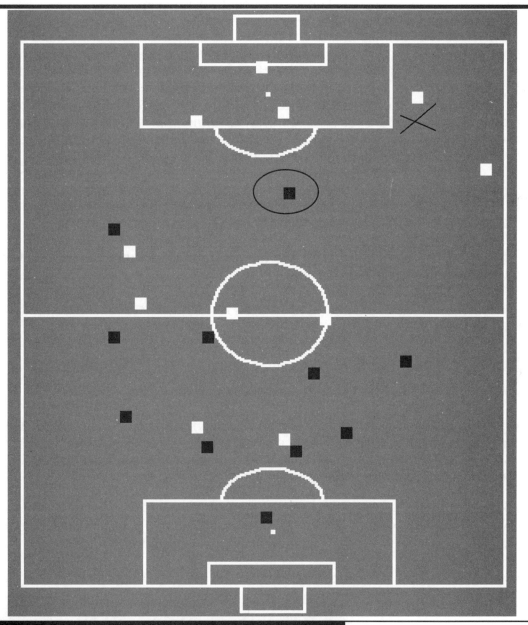

Key coaching tips– don't go forward into space after the ball without support you leave space behind you the opposition can exploit

The answer is no. To Close the ball down you need support. The player above does not have this and so should wait at the half way line.

How far up the pitch should you try to regain possession?

Theory

What you will learn

♦ How far up the pitch players should try to regain possession. This is different from pushing your back four up and leaving space in the danger zone.

Whilst a player who is near to an opponent and has a chance of winning possession will always try it is worth considering what happens if they have 'good possession'.

> *Good possession is where a player has enough time and plenty of passing options. For example when a full back has asked for the ball off the keeper and the team are playing out from the back. If a player has good possession then a team has to re-group and retreat or they will be passed around and are in danger of conceding a goal. Some teams are really effective at using the transition and it is important that agaist these teams you organise defensively and decide where you are going to start defending from when they have good possession.*

The days of English teams and Ireland trying to regain possession of the ball at the opposition's penalty area are gone. The tactical and technical ability of teams means that they just played round them and exploited the space they left. Roy Keane identified this point (see section on long ball game)

So where do you start to pressure the ball? At a higher standard around the halfway line but how good the opposition are does have an impact.

♦ As a general rule, if you are significantly better than your opposition you can try to win the ball back by their goal.

♦ If you are similar, around the halfway line.

♦ If they are better than you, around the back edge of the centre circle.

The reason is simple: you need to deny space and have support for each other a lot more against a better team. You can push up and have a greater chance of winning the ball against a technically/tactically weaker team. The Irish of Charlton's era also used the poor surface of Landsdowne Road to create situations where the opposition would make mistakes (see module on Pitches)

Teams often try to push up to deny the opposition space. The biggest danger of this is that you leave space centrally (see Danger zone) for a ball into a fast or clever forward who is through on goal - 'one on one' with the keeper. Football is a game of too few goals to risk this strategy.

No matter how far up the pitch the midfield is trying to get the ball back, the defence should always try to keep play in front of it.

The defence should always try to keep play in front of it. If the opposition is successfully delivering balls in behind to forwards you are too far up

If a forward is to try to re- gain possession he/she must have support. One player chasing round after a back four is a waste of energy

What do we mean by 'too deep' or 'too flat'?

Theory

What you will learn

- The only way a defence push up safely is if their own team attacks and has possession further up the field

These two terms are often misused and misunderstood on a regular basis.

You may well have heard the criticism that a team is defending 'too deep' (too far back). The implication of this is that the defence should push further forward. It is important to recognise that the only way a defence can safely push up is if their own team attacks and has possession further up the field. The fault therefore is with the lack of successful attacking (holding the ball up).

Another commonly heard criticism is that 'the back four were too flat'. This is also confused by the term 'play a flat back four'. In fact, a back four should never be flat, except for the brief purpose of playing offside. Someone should always be covering (drop off a couple of yards): this varies depending on where the ball is. If a forward spots this and moves in behind another defender, the player simply steps up to catch him offside (see the diagram on the next page for an explanation). For this brief time the back four is flat but as soon as they can a defender will again drop off to offer cover. It is a 'cat and mouse' game between the defence and forwards. The advantage is with the defence as they can determine the offside line and trap forwards who try to exploit the space provided by a player dropping off to offer cover. How far back to drop depends also on the speed and ability of the forwards of the opposition. It also presents problems for a team when mounting an attack.

These two points are emphasised by Ron Atkinson (Monday March 10, 2003 The Guardian)

> *Thierry Henry's substitution played a massive part in helping Chelsea to equalise. When the Frenchman went off with cramp in his calf it not only took something away from Arsenal but made it far easier for Claudio Ranieri's team to mount the pressure that earned them a replay. The key is that Chelsea's back line was able to squeeze up a lot more, making the team more compact and giving them less distance to cover to mount a real threat ohad to defend deep because of the danger he poses with his pace if he's given acres n Arsenal's goal when they went forward. While Henry was on the pitch, Chelsea of space to run into over the top. The problem of holding a high line against Henry was shown with his goal. Defending deep meant Chelsea were stretched as a team and had a long way to travel with the ball to trouble Arsenal when they won possession at the back.*

Ron Atkinson also identifies the dangers of a high back line and the need for a solid defence (Monday February 24, 2003 The Guardian)

> *Manchester City gave the worst display of defending I have ever seen … their back line held a dangerously high line and I can't remember City making one decent challenge for the ball … but it's interesting to note that it was the team with the best defence, Valencia, who won the Spanish league last season. At the end of the day people know it's very difficult to win things with a ropey defence.*

A back four should never be flat except for the brief purpose of playing offside

Always try and keep an eye on all of the back four. One will try to drop off. Use the space. It's about timing

The next time someone uses these terms ask them what they mean. It is often the case that they are talking nonsense!

SPACE Practical Drill – the danger of the wrong offside line– *The need for a Covering player*

In this example player 1 is offering cover. If player 2, from the opposition, moves into the area shown by the arrow before the ball is played, then player 1 steps up and, for a brief moment, the back four is square. If the player 2 then realises and comes back to an onside position player 1 would once again drop to cover. The secret is to drop without being seen but if you are seen, and someone uses the space, step up.

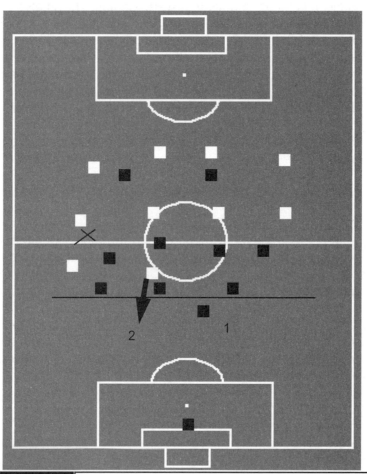

Key coaching tips– a defending player must be ready to cover the danger zone

A back 4 is only ever flat to catch a player offside. Someone is always covering the space. They are not covering the space if the opposition moves into it so they will briefly move up **(flat)** to catch that player offside. As they move back and become onside the process starts again. The secret. Don't be seen. In the example above the whole back 4 have left too much space, allowing an easy ball into the danger zone for the player with the ball BUT the covering player 1 should see off the danger.

'Going to ground' –
wastes time and frees up space for the opposition

Theory

Going to ground may give away a free kick (Up to sixty per cent of all goals come from set plays)

♦   Valuable seconds are lost (around 2.5) as a player gets up.

Going to ground means defenders sliding on the ground (slide tackle). This has three impacts
1.   It may give away a free kick (Up to sixty per cent of all goals come from set plays).
2.   Valuable seconds are lost (around 2.5) as a player gets up.
3.   At full back it may cause one of the centre backs to come across, leaving space in the scoring zone.

The following quote from Dario Gradi shows this

> *On the third goal David Walton **went to ground** and I am finding it hard to get through to him that quality centre-backs do not do that. I'm also always on at Dave Brammer **not to give free-kicks away**.* (Up to 60% of all goals come from set plays).

Another really good example of how costly going to ground can be was in the 2003 Champions League semi-final between Juventus and Real Madrid. The Italian defender slid in on Raul. He got the ball but it went to Ronaldo, who moved past the defender on the floor and scored. In other words, you can win the ball but, unless it goes to one of your own players, this can cost you.

DRILL – time 'spent lying down'- get everyone in the team to go into a slide tackle with no-one there and get back up again. Do this a few times, shouting out how long it takes (2.5 seconds ish). Next, get them to see how far they can run in this time (12-15 yards).

In pairs, tell one player to go down, and as he is down tell the other to run. Now add in the fact that they will be tangled up with an opposition player. In threes, two come up with a slide scenario in which they both end up on floor. Practice this using a ball and see how far the third player can get. Point out that on the ground, they are not in a position to stop a pass. Using an 11-a-side setting, create three scenarios when going to ground can cost.

If a midfielder goes to ground and the ball breaks to a player who can pick a pass into the danger zone for a fast forward.

The Juventus example (above). English players and in particular younger players are far too willing to 'slide'.

The simple message is stay on your feet. In last year's Champions league final (2003) there was only one free kick from a goal scoring position. Don't give away free kicks

As the game goes on defenders will get tired and slide in more. Utilise this

Don't concede the first goal!

Theory

What you will learn

- In football goals are precious. Scoring the first goal is critical.

Football is complicated by two other factors.

Firstly, football, unlike, for example, basketball, is a game of few goals. It is very possible to dominate a team in terms of possession and chances and still lose. Statistics do, however, show teams who have more possession are slightly more likely to win. Perhaps the analysis should cease after the first goal, when teams often sit back or are forced back (see below).

Secondly, scoring a goal, even with a reasonable chance, is not as easy as basketball or rugby. Centre forwards who take the few chances they get are rare and, at top level, expensive.

Having outlined how difficult it can be to score, it is worth noting that if you do score the first goal you will probably win. Research has consistently shown that scoring the first goal will go on to win a game in over seventy five per cent of matches.

The first goal is important because, against a team who is better than you, at some point you will commit players forward searching for an equaliser, this leaves you vulnerable to a counter attack. Against a team you are better than, the first goal to them boosts confidence, their 'tails' are up. They will defend their lead with gusto.

In fact, if you consider that a team will draw sixteen per cent of the remainder you will only lose in ten per cent of games having scored first. The most Common score is 1-1, so if you get a goal ahead, don't simply sit back.

A sound defensive tactic is simply not to commit players forward on an attack. This makes you ready to mark space on the transition

You won't score unless you create chances

Practical Test – mark on the following

Mark on the following.

- Scoring zone
- Danger Zone
- Thread zone
- Where would you 2 up on attackers
- How high you would try to win the ball back versus a team you are better than - 1
- How high you would try to win the ball back versus a team you are the same as - 2
- How high you would try to win the ball back versus a team who are better than you - 3

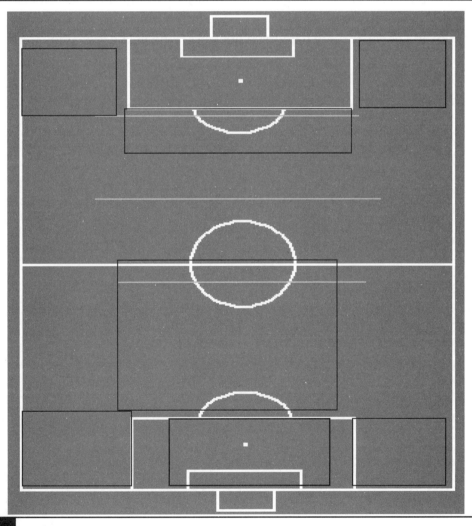

Key coaching tips

Go through the three different options. Discuss in relation to how good the opposition is. There are two points. Firstly, are their defenders good enough to keep possession and pass round you?
Secondly, does the defence need close support to deny the opposition space?
Remember, the better the player the less space s/he need .

What is meant by being 'sucked in'?

When marking at a set play the best tactic is a mixture between 'zonal' and 'man for man', Why?

Fitness and how good the opposition are determine how far up the field a team tries to win the ball back or if forwards try to win the ball back. Why?

What advice would you give to a forward about when to close down an oppositions full back with the ball.

What do we mean by too flat?

What do we mean by too deep?

What is wrong with the way most people use the terms?

What is meant by going to ground? What is the problem with a player going to ground often?

What % teams go on to win who score the first goals?

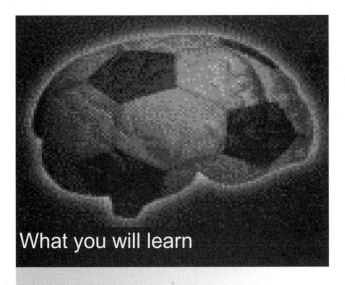

What you will learn

♦ **How to exploit time and space**

Here is a list of tactics that all sides should be familiar with if they are to use a variety of attacking tactics.

- The six ways to score a goal
- The first ball to look for is always forward
- If the ball into the danger zone is on do it
- How to play out from the back
- Winning the second ball
- What Holes are
- What Passing lines are
- What Bounces are
- The need to Switch often and fast to beat the gain line
- The Thread zone and how to use it
- Creating numbers up
- One touch– why it works
- 'Overs'
- Straight ball diagonal run, diagonal ball straight run
- Third man run
- Offering a good angle
- Good body shape to receive ball
- Having the run
- Going off the radar
- Timing and movement, shifting players, inside out

The crucial thing is that England are moving defenders about and making space for themselves.

Strachan June 17th Guardian

The 6 ways to score a goal

Theory

To understand and develop a teams attacking ability requires looking at 2 factors.

1)   How goals are scored. There are 6 ways to scorer goals and good team is able to exploit all of these.

2)   How the ball is moved to the oppositions goal. This can be quickly on the transition or more slowly from the keeper– played out from the back, a long kick and winning the second ball. Attacking teams will work the ball quickly or slowly up to the opponents penalty area. As they do this they will be testing the defence often by switching the ball. They are looking for a defensive player slightly out of position to allow a ball or run into a key space. They are testing the concentration of the defence. The more variety the more they are testing the defences concentration. The success of a team going forward is always going to be determined by tactics and other key factors such as how technically able a side is and having goal-scorers in the side. Goal-scorers come in all shapes and sizes, Some have pace others not, but all share the characteristics of being good decision makers, having excellent timing/movement, being cool in front of goal, and playing in teams that know how to get the best out of them by giving them the ball and creating the space they need.

The starting point is to try and analyse how goals are scored, By doing this we can look at out own teams and try to develop these methods. The table on the next few pages takes a look at this.

There are 6 ways to score goals. By looking at these it is possible to analyse if your team uses these tactics and if not develop them.

1.   Set Plays
2.   Crossing
3.   Ball played between defense and keeper– danger zone
4.   Ball played through the thread zone
5.   Long shot outside the area
6.   Skill

We will now look at each one of these and the defensive response.

1) Set Plays- Free Kicks /Corners/ Penalties NUMBER OF GOALS = 40-60% goals

Try to earn free kicks- encourage players to dribble when appropriate. Practices corners and free kicks. **KEY point** players have to accept that their role is to make false runs move opposition players around to create space for the intended recipient of the ball. At least tell the person taking the kick to aim for one person and try and get the timing right. Ask everyone else to do what they can to free up the player and space.

DEFENDING

Don't tackle unless you are sure you can win the ball. It is more dangerous to give away a free kick than let open play carry on- which is less likely to result in a goal. KEY point tell defenders to stay on their feet, not go to ground.

2) Crosses– there are 2 types of crosses NUMBER OF GOALS 30% in open play
Crosses from the wide area level with the penalty are often lead to goals. Especially those from near to the are at the touch-line delivered centrally. Work on overlaps and balls in to the space behind full backs for a diagonal run from a forward.
DEFENDING
Make wide players come inside. Double upon wide players with the ball.

The 'Shearer' cross- a diagonal ball to the far full back which is played back in to the penalty are for a forward to score from- occasionally leads directly to a goal but only if close in as it is a difficult angle top score direct from. Accounts for 5/6 % of crosses.A ball played from deeper diagonally on to the far opposition full back has 2 advantages for an attacking side.
1) Full backs are less able in the air than centre halves
2) The attacking player can be out wide and time their run to have a good jump at the ball- they are moving have the run.
Alan Shearer (Newcastle) does this very well.
DEFENDING
Ensure defenders react to second ball. Ensure the defensive line is not too deep and the keeper reacts.

3) Over the top- NUMBER OF GOALS 10%
If the space between the oppositions back line and keeper is available a ball should be played in to it. A second option is to flick the ball in to this space from a forward. A keeper should always have a look if a ball is available in to this space or to a centre forward who can flick the ball on.
DEFENDING
Never allow an easy ball in to this space as a defence this is your top priority. Make the opposition work for their goal. A defence needs good shape with one centre half will go for the header the other drop off to cover defenders should adopt this policy regardless of the threat. When the ball is at the other end e.g. your team has a corner- be aware of the keeper getting the ball and delivering in to this space.

4) The threaded ball– NUMBER OF GOALS 10% more in Italy
Add an area approx 10 yards long the width of the area and this is the space that teams- especially in Italy my research has shown will try usually using one touch to deliver a threaded ball in to the area for a forward to run on to.
Practice playing a ball in – on the floor if you can, to this area. Players thread the ball through. It's about timing. Sometimes players will have to play the ball out of the area backwards for another try. Space for this move is often found halfway through a switch from one side of the pitch top another when a defensive team is readjusting. Arsenal are expert at this. If a team only has between 0 and 18 occasions in most games when they have 3 or more passes in the oppositions half this ball is one part of a teams armory.
DEFENDING
Defensively teams that defend deep and are centrally compact are very hard to break down. Arsenal manage top break down defences regularly using this tactic s but a Champions League level defences are better at dealing with this (see below). This is part down to concentration and organisation.

5) Long shot 18 yards or more NUMBER OF GOALS 5%
Practice this and try to shoot. Successful teams put more shots on target not have more shots so it needs working on.
DEFENDING
Try to get players on their weaker foot even at professional level many many players really favor one foot. Be aware of players from the opposition who are dangerous at long shots.,

6) Skill– NUMBER OF GOALS 5%
Try and switch the ball or move it quickly to get players who dribble well in 1 v1 situations and encourage them to take these opportunities. A second player trailing them often will pick up a second ball as a defender gets a foot in but goes to found and leaves a free run, shot. Players that dribble and have skill distort defences shape and create space for others, Players that run distance well with the ball often a different attribute are good at breaking fast and turning defence into attack. Encourage defenders to look for these players as possession is re- gained and get them to run intelligently.
DEFENDING
Often the opposition players skill is down to players diving in of over committing. If a defence doubles up stays on its feet and has cover very few goals come from skill.

Analysis of goals scored in the English Championship weekend 13th March 2005

I have looked at how goals are scored and identified various categories that they fall in to. This is a useful exercise in terms of working out how to defend against goals and score goals. There were 82 goals in all. They were scored in the following ways. Some interesting

TACTICAL CONCLUSIONS The number of goals from set plays was lower than expected (stats usually point to between 40-60%). Although crossing is not an essential factor in terms of success- Arsenal are successful and do not score from crosses (Finkelstein has pointed out it is a matter of style) many goals were scored as a result of crosses.

How goals are scored	TOTAL 82	
SET PLAYS	31	37%
Corners	11	14%
Free Kicks	12	14%
Throw in	1	1%
Penalty	7	8%
OPEN PLAY	51	63%
Crosses	22	27%
Ball over top- *in between defence and keeper*	8	10%
Shearer- *ball played diagonally in air from deep to back of area for a player to head back into the centre of the penalty area to create a chance.*	4	5%
Skill- Dribble	4	5%
Long Shot from Outside the area	7	8%
Thread zone- *a ball centrally threaded through for a player to run on to or shoot to score*	7	8%

There are various tactics a team can use get to the oppositions goal

The keeper will have the ball on average around 30 x in a half. The first ball a keeper will look for is the ball in to the danger zone. If this is not on then there are 2 choices.

- A long ball from the keepers hands. If a team does this then they need to work on the second ball (see later). Any long ball is unreliable and the opposition often have as much chance of wining the ball as the team whose keeper kicked it. It is important to treat a goal kick or drop kick as a defensive situation– be compact and central.
- Play out from the back– it is essential a team can do this and the work on the movement to do this (see later). This is the most reliable way of mounting an attack and at top level teams will do this most of the time. As was mentioned earlier in this manual it is essential to play out from the back if you are to develop players.

A team needs to work on a variety of tactics to move the ball forward the common characteristic of all of these is movement..

- Creating passing lines
- Deciding how many players to send forward
- Switching
- In to feet
- Using the holes
- Creating numbers up
- Moving the ball quickly using 1 touch
- A ball in to space
- Working on crossing

All of these are covered in the following section.

A teams attacking tactics vary, unlike defensive tactics which are similar, as they have to get the best out of the players they have especially the forwards, and reflect their managers priorities. The following demonstrates some of the different priorities.

- Manchester United go out to win and attack as do Arsenal.
- Blackburn go out and prioritise not losing so they commit few players forward.
- Chelsea have the most flexibility and can win 1-0 from a set play or go out and score goals.
- Manchester United prioritise getting the ball wide and crossing the ball into the scoring zone where they have plenty of players.
- Arsenal use the thread zone constantly switching the ball then using the thread zone.
- Tottenham concentrate on defending and do not push many players forward instead relying on their forward talent to create something.
- Portsmouth like to go to feet down the middle.
- Sheffield Wednesday play a long ball game never playing out from the back
- Greece in winning the European Championships concentrated on defending and stopping the opposition and then kept the ball and relied heavily on set plays to score.
- Champions League winning Porto often played a 4-5-1 and followed a similar pattern.

We will firstly analyse how teams attack and goals are scored.

Then move on to look at some tactical considerations.

PLAYERS WITH POOR TECHNIQUE CAN DEFEND BUT NOT ATTACK AS WELL

TEAMS FOLLOW SIMILAR TACTICS WHEN DEFENDING
BUT THEY VARY CONSIDERABLY IN ATTACKING TACTICS

ALEX FERGUSSON TRIES TO WIN GAME BY COMMITTING PLAYERS FORWARD AND TRYING TO WIN AS OPPOSED TO NOT LOSE – THERE IS A DIFFERENCE

A TEAM NEEDS TO WORK ON MOVING THE OPPOSITION PLAYERS OUT OF SPACES FOR OTHERS

THE MOVEMENT OF PLAYERS WHO ARE NOT GOING TO RECEIVE THE BALL MATTERS AS IT CREATES SPACE FOR OTHERS

Attacking – how does your team attack?

It is worth considering two things if we are to analyse a teams use of attacking options.

1)   Firstly, **how your team attacks.** This should be part determined by the strengths of your forwards. **Be clear about what the strengths of your forwards are.**

2)   Secondly, does this work or need changing/do you need more variety?

To measure how well your team attacks, need to devise a set of criteria to look at. This helps us **test the variety of attacking tactics and their success.**

When watching Sheffield Wednesday in 2004 I noted they did not play the ball out from the back until the 53rd minute. They worked on a set goal kick routine with mixed results. They had no variety in how the attack began from the keeper. Watching the Sheffield Wednesday and United academy under 19's, neither side passed the ball out from the back for the entire game. The result, very scrappy games with a waste of the opportunity to launch an attack with a high degree of success. I chose a Local League game at Stourbridge to form a set of criteria. I watched the first half then devised a set of criteria to look at for the second. I looked at some attacking options to help devise a checklist. I measured the start of an attack by looking at the times that a team had the ball and are able to dictate what happens next . This can be divided into two.

1.   Set plays, goal kicks, drop kicks from the keepers hands, throws from the keeper, free kicks taken by the keeper e.g. for offside, throw ins, and free kicks. These are your best chance of launching a predictable attack.

2.   The opportunities in the game when the ball is in open play when a player has a choice over what to do with the ball. TIME. A player then needs to adopt an attacking tactic often faced with a great deal of choice. These choices are listed below.

	The Stourbridge Game– 2nd half	X = failure + = success
Goal Kick, offside foul GK if your side won second ball deliberately this counts	14	2 + 12 x
Drop Kick DK **if your side won second ball deliberately this counts**	3	3 x
Throw out from the keeper TK	3	3 +
Long ball in the air to feet or space 20 yards	20	7 + 13 x
Long ball on ground feet 20 yards +	3	2 + 1 x
Pass, Pass, Pass Dribble, long – put a d in if dribble or L for long	20	16 + (3d 2 ppl) 4 X
Free Kick FK on goal – attacking team got first touch	4	2 + 2 X
Corner – good delivery timing failed is a plus/ chance on goal is a plus	7	3+ 4 X
Switch – did the switch result in ground being gained	4	3 + 1 X
Crosses from 18 yards or in – attacking player first to ball	7	1
Threads	6	7x 1
Missed the pass – a player chose the wrong option, they may have kept the ball but they had a better option, e.g. ball to forward	8	Number 2, 7, 11, 9, 7, 2,3,8,2

We can see from this neither team passed the ball out from the back. Long passes were used frequently and with little success. The ball was not switched often. **What can we learn from this?** It tells us how a team attacks – in this case, using a balance between long passes and short passes. The balls from the keeper were very ineffective in terms of launching an attack. Some attempt has been made to identify players who chose the wrong option. A video of the game would allow them to identify their mistake, you would be surprised how well you and them will remember incidents. **This analysis could now form the basis of devising better attacking tactics.** Further useful analysis would be the speed between a team gaining possession and the ball arriving at the scoring zone - use of the thread zone.

The Long ball in the air 'LBA'

The Long ball in the air (LBA) tells us much about the nature of a game. The LBA could be a long ball from the keeper or a long ball when a player has a choice. The distance is approximately twenty yards plus. The table below shows how many times such a ball is played. Both Stourbridge and AC Milan played a similar number. AC Milan had a 'traditional' big strong centre forward, Stourbridge a forward who held the ball up well. Even with these two success was limited. The disappointing thing was the lack of variety, **predictability is the friend of a defence**. Stourbridge scored from a set play, shot from outside the area, the opposition a danger zone ball. In another game Manchester City dominated the game when they played a short passing game. As soon as the longer game came in they lost their way. Both goals in the game were a result of errors. Barcelona played a breathtaking game predominantly of short passing and trying to thread the ball through. They played out from the back through the midfield, switching and probing. The long ball they played was often a diagonal one to a forward wide player. One long ball that did lead to success was a perfectly weighted ball into the danger zone by Inter Milan to a forward who scored. In a game dominated by the ball being played out and around at the back, the one chance for this ball into this key space was taken. Barcelona goals came from a moment of skill and a thread zone ball.

How often and how successfully does your side use the LBA? Could your side emulate Barcelona whose keeper kicked the ball once in forty five minutes and had a fifty per cent success on their LBA's. They had over sixty two per cent of possession. A team having more possession is not, as a rule, a good indicator of success, but it does show that a team plays a more measured possession-based attacking game. As the ball into the danger zone is rarely available this is the norm for the best sides.

Stourbridge	37 (45 mins) LBA 7 successful 30 failures
Man City V Norwich	39 (45 mins) LBA 9 successful 30 failures
Barcelona v Inter Milan	18 (45 mins) LBA 9 successful 9 failure
AC Milan V Valencia	40 (45 mins) LBA 6 successful 34 failure
Total	134 31 success 103 failure

An analysis of goals in the Champions League (November, 2004) showed chances on goal to fall into the following categories. This analysis may help you prioritise development as it raises awareness of where chances come from. **Does your side use these attacking options?**

Mistake	4
Skill	5
Thread zone ball	8
Danger zone ball	6
Cross () further than 18 yards delivery	8 of which (2)
Set play	10
Shot outside area	5

Passing Lines

A passing line is the line between the player with the ball and another player on their team along which the ball can be safely played. The passing line may involve a ball into space and it is important that players create a passing line that offers support with correct distance so that when the ball is played and received they have enough time to control or chose a pass without the opposition players closing them down.

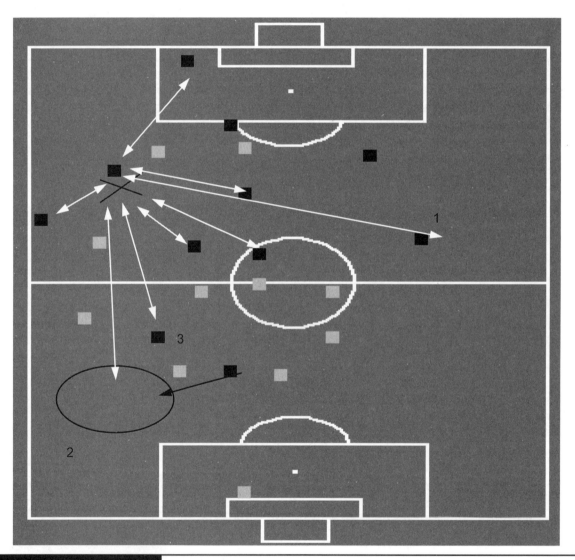

The shaded players team-mates have created a number passing line options. The choice the player with the ball makes should be based on 2 criteria.

1) Can they deliver the pass safely– have they the technical ability hence 1 and 2 *may not* be viable.

2) A forward ball. In this case 3. The rest of the team then has to react to this pass and create more passing lines

Moving players out of spaces

Players must be aware that their unselfish movement can create space for others. Try telling young players that they need to make a run with no real intention of getting the ball but simply to create space for other players and you are asking them to be very unselfish. To expect this without firstly making the whole team aware of the need to do it and secondly give them praise for it, recognise it, is unrealistic. Coaches need to 'look away from the ball' to spot their teams movement. This is not easy to do. Lets firstly look at some examples of movement.

The first thing to appreciate about attacking tactics is that players need to be aware of the value of movement that moves players out of spaces. When a goal is scored the scorer deserves recognition as does the person who provided the pass prior to the goal. However until teams and coaches start to appreciate the role of players who simply made runs or occupied spaces to create space for others we will not fully appreciate the game

The shaded player has run with the ball centrally from the position shown (thick arrow). The full back has followed. This has left space. The player with the ball plays it to a team mate who plays it into space shown for the wide player to run on to (thin arrows).

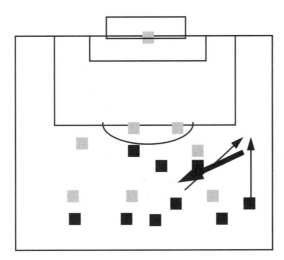

The full back has played the ball to the wide player (thick arrow). The opposition player is drawn to the ball and out of the space protecting an easy ball to the forward. The ball is played back to the full back (thick arrow) who can now play the ball forward (long thin arrow)

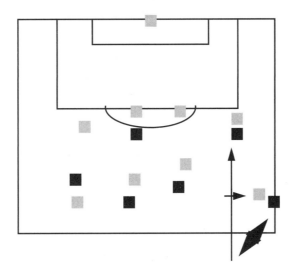

The shaded player moves into the space (the hole SEE LATER). The defender follows. Before the defence can adapt and become a back 3 shape the ball is played in to the space. The player has not touched the ball but created the space for the ball to be played. This quote from the professional game sums up the value of this movement *my job is to move defenders around and create space for Michael Owen.*

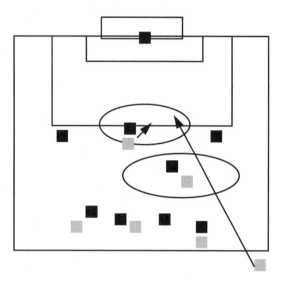

In this example the wide midfielder has moved centrally towards the ball x. This creates space behind him/her for the full back to exploit.

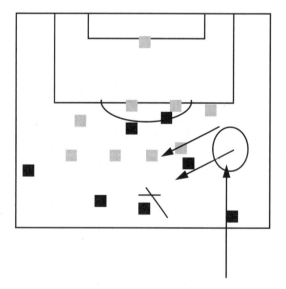

A team needs to create space. The first step is to appreciate players who do this. Once a team appreciates this they can exploit a whole range of tactics. Before we look at these we will firstly look at some facts about goals.

Shift him/her– creating space

At the start of this manual it was emphasised that movement is the most important factor in a game. It is therefore important to develop communication to improve this. The term shift him/her asks a player to try and move a member of the opposition.

The fact that the term exists raises awareness of the importance of movement.

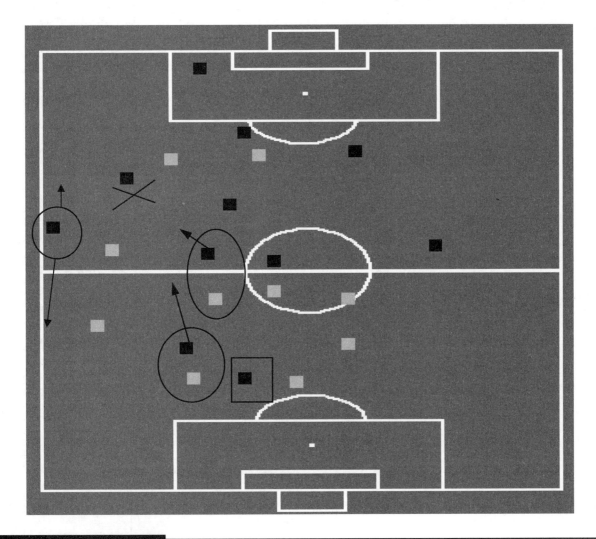

Key coaching tips– The important thing is the term SHIFT gets players thinking about movement and creating space

The 3 circled areas all contain players who can move and shift the opposition players. They are all on passing lines. It may be they have to actually receive the ball and then give it back as they attract-shift a member of the opposition. Remember attracting an opposition player forward leaves space to be exploited behind. The player highlighted by a square could ask the 2 nearest players on his/her side to shift the defending players so creating space for them to receive the ball

131

How to disappear as a forward– 'going off the radar'

Defenders watch the ball, players in their zone and players near the ball that may become involved. This means they are less aware of where other players are. It is possible to disappear off the radar and by timing a run, find space. Forwards often do this. Michael Owen (England V Azerbijan13th Oct 2004) did this and scored. He was not in the defences zones, he was not part of build up play, he arrived in the scoring zone at the same time as the ball. He was undetected by the defences radar until the ball arrived. Many other players do this. However it is essential that all the team is aware of this tactic or players will look for forwards and may criticise their lack of availability. The attacker has gone off the radar and will re-appear. They need to know this.

This player is 'off the radar' the nearest defender will be concerned with the scoring zone and the ball. He/she has 3 things to concentrate on and the wide player has moved to his/her 'blindside' ready to time their run as the ball is crossed in. With the attacking side having a numbers up situation is likely to happen.

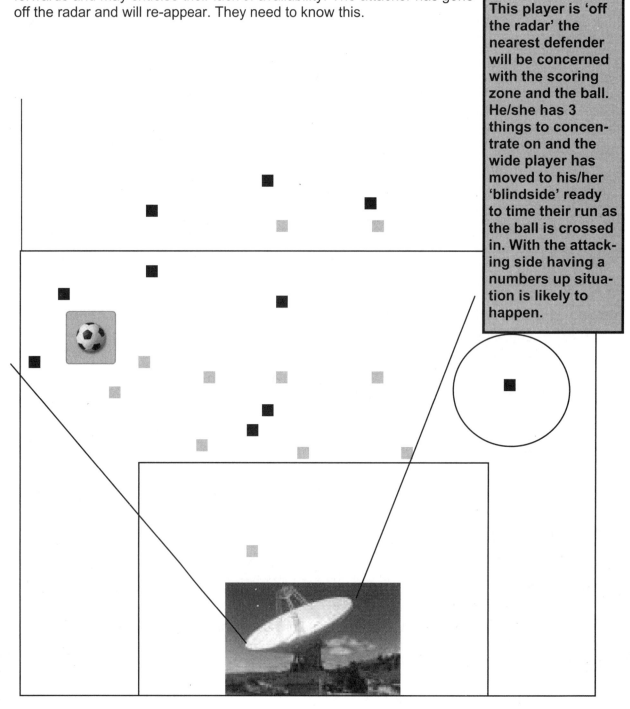

Theory

The timing of runs, especially to beat an offside trap or find space in the scoring zone, needs to be worked on.

The interchange between players in midfield and front has been highly developed and leads to many goals.

Players from midfield exploit the space created by the strikers.

Morientes, the Spanish forward, used this tactic against Chelsea in the Champions League semi final 2005. Chelsea stepped up their eye on the forwards, Morientes was just behind and ran through onside to score. The new rule regarding offside players who are not interfering not being offside also helps to distract defenders who will be focusing on them at the expense of a midfielder running through.

The England full back Gary Neville, has recently in Euro 2004, matured into a player whose timing to receive the ball on an overlapping run as he arrived level with the oppositions back four was, therefore, onside and in space in the scoring zone.

A full back who is overlapping needs to time his/her run to receive the ball and make use of the space too early or too late. Timing for a full back, as a general rule, means don't go beyond the player with the ball until it is played.

Forwards try to time their run to arrive in the closely guarded scoring zone at the same time as the ball so the defence can't react.

A forward dropping into the hole tries to time the movement to receive the ball unmarked and turn. The effect on the defensive shape, they will become a back 3 and close up in the central area, leaves space wide which can be used by a wide player or midfielder going beyond the attack.

When coaching timing, try and get players who play near each other to think about the timing of runs and be aware that often movement is designed to move opposition players to create space for someone to run into. Full backs need to work with the wide midfielder and forwards to see how to create space. The timing of a pass to meet a diagonal run needs to be worked on.

If players are aware of the runs and passes available, and communicate, it is possible to attack successfully.

Beware, the space you are guarding may be attacked by a late run

Timing is essential for overlapping fullbacks, centre forward arriving in hole, mid field running beyond the opposition back four and staying on side

Some facts about goals

Theory

What you will learn

♦   It is worth analysing some facts about the game to see how they can help us score goals. This module then goes on to look at the team strategies to utilise this information

Are goals scored as a result of defensive mistakes or are there 'good goals' which the defence could not stop?

♦   Some goals are due to mistakes. Either a defending player is in the wrong position or gives away a free kick/goes to ground.

♦   Some goals are the result of the attacking team finding a player in space with enough time (the defenders are still reacting but are in the correct position) to score. Good timing and a good goal.

♦   A well struck shot from outside the area.

♦   A moment of brilliance, for example , a winger who gets round the two players marking him/her using skill and crosses for a player, who has timed his/her run well, to score

♦   Analysis of thirteen goals in a Premiership on a weekend in April 2004 reveals some interesting facts about goals.

♦   two goals from a set play,

♦   five were 'good goals',

♦   six were defensive mistakes.

Was pace a factor?

♦   For five out of thirteen goals, a player needed pace.

Was height/aerial ability a factor?

♦   Two goals were the result of a flick on or a direct header off a corner.

Pace or height were a factor in around fifty per cent of goals. Whilst these conclusions are useful, more research needs to be done on this.

Where do moves that score goals start from?

The next thing to look at with a critical eye is where the moves leading to goals start from: again research shows (Premiership)

♦   from the attacking third it is around fifty per cent

♦   from midfield thirty per cent

♦   from the back twenty per cent

If we look at these figures at a higher level (World Cup) more goals originate from the back (fifty per cent).

What is the relationship between goals and passes?

In analysis of over 5,000 games (INSIGHT), several studies indicate that approximately eighty per cent of goals are scored from five passes or fewer (often three or fewer). It is also interesting to note that, in the 1994 World Cup, fifty per cent of Brazil's passes leading to goals were "one touch" passes. However, as I mentioned above, the key point here is the speed (time) between regaining possession and the goal for which statistics are not available.

How does this affect your attacking strategy?

I would, therefore, argue that a coach's commitment to develop players along with greater tactical awareness and technical ability, means that teams that more successfully play out from the back will, inevitably, be more successful. The high proportion of goals scored from midfield and attack show that

•   teams use the transition well to attack

•   teams defend badly from the transition.

It is essential for coaches to concentrate on how well their team reacts to the transition.

Whilst it is desirable to play out from the back, this must be varied and the whole team be aware of the position they should adopt to do this

The speed that a team does things at is more accurate as a measure than number of passes (which implies long ball soccer)

How much time do you have to attack?

The ball changes hands every 15

- Research has shown that the ball is in play, on average, approximately sixty minutes of a ninety minute game.
- Contact with the ball by outfield players has been estimated to be between one and a half and three minutes. This may not seem much, but it shows the speed of the game, the importance of making good decisions, and the necessity to use time and space well.
- How often does possession change? On average possession changes around once every fifteen seconds, so you will have plenty of opportunities to attack.

The ball changes hand so often that a team is constantly either attacking, defending or at some point in transition. If good decisions are made, then the time between your team regaining and losing possession should increase. This is a good analysis but your team must not simply keep possession for possession's sake it must still be intent on scoring. Obviously, if you are ahead priorities are likely to change.

How many goals come from crosses?

- Around one third of all goals come from crosses
- The wider the area the ball is crossed from, the less the chance of scoring. Between the six yard box and just outside the penalty area is the most effective place to cross from
- Crosses to the middle, as opposed to far post, are the most effective (the near post is the least effective) and attacking players need to make contact with the ball first

You will not score unless you create chances. The key points is therefore to create chances.
This is highlighted by the ex Liverpool manager

'As a manager the most important thing to ask is do we create chances? Yes we created 29 against Palace and battered them. So are we playing well? Yes.' (Gérard Houllier, The Guardian, 8th February, 03)

Houllier added to this in November: *We have 15 to 20 attempts on goal every time, Liverpool have the most shots on goal of all premiership teams this season… he goes on but if you take the game to the opposition, taking that risk, sometimes it gives space to the opposition'Gerard Houllier Observer 2nd Nov 2003)*

How many players you commit to an attack - 'The numbers game'
As we have mentioned before, breaking quickly is essential. If an opposition team has the back four and a midfielder, then committing six players is desirable if the midfielders work back.

Set Plays - How many goals are scored from set plays?
- Analysis from the 1994 World Cup shows that
- Forty per cent of goals were from set plays
- For the winners, Brazil, fifty per cent of goals were from set plays
- In all competitions the figure can vary from forty per cent to over sixty per cent.

Players dribbling with the ball often win free kicks, so this should be encouraged, especially in the opposition's third. Many teams at all levels maintain their status by scoring goals from set plays (spend time working on free kicks and corners, as up to sixty per cent of goals are scored from set plays). Do teams spend sixty per cent of their training time working on them?

The value of set plays is highlighted by an ageing side of limited tactical or technical ability which stated this in a newsletter.

The game changes all the time. Concentration is essential

You need to use the transition time well. Crosses are an effective weapon, but try to get close to the area and to the touchline

> *Wombourne started the second half as they finished the first and went about trying to win corners and free kicks towards the opponent's box. The one area where Wombourne dominated was on set pieces and it looked like this was the most likely avenue to produce a goal*

Teams such as this then sit back on the seventy five per cent (first goal wins game) rule and try and sneak another in the space left as the opposition pushes forward to equalize.

Analyse a video and look at the numbers of players a team commits forward.

Time the speed between regaining possession and an attack.

Are goals scored as a result of defensive mistakes or are there 'good goals' which the defence could not stop?

Was pace a factor?

Was height/aerial ability a factor?

What is meant by 'going off the radar'?

Where do moves that score goals start from?

What is the relationship between goals and passes?

How does this affect your attacking strategy?

How much time do you have to attack?

How many goals come from crosses?

You will not score unless you create chances. The key point is therefore to create chances.
How many chances did Liverpool create (Premier Division club) against a side from the division below? Guess

How many players you commit to an attack-'The numbers game'

Set Plays-How many goals are scored from set plays?
What wins free kicks. What does this tell us about out tactics?

'Sucking' a team in – short, short long/slow, slow quick

Theory

What you will learn

• That sometimes an attacking team may play the ball around at the back or in midfield to attract opposition players to the ball before playing it long into the space the opposition have left

Dario Grady observed in a comment reported in the Observer, April 2004, that his team 'got sucked in' and that it cost them a goal. What does he mean?

The opposition had possession in a particular area (for example, the back five). They played the ball between them often slowly to encourage the opposition to move forward and try and gain possession.

Once they had attracted players to the ball they played a longer ball into the space that was left and exploited this.

This was done quickly before the opposition could re-group. So another way of describing the tactic would be slow, slow, quick (this relates to Time).

A simple coaching strategy to employ this is short, short, long. This implies two short passes to attract players to the ball and then a long pass to the space that this creates behind them. It obviously could be a case of short, short, short, long (this relates to space).

A team may use its defence playing the ball around in their own half to try and attract the opposition forward to gain possession. They then play round them, or switch the ball to find space and attack. In general, when attacking, the ball needs to be moved quickly. On this occasion the ball may be moved slowly as bait for the opposition's players.

If a team adopt this tactic at the back, the opposition have to be very disciplined. The crowd may be baying them to push on and get the ball, other players in their team may be demanding this. The inherent need to gain possession has to be abandoned or the oppositions may punish them.

If a team is to push forward on re-gain possessions high up the field it is important that players go forward as a unit with a high chance of success. A lone forward trying to regain possession off a back four is a waste of time and energy.

When defending, teams need to be aware of over committing players and leaving space that the opposition can exploit

As an attacking strategy a team can try to create space by, for example, the defence playing the ball around with the specific intention of drawing players towards them to create space elsewhere

'A Winger should always get the ball'

Theory

What you will learn

- A winger (wide player) should always get the ball if he/she uses space well.

A winger (wide player) should always get the ball. Good defensive play always leaves more space out wide. Priority is given to defending the space centrally (this is why switching play quickly will always find space).

A defender with a wide player without the ball in their zone will
- Allow him/her to receive the ball, as long as the attackers are in front of him/her
- The defender is advanced marking. The defender will not close the wide player without the ball down as this would mean leaving space in a dangerous central area. The wide player may then move into this space and receive the ball.
- If the defender moved over to mark the wide player and left the space it could also be exploited by the oppositions forwards.
- When the wide player has the ball the defender will close him/her down. The defender may delay this to allow his/her team to move over and cover the space he/she is about to leave.

Using wide areas and switching the ball well stretches defences and create space, as well as providing crosses.

Wide players need to practise, especially with the full back, the movement required to get possession. Wide players will go wide and deep to receive the ball. If a defender follows (as mentioned above) he can move into the space to receive the ball, or another player can use this space. A wide player can create space and allow a player from his/her team to gain possession without even touching the ball.

These points really need demonstrating in an 11-a-side match situation as they are very hard to describe. Chess pieces can be used or other chalkboard techniques, but practical with questions is the best way to aid understanding. The practical drill on the next page will help.

Good defenders leave players out wide. This means wide players are able to get the ball

Use the fact that a defender will leave you if you hug the touchline to get the ball. Go wide and deep

Practical Drill – *offering a good angle*

Drill– The wide player is not offering a good angle (1). The player with the ball should not pass. If the wide player (1) moved back to the position shown (2) the defender should leave him. S/he can now safely receive the ball.

If the defender follows the player to position (2) a ball into the space is a race. The 2 centre forwards can also use the space vacated.

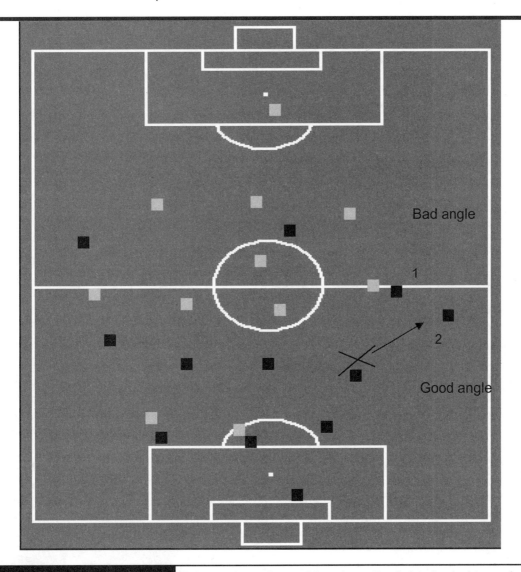

Key coaching tips– make sure receiving players are at good angles making it a safe ball and testing the positional sense of the opposition defender

Other points above. Note how the light shaded team have left the wide player for the shaded team (this is correct).

Note how the shaded team full back has moved into midfield and the remaining three have adopted a three at the back formation.

'Playing in the Holes'

Theory

Many teams play 4-4-2 with the defence and midfield broadly in lines. Certainly the defence will try to be in a line. This means that between the defence and midfield there will be space and between midfield and attack.

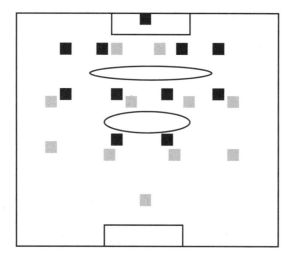

There is space to be found in 'the hole'
- ♦ between midfield and defence
- ♦ between defence and midfield.

Centre forwards often drop off the defence into the area between the defence and midfield. There is space here. Defenders are reluctant to leave the back line. Attackers who do this, and time it well to receive the ball, create problems for the defence. Alex Fergusson- *we spoke about Zidane because great teams invariably have an axis. He can be hard to play against when he drops into the hole behind the strikers.*

Does one of the centre halves go with the player so leaving space? If this happens it is essential that the defence closes into a back three shape. If this happens it leaves space on the wings, as with a back three shape there is twenty five per cent more space for the remaining forward to use. This space will be wide. Although this space will be away from the danger and scoring zones (out wide) a third of goals come from crosses. This space can therefore be exploited to move the ball forward.

The second hole is between the defence and midfield. A central midfield player will often use this space to receive the ball and look forward or switch the ball. If the opposition close this player down it creates space in the midfield and, in particular, out wide, which full backs can exploit by pushing forward.

The defence likes to have all four players at the back. As soon as one moves into midfield there are three and so more space for the attack

Moving back in to the hole often finds space

Practical Drill – the holes

The holes exist in between defence and midfield and midfield and attack. One obvious tactic to use these is a forward dropping off to find space. Another is by playing a diamond shape in midfield, as opposed to a more flat shape, the central midfielder at the forward point may find space in the hole. However this may mean it is not available for the forwards. If the 2 forwards play pushed up on to the defence centrally then the hole can be used if the oppositions midfield do not react and drop in to cover the space. A wide midfielder such as Paul Scholes of Manchester United can exploit this space. It is important to realise how a teams formation dictates where space is. It then has to be used.

DRILL simply play a game with all forwards told to try to use the hole. Stop the game when a player uses the hole and discuss what happens. It may be that a defender pushes on. Highlight the new space this creates which may be out wide as the defence adapts to a back 3. Players who use the hole successfully must have excellent control (first touch) and be able to move forward at the right time (timing).

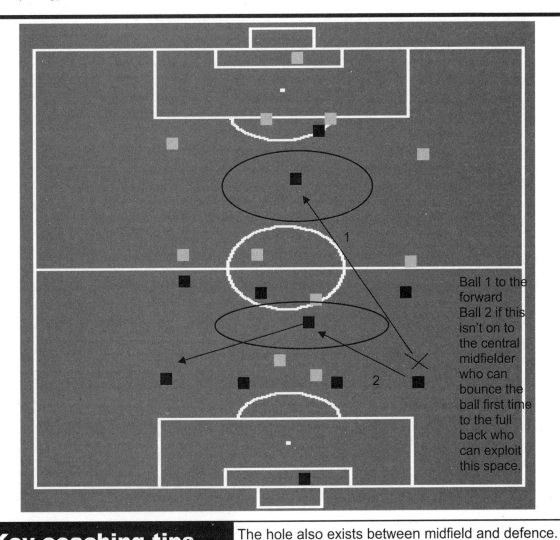

1

Ball 1 to the forward
Ball 2 if this isn't on to the central midfielder who can bounce the ball first time to the full back who can exploit this space.

2

Key coaching tips– as a coach look away from the ball to see how the holes are used. There are 2 obvious holes to exploit

The hole also exists between midfield and defence. You will often see a midfielder dropping into this space to 'bounce the ball' – help play the ball out from defence. 1 plays the ball into the forward who has moved into the hole. The forward is closed down.

141

Practical Drill – 'the third man run'

Drill– 1 plays the ball into the forward who has moved into the hole. The forward is closed down. The forward plays the ball back to 1 who plays it into the space for the midfielder to run on. He is the third man. He benefits from the play by the creation of space.

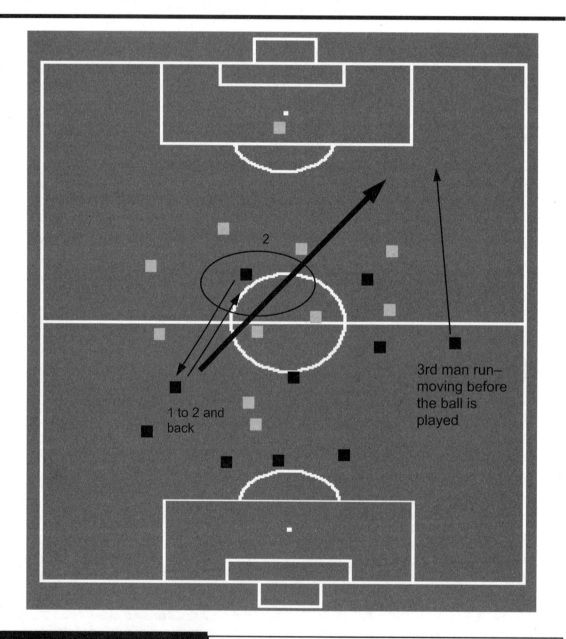

2

1 to 2 and back

3rd man run— moving before the ball is played

Key coaching tips– make your team aware of the third man run. It combines timing with 'going off the radar'

The defence will watch the ball and players around it. This means a player other than the passer and receiver can 'have the run' and using good timing find space and beat an offside trap. By using the hole it is possible to make the time to play a ball for a third man run.

Straight run to diagonal ball, diagonal ball to straight run

- The best passes to release players into space

Theory

Straight run to diagonal ball means a player with the ball plays a diagonal ball (cross field ball) to a player who is doing a straight run. The player doing a straight run can time this run whilst being able to see the defence and, as is often the case, the offside line.

Run– straight

Pass– diagonal

The straight ball to a diagonal run is also based on the ability of the attacking player to see the opposition, and the space. Timing is essential.

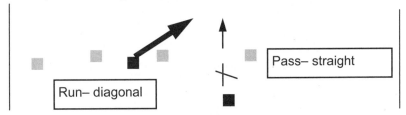

Pass– straight

Run– diagonal

If you imagine a straight run to a straight ball, a player receiving the ball would have to keep turning to watch the ball and hence not see the space or the opposition as well. It is a much harder ball to control.

This whole tactic is based around being able to see the ball and the space that you are trying to run into.

The key is to arrive at the correct time to beat any offside trap and not give the defence the chance to adapt its position.

These two balls are really useful when playing around the opposition's penalty area, as the longer ball over the top is no longer an option, and the keeper awaits any straightforward over-hit ball.

A straight ball to the forward who has made a diagonal run to receive it has the following advantages

1. He is already running while the defenders have to get up to speed

2. He can see the ball and the space he is exploiting, as well as the defence and their offside line.

3. As he moves between zones defenders have to react - this can take a split second.

A diagonal ball to the straight run has the same advantages. Both these balls are used throughout a team. A wide player will exploit a ball played straight between the full back and centre half (sometimes called a channel) .

Defenders need to be aware of the two runs in order to deal with them

Attackers who time these runs well will be most successful against teams

Practical Drill– Straight run to diagonal ball, diagonal ball to straight run

DRILL– 1 plays a straight ball in to the forward 2 who has made a diagonal run to receive it. The advantages of this ball to the forward are that
1. He/she is already running, while the defenders have to get up to speed. *Has the run.*
2. He can see the ball and the space he is exploiting as well as the defence and their offside line.
3. As he moves between zones defenders have to react; this can take a split second.

2 plays a diagonal ball to the straight run as shown. The advantages are the same.
DRILL Mark the pitch off with 2 lines -one at each end at the position shown. Play a game in which no one can enter this area until the ball is played. The most successful balls will be straight to diagonal or diagonal to straight. Discuss.

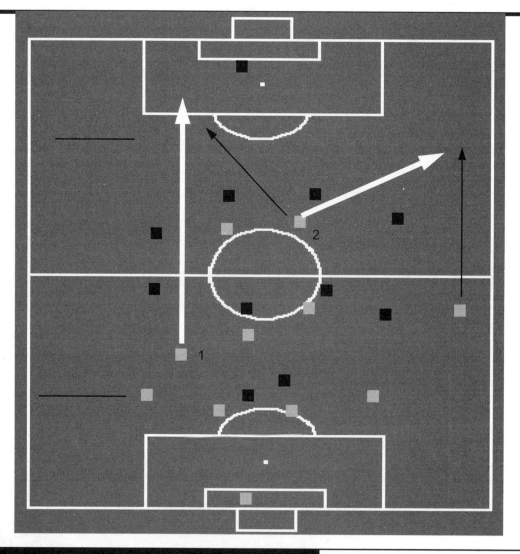

Key coaching tips– attackers can see the ball and the space they wish to run in to as well as the opposition, who are holding an offside line, if they choose the correct runs. The also 'have the run' on the defence

If a player receiving the ball is running when she/he receives the ball she/he always have the advantage that the defender has to get up to speed. Reaction time/thinking time. This split second can make all the difference.

'One touch' soccer exploits time and space best

Theory

What you will learn

- Playing one touch soccer moves the ball quickly and hence exploits space. If done well it is very difficult to defend against

This is demonstrated by looking at Brazil. In the 1994 World Cup fifty per cent of their passing prior to a goal was one touch. One touch moves the ball quickly, so exploiting space.

One touch football is also a fantastic way of developing players and perhaps the best means to judge how good they are.

If you put players into a one touch situation they have to do the following
- Get good body position
- Have a good first touch
- Be aware of what is happening around them (where the space is)
- Deliver a well weighted ball to their own player which gives him/her the chance of making a good pass
- Having passed the ball, find space/have good movement to offer a passing line

Good players are appreciative of time and space.

Far too often teams play too much two touch. As you will see later, the extra touch changes everything and is a lost opportunity to exploit space (this is also dealt within the chapter on playing the easy ball).

Put simply, if you use two touches instead of one it will take twice the time to get there.

The defensive team should try to speed things up if it leads to mistakes, but against good teams make play slow and pre- dictable

One touch moves the ball quickly so exploiting space

Practical Drill – 'one touch' passing exploits space best

One touch and switching are the 2 most important tactics to practice even if it is in training in a sports hall etc.

DRILL Use one touch in your warm ups and in game situations. Vary the numbers and the space. Play will break down but this exercise really develops players. Choose areas of the pitch to practise. Have the aim to move the ball to the forward line in the grid. Do it in the area with the aim to score when you have the ball. This is good practice for the transition Houllier talks of mastering. Have the team working in 2 different areas, then change. Introduce offside. If you catch the team you get possession.

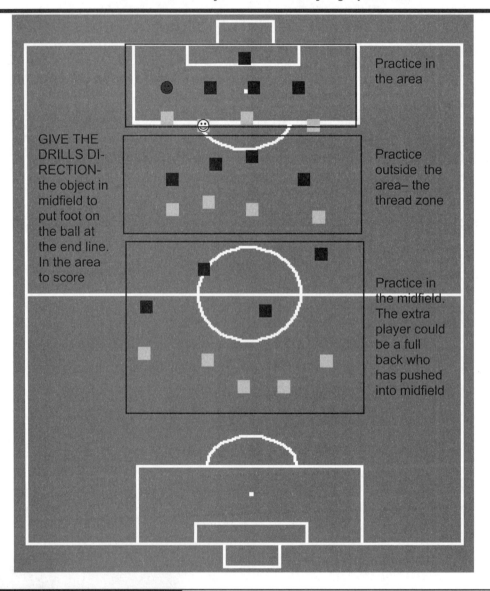

Practice in the area

GIVE THE DRILLS DIRECTION– the object in midfield to put foot on the ball at the end line. In the area to score

Practice outside the area– the thread zone

Practice in the midfield. The extra player could be a full back who has pushed into midfield

Key coaching tips– one touch can break down defences

You may not be able to use a pitch all the time, there maybe no light , or it would damage the surface.

But if you start off on a pitch then players can relate to the key spaces. It gives greater meaning to drills .

Switching the ball

Theory

Switching the ball means moving the ball from one side of the pitch to the other to find space and ideally move forward. It is useful for coaches to borrow the term a gain line from rugby. The gain line is a line from where the ball started across the pitch. If in switching the ball is further forward than the gain line it has been a successful switch.

Any analysis soccer would conclude that the best teams switch the ball well. The best way of switching a ball is using first time passing because this takes the least amount of time. In addition, use as few players as possible as this also saves time.

The section 'playing out from the back' describes more extensively 'bouncing' the ball' off midfielders and attackers. This basically means playing a ball to them which they (first time) play into an area of more space (see this section for the range of options). Once the ball is played into space this must be used to move forward . Then switch the ball to the other side as the defence closes to reduce the space around the ball.

A defending team will always try to compact but this takes a few seconds. If the ball is on the left, there will be space on the right. If the ball is central, there will be space on both wings. This space needs to be used, then the ball moved to find new space as the defence becomes compact around the ball. Here are two examples of where space is in a game.

The Champions League final 2003 (Milan v Juventus) had two Italian teams who spent the whole game switching the ball to get near the opposition's goal. There it would break down (as time and space ran out) and so the other team would attempt the same.

In terms of time, the golden rule is usually to do things quickly - hence using space before the opposition fills it. What is the advantage of switching the ball? Let's look at **Ron Atkinson, Monday, September 1st, 2003, The Guardian**

> *Liverpool have often lacked width under Gérard Houllier and benefited from using two players who got chalk on their boots at Goodison. Everton's defence and mid-field were pulled about far more than they'd have wanted and Steven Gerrard had much better passing angles.*
>
> *With El-Hadji Diouf wide right, Harry Kewell wide left and Vladimir Smicer getting forward from central midfield, Houllier put out the most adventurous line-up I have seen during his time at Anfield. Kewell drifted infield cleverly at times and, while there wasn't a stream of crosses from him and Diouf, they drew opponents out wide, pulled people about and created space for Gerrard, Smicer, Michael Owen and Milan Baros. When Liverpool play narrow, teams can basically defend just the width of the penalty area and keep things very compact at the back and in midfield. Then it's hard for Liverpool to break them down. Their forward players are tightly marked and Gerrard ends up playing little poky balls which teams can scramble out. With the wide players, Everton couldn't stay so compact .*

When switching the ball along the back four, it is better to have your centre halves in position B. It offers two options to switch and involves fewer touches

When switching the ball try to use one touch - it is faster and exploits the space better. There will be little space in the area where the ball is. Players need to think- I need to switch the ball away from this area to find space

Switching and using width creates space in the centre. If the switch is fast enough and the ball is played via a player in the centre s/he may find space centrally. They can use the player in the space as a 'foil'. Arsenal do this particularly well.

Practical Drill– 'switching the ball' to find space

DRILL Set up the position below. The defence is positioned correctly. Ask players to identify where the spaces are. X = the ball

The best teams switch the ball continuously looking for space and probing the oppositions defence for an error. As you can see, there is little space in the area the ball is in. The area with space is marked by the x or above by the O.

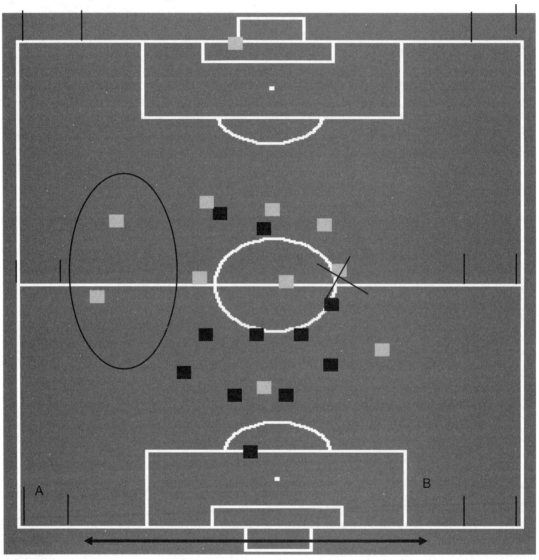

The best teams switch frequently. Do an analysis of how often your team switches in a game. A worthwhile drill is to have 6 small goals as shown. A team gets a point if it gets a player to run through the gates in the middle when playing out from the back or 2 points for passing through the end gates. This encourages switching. ALWAYS play offside it keeps it realistic. Make the gates/goals wide enough to mean there is no use simply putting a player between them to stop a run or pass. An added alternative is at the goal-line have one player who runs from goal, A to B, off the pitch if they are in the gate the opposition cannot score. They could, of course, also act as keeper.

'Bouncing' the ball

Theory

- The ball can be moved into space by playing a one touch pass off various players

'Bouncing the ball' means a player passing to another player who, first time, plays the ball to a player in space.

This pass is unavailable to the player with the ball as the opposition are in the way.

'Bouncing the ball' as a term is an apt description of the tactic: the pass is not a 'one, two' with the same player passing and receiving the ball, but a pinball type first time ball to a player in space.

The player delivering the ball will see the destination and so should deliver a well weighted ball to the correct foot and also communicate the bounce. In certain positions this will be an obvious ball. The tactic can, however, be developed successfully in really tight areas, such as the opposition's penalty area.

As a defender, having the opposition bounce the ball using one touch is very hard to deal with.

One of the most useful bounces, as it switches the ball to space, is the use of the two central midfielders by the defence.

The defence must use the goalkeeper. When playing out from the back, or when bouncing off a midfielder, the keeper should always make himself or herself available. There are various reasons for this
- If it's getting tight and a player is under pressure, then a ball to the keeper, and a first time clearance, can take the pressure off.
- Remember the keeper has a great view of what's going on so s/he can often start an attack or switch play. The keeper has time and is in space.

Put your players in this position on the next page or talk through the options in a class based situation .

Watch a top level game and identify as many bounces as you can.

It is impossible to defend against a good bounce

Bouncing is essential to good attacking play

Practical Drill – various 'bounces'

BOUNCING the ball means playing the ball to a player who first time plays it to another player. This ball is not available to the passer due to oppositions players being in the way. The player 'bouncing' needs to do it first time to avoid being tackled. The passer needs to make it easy for the receiver by passing at the right weight and to the correct foot. Communication is essential but when players are aware of the concept of a bounce they will soon pick it up. The timing of the receiver allows them to always be able to 'bounce' the ball. The opposition will still be reacting and can do nothing about it. Drill– put your players in this position and talk through the options. Answers are on the next page.

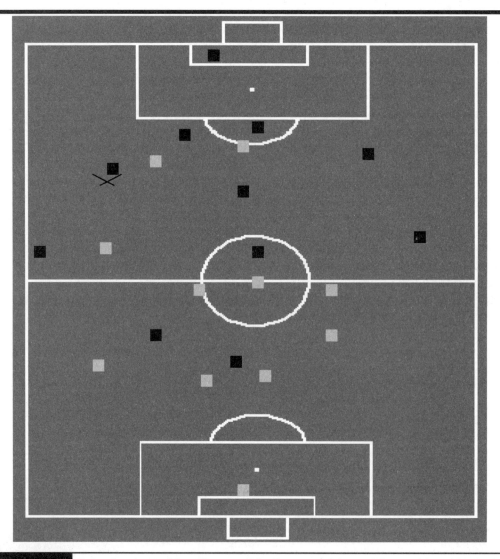

Key coaching tips- bounce the ball to find space	Ask players to identify possible 'bounces' from this position. Walk through them. Try them 2 touch then 1 touch. Ask the player with the ball what considerations he/she has to make when passing the ball. Needs to be well weighted at a good height– on ground. Try doing bounces using headers as this is also a possibility. Move the whole position to around the opposition's area. Identify and execute bounces to release a forward. These bounces are often to an outstretched leg, chest etc.

ANSWER Practical Drill – 'bounces' highlighted

Drills– put your players in this position and talk through the options. The most obvious ball for a bounce, as it has the greatest space, is the use of the 2 central midfielders by the defence to switch the ball

Bounce 1 Full back to Keeper to full back
Bounce 2 Full back to Centre midfielders to full back/wide midfielder
Bounce 3 Full back to Centre forward to midfield who moves in to space
Bounce 3a Full back to Centre forward to centre mid who makes run shown
The ball may be switched to the opposite wide mid player who often may have to bounce it back to the full back

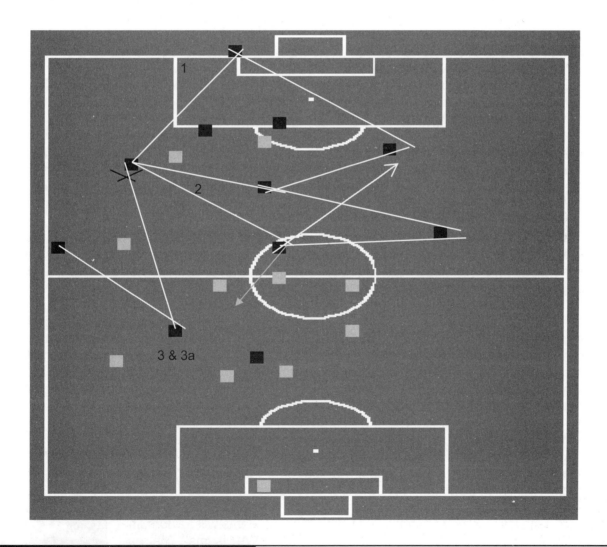

Key coaching tips-There are bounces all over the pitch. All the players above are trying to create passing lines.

Try from other areas such as midfield. Vary the starting position. Maybe introduce a call 'bounce right'

Playing out from the back – the numbers game

What you will learn

- How to play out from the keeper
- How to create a numbers up situation in midfield. How a defence may play the ball around to 'suck' in the opposition before exploiting the space they have left

Theory

Why play the ball out from the back? Daniel Finkelstein (Times, November, 2004) a statistician, observes that

- Good teams play the ball out from the back
- The keeper plays a critical role with good teams having keepers who, often using a throw, keep possession and start another attack.

It is important for any team to have a clear purpose. Simply passing the ball around without the intention of getting it forward is not an effective tactic. This point is emphasised by a quote relating to the England Rugby team *England have been too lateral for too much of the time in this six nations. Its been pass, pass, pass, I pass, he passes, we pass rather than … trying to get round the back of the line.* The main objective when playing the ball out from the back is to get the ball in your teams possession as far forward as possible. Playing out from the back is a lot more reliable than a drop kick or goal-kick, which are fifty/fifty situations (that is not to say you should not use these sometimes). The purpose of playing the ball round at the back is to find space for a player, usually full back, to move into midfield.

This should be easily done

- The back five are up against two forwards.
- If the ball is switched quickly a team will find space. Players need to move forward into this space quickly before it is closed down. They can move into the midfield. This creates a 'numbers up' situation in midfield (further forward).

Football/soccer is therefore often a numbers game. The need is to create situations where you have numerical superiority over the opposition. You now have five in midfield, the opposition has four. You can play round them. This is not as easy as at the back, four versus five does not allow as much space as five versus two.

Using 'bounces' and, if needs be, going back again to launch another attempt a team now can begin to more effectively probe the opposition's defence. One simple tactic to ensure you create numbers up is to get full backs to take throw ins. This means that the back four now adopts a defensive back three shape. The full back can join in general play and create 'numbers up'.

This is logical as teams are more vulnerable during the transition. A team, at the point the oppositions keeper receives the ball, are committed forward and spread out. An intelligent use of the ball by the keeper can effectively launch an attack by for example releasing a player who runs well with the ball to exploit space and create numbers up at the other end. Sometimes this 'fast break' is not available. In this case a team needs a more measured slower approach. Playing out from the back or maintaining possession to launch another attack requires good technique. Dario Gradi highlights this point.

> *We weren't playing for a draw, we were just trying to get our passing going. But unfortunately we just went backwards and our players at the back aren't technically good enough to play it around and get a counter attack going. Dario Gradi, The Observer, 30th September, 2001..*

A defender moving into midfield with the ball creates numbers up. The remaining three adopt a back three line up

The keeper can effectively start attacks– good teams use this fact

If we watch any high level game of football you will notice that teams will seldom, if ever, try to stop the opposition from playing out from the back. Why is this? The reason is that, if coached correctly, it is very difficult to stop teams playing out from the back. To commit the players forward in order to stop teams playing out from the back leaves a team vulnerable to a long ball- from the keeper or member of the back four into the space left.. This tactic is called sucking a team in.

Playing out from the back or around at the back has two clear purposes
1.   Release a player, usually a full back, into midfield
2.   Suck the opposition into the space and create space further forward which can be exploited. This second purpose is examined in more detail in the section on 'sucking players in' but it is briefly worth considering it here

The defence play the ball around, pass for the sake of it, in an attempt to draw as many of the opposition as possible forward into this area. The ball is then moved quickly to exploit this space. The purpose, therefore, is to 'suck the opposition in'.

By using the rules regarding goal kicks it is easily possible for the keeper to launch attacks.

Using the area rule to play out from the back from a goal kick

If the goalkeeper passes the ball to a full back who is positioned on the edge of the penalty area and the player goes into the area to touch the ball the goal kick is taken again. This rule effectively means that a player who has asked for the ball, and then realises that the ball has been under hit or an opposition player is closer than he/she thinks, can simply step into the area. The referee (and usually the opposition) will blow for the kick to be taken again. The ball is then played quickly back to the keeper who can then pass to the other full back (who is usually in space) as both forwards have been drawn towards the ball.

Put simply, the rule means that the keeper should always find someone to pass to and defenders can decide if it is a good time to have the ball.

The role of the keeper

Keepers must be told to want the ball. Take the pressure off them by saying 'it doesn't matter if you mess up trying to do the right thing'. In my experience, in three seasons we have only given away one goal due to a keeper being overconfident and delaying a clearance. Keepers can communicate the best option and they can also offer support and switch the ball. A team without a keeper prepared to receive the ball will struggle to play the ball out from the back.

By looking in detail at the positioning of players from a ball out to a full back it is possible to work out the movement and options of the whole team. It is important to understand

♦   Knowing where to position the team after the full back has the ball off the keeper.

♦   Being aware of the relatively low risk of a full back losing possession, as long as it is outside the scoring zone, and when the full back has the ball.

♦   The whole team must be positive about doing it and have no fear of failure. You will score more goals as a result of doing it well than you will ever concede.

♦   A back five that has reasonably good technique can control and pass a ball well. The back five must also make themselves available to receive the ball, as well as supporting the player with the ball, and communicating options to each other.

♦   Both full backs must develop the following
Have the technique of opening their body out to see space.
Using the goalkeeper and the keeper being confident in possession.
 Understanding how to use wide players (see page 'why a wide player shouldn't fail to get the ball)

Practical Drill– the full back creating 'numbers up' in midfield

Drill– Walk through the full back moving into midfield using a switch and show how this creates numbers up (this is highlighted by the enclosed area below). Ask the team to identify how this could be used to attack and how to deal with it defensively.

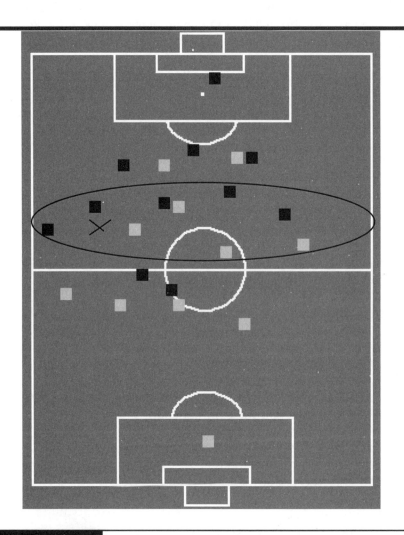

Key coaching tips– make sure your team understands numbers up

The midfield working with the forwards needs to use this numbers up situation to pass round, and forward.

The full back plays an essential role in this process: defensively his/her team must take up the shape of a back 3 to cover.

Practical Drill – full back passing options–passing lines and bounces

Drills– Firstly (1) the full back receiving the ball has let it run in front of **him (good body position)** so he can see the forward options.

Secondly (2) the centre forward has made a diagonal run for a straight ball over the top of the opposition full back. The player with the ball may decide this is not on, as the defence adapts and drops and he can't be sure of getting the ball over the top and turning the defence.

The wide player (3) has dropped back and offered a safe ball. If the opposition midfielder closes him down he can come deeper: if he/she is followed, the option of a ball into the space left by opposition (4) to the winger (3), or the feet of the centre forward (5).

Player (5) is offering a ball to feet. He can 'bounce' (play the ball first time) the ball to Player (3), or back to Player (1), or to a free midfield player (7) .

If the full back had the technique to deliver a diagonal ball for the wide player (6) to run on to, this is an option. This is unlikely at this point but as play moves forward it may become an option.

Player (7) offers a first time ball bounce/ to switch play (the ball needs to be first time and played to him at a suitable pace on the correct foot at the correct angle).

Player (8), the keeper, is offering the possibility of a switch to the free space developing on the other side, or a long ball

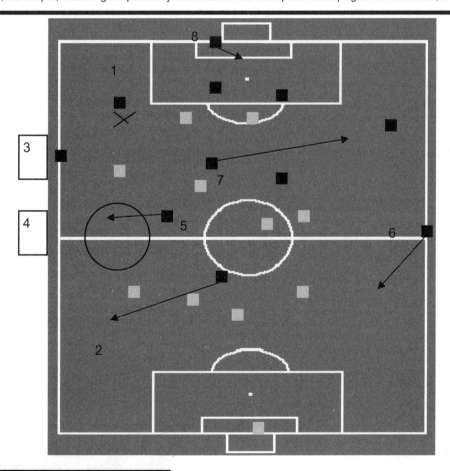

Key coaching tips–
full back and others should
have numerous options

The full back has plenty of options if players make themselves available.
One forward has come into the hole (see later); the other is making a diagonal run for a straight ball. If the full back loses the ball the centre halves covering positions.

155

Set plays – corners, free kicks, etc

Theory

No one in football/soccer should underestimate the value of set plays. They determine the majority of games. Bobby Robson observed (Newcastle v Marseille, semi final, UEFA 2004) that his side had to concentrate on not conceding a goal and wait for a free kick/corner/throw in to try and get a goal, if they were to win. They had got through the previous round by again relying on set plays. Alan Shearer when interviewed claimed that they spent hours in training working on set plays and it had paid off.

Forwards who score regularly are hard to come by. Teams without one rely on set plays to maintain their status. The most successful teams have goal scorers and work on set plays: Brazil are expert at them.

The key to all set plays is delivery. If the ball is delivered to a key space in the scoring zone, at the time a player arrives s/he will probably score. Whilst there are numerous free kicks and corners that teams plan, the key point is they are planned. The deliverer makes it clear what they are doing and the rest of the team try to get a player or players into this area to meet the ball as it arrives and score. A team needs to be aware of the need to deceive the opposition. Players have to make decoy runs give false communication. This is essential. Below are some general rules.

Corners

Always have a player in front of the keeper. The aim is to reduce the view and cause confusion. **The near post corner.** The aim to deliver a ball into the near post area which is flicked on and converted by an oncoming player. If the defence put a man in front of the player flicking the ball on the attack can put another man in front and so on.
Short corners– do them quickly. The corner taker plays the ball to a player on their side who holds the ball drawing the defender, the ball is then played to the corner taker who has moved outside them to offer an easy ball.
Variation Short corner If the player with the ball moves outwards away from the byline, pretending to cross /shoot, as a defender arrives the player with the ball back heal to the corner taker. This gives him/her the ball around the 6 yard box, a very good position to be in.

Free kicks

Champions League Magazine, April 2004, had an article 'The art of free kicks'. The writer observed that the nine free kick goals in Japan and South Korea came from one hundred and six attempts on goal. In other words the worlds greatest players score from fewer than one in ten set pieces.
The number of goals scored in world cups is increasing: 1930 -1, 2002 - 9. Berd Schneider of Bayern Leverkusen (best free kick taker) spends twenty to thirty minutes practicing during training and scores between seventy to eighty per cent. In a match, however, you seldom get the kind of   free kicks you like
Free kicks loosely fall into three categories:
1.   the swerver
2.   the power kick
3.   the unexpected.

Missing the right spot by less than a centimeter can lead to a shot missing a target by a metre or more than twenty metres.

Defenders will mark key spaces/ zones and often match players up, e.g. a dangerous header of the ball is matched with a similar player

Work on set plays and on winning set plays. Ensure you have a plan. Short corners work well if taken quickly. The delivery is the key. Practice this and the timing of runs. Believe you can score, attack the space and hope the ball arrives

Practical Drill – The 'Robbie Keane conga'

DRILL– Set up the situation below. The midfield players plays the ball on the floor to the 2 forwards in line. The first forward lets it go the second plays it as shown for the first forward who has turned to shoot or take the ball forward.

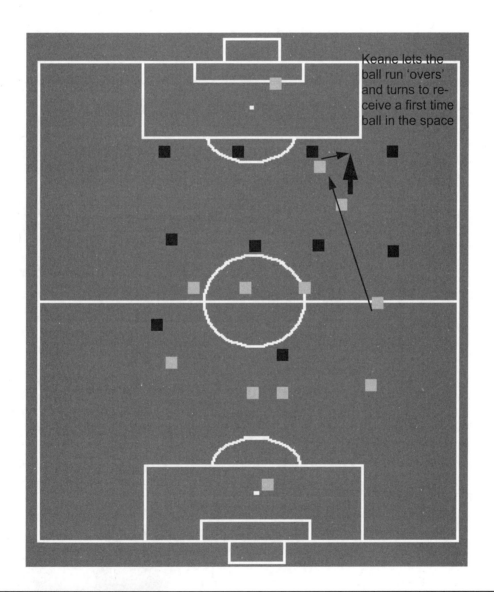

Keane lets the ball run 'overs' and turns to receive a first time ball in the space

Key coaching tips–
Use another player as a shield to create space

This move can be used all over the pitch but is most effective around the area. Players must do things first touch or the defence will react.

Practical Drill – making the most of a drop kick from keeper – the 'second ball' 'PUT THE BALL IN THE HOUSE'

Drill – show the team the position below. It offers the keeper a large area to aim at and has the advantage of having plenty of players in the area where the ball will land if the oppositions centre half was to win it. Work out the length of the keepers kick. Chelsea also did the same using a diamond shape. The other forward is in place where he is to react to a ball that is flicked on. The team can move into this shape as the ball is kicked so not making the tactics too obvious.

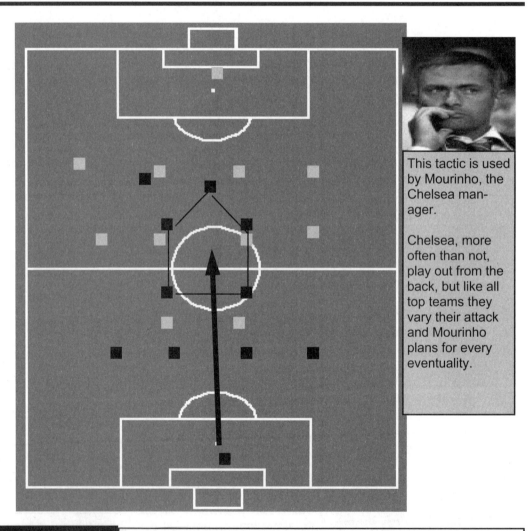

This tactic is used by Mourinho, the Chelsea manager.

Chelsea, more often than not, play out from the back, but like all top teams they vary their attack and Mourinho plans for every eventuality.

Key coaching tips– work on the second ball	The keeper should practise delivery and the forward most player receiving. The forward can work on ensuring the defender who 'has the run ' doesn't get a good contact/clear and easy header. Players around the house can work on reacting to the ball and using it well.

Practical Drill – making the most of a drop kick from keeper – the 'second ball'/ 3 player gamble

Drill – show the team the position below. The key is the timing of the three runners. Liverpool academy send 3 players forward in a similar way if their keeper gets the ball off a corner. They are relying on winning the second ball and the fact they are moving at pace and clear in what they are doing makes this a very effective tactic for turning defence in to attack. The example below is a long ball to centre forward who tries to flick on. 3 players gamble/guess on success and move to cover the space the ball will arrive in (used by Chelsea against Bayern Munich in Champions league 2005). Note the cover if the defender knocks the ball back.

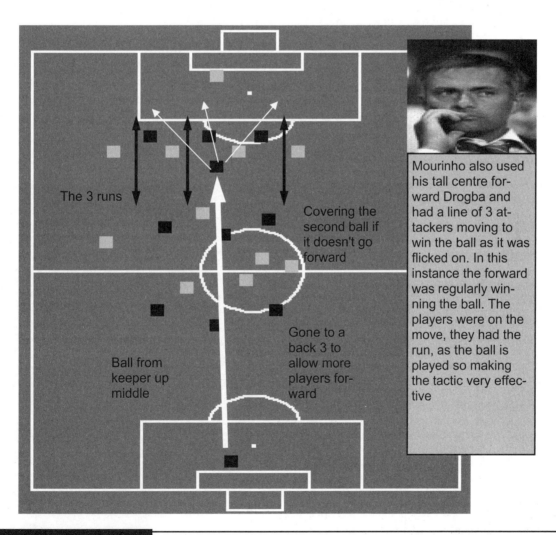

The 3 runs

Covering the second ball if it doesn't go forward

Ball from keeper up middle

Gone to a back 3 to allow more players forward

Mourinho also used his tall centre forward Drogba and had a line of 3 attackers moving to win the ball as it was flicked on. In this instance the forward was regularly winning the ball. The players were on the move, they had the run, as the ball is played so making the tactic very effective

Key coaching tips– **work on the second ball**	The keeper should practise delivery and the forward most player receiving. The three players have timed their run to be on side and are guessing that the ball will go to one of them. Remember heading under pressure is not an exact science. The defence have gone to a back 3 and the midfield is central and ready in case the ball is headed back in to this area.

Practical drill- A How many players and which players to send forward– The FAST break

The answer to this question depends on the players you have available and their attributes, the score, and most importantly the position of the opposition when you regain possession.

A team is vulnerable to a FAST break (move the ball quickly) if they lose the ball when trying to deliver a cross and have committed players forward in to the opposition scoring zone. These players are a long way 'from home'.

At top level teams will decide how many players to commit on a fast break, or a slower build up. The emphasis will be on having players in midfield who are fit enough to get back and players who are left behind able to defend and slow the game down enough for those who have gone forward to return. Ball travelling time allows attacking players to move from box to box.

A manager/coach needs also to decide how attacking they wish to be. As a general rule most teams will commit a minimum of 4 (defensive approach) to a FAST break, a slower build up would involve 5 or 6 as some of these players are in a semi circle ring around the opposition to switch the ball and look for a ball into the thread zone. Real Madrid who have full backs who like to get forward but this is a matter of style and the attributes of players.

FAST BREAK (5 players involved)

A fast break happens on the transition often when a team is about to or has crossed the ball in open play or for example off a corner.

In the example (right) the player with the ball has gained possession and is moving forward. The team has to decide who goes forward too. The 2 wide midfield players circled are going to support. The logic to this is that often players in these positions are more attacking. They do not guard key central areas although if one or both of the central midfielders was to go then they may stay and drop into the centre.

One issue that often arises is if the opposition leave many players forward. This could be tactical, Terry Venables organised his England team to leave central midfielder Platt up the pitch as this is where he was most dangerous. Or it could be they are tired or lazy (they are 'cheating') usually players who stay forward for this reason are easy to deal with . The shaded team has to decide who is in the best position to support and who has the fitness to get back when the ball is lost. As the rest of the team push up to halfway and if the attack is slowed then we may get the position below. To only commit 4 players to this attack would be viewed as very defensive minded. And reliant on forwards. Some teams Tottenham 2004/5 adopt this.

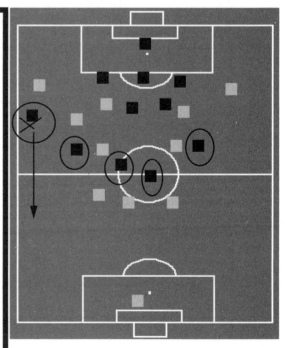

The slow break needs to probe and switch with the ball testing the defence. It is a lot harder to create a numbers up situation and a team always has to be careful in how it positions itself. Giving the ball away centrally is especially dangerous and a team needs to be very careful here. Teams who do not work on using the thread zone are limited and too reliant on a complete switch from one side to another. The best teams , when switching are always looking for the possibility of delivery in to the thread zone.

SLOW BUILD UP (7 players involved) The slow build up is more typical of play in most games. Even if initially the play was a fast break the position is now of a slow break. The opposition is defensively set. It is worth considering a number of defensive factors. The white team have retreated to the edge of their area. They have 'doubled up' on the wide player. One of the white forwards has moved over to offer an easy ball up the line if the full back wins the ball. The shaded team have pushed up a full back up and the rest of the back 3 have adopted a central back 3 position. The white team have now got themselves in to a solid well organised defensive shape. They have cover in the scoring zone, have taken away the ball into the danger zone by retreating to the edge of the area and left the hardest zone to exploit , the thread zone, well guarded. In this instance the shaded team need to commit more players if they are to keep the ball and switch the ball. This may create an opening centrally in the thread zone or allow the shaded player shown to get to the 18 yard cross area.

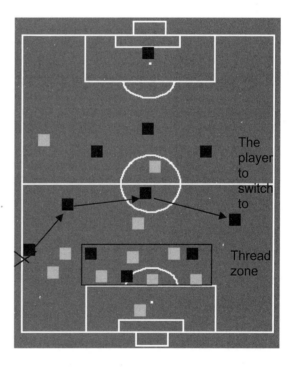

The player to switch to

Thread zone

Analyse a video and look at the numbers of players a team commits forward.

Time the speed between regaining possession and an attack.

Are goals scored as a result of defensive mistakes or are there 'good goals' which the defence could not stop?

Was pace a factor?

Was height/aerial ability a factor?

Where do moves that score goals start from?

What is the relationship between goals and passes?

How does this affect your attacking strategy?

How much time do you have to attack?

How many goals come from crosses?

You will not score unless you create chances. The key points is therefore to create chances.
How many chances did Liverpool create (Premier Division club) against a side from the division below? Guess
How many players you commit to an attack-'The numbers game'

Set Plays-How many goals are scored from set plays?
What wins free kicks. What does this tell us about out tactics?

What is meant by 'benefited from using two players who got chalk on their boots at Goodison'?

What is the disadvantage of Liverpool playing narrow?

What advantage do wide players give? What problems for

A full back is the link between defence and attack. Explain this statement.

A 4 4 2 is fluid and when attacking as when the ball played out from the back the formation changes.

Explain in a team talk how your team can use the goal kick to start play out from the back

Watch highlights of a weekends goals. Work out the percentage of goals from set plays. Identify why the goal was scored. Devise 2 free kicks, corners and some general rules for throw ins.

What you will learn

- What is meant by a formation?
- How teams have two formations – one for defending which is the one stated in newspapers, etc, and one for attacking
- Key issues that arise when different formations play each other
- When to change your formation
- Why most teams play 4-4-2

'I'm not sure how important the formation is. What I do know is that players need to feel comfortable with the job your'e asking them to carry out.'

Brian Clough, Walking on Water

Formations

Theory

It is firstly important to determine what we mean by a formation. As you are aware teams are either attacking, defending or between the two (in transition). So which of these situations does a formation relate to?

Essentially a team who, for example, play 4-4-2 actually tries to play 4-4-2 when defending. The 4-4-2 is the best formation for this as it puts four players in the key spaces when defending. It also gives clear responsibility for spaces to players. However, a 4-4-2 when attacking often becomes 3-5-2 with a full back pushing into midfield. This is particularly true when the ball is played out from the back where the intention is to release a full back with the ball into midfield.

The midfield in a 4-4-2 may be in a different shape when defending. In transition the team is between the two. The midfield may also play a diamond shape or more flat. One of the forwards may drop back in 'the hole'. The formation is fluid and depends on how a team attacks, defends and how quickly they deal with the transition.

The key point is, therefore, where players are when defending and attacking. The issue is where your formation leaves space to defend and how it releases space to attack. This is, of course, to an extent dependent on the formation and tactical strength of the opposition.

In February 2004 Chris Turner, the Sheffield Wednesday Manager, changed his normal formation from 3-5-2 to 4-4-2. The Sheffield Star observed 'Turner admitted it took the Owls around 20 minutes to get used to the change but he explained' I know Hartlepool's strikers …with their pace we couldn't allow balls to them down our sides of the centre-halves (in a back three).

A formation also has numerous variations. Do you play a diamond shape in midfield in a 4-4-2 bringing wide players more central? If you play 4-3-3 are you in effect asking 2 players to be wingers who drop back so playing 4-5-1 when defending? You can ask a forward to drop back in either 3-5-2 or 4-4-2.

A key player in 4-4-2 is the full back. When attacking, one full back (especially if playing out from the back) will move into midfield. This creates a numbers up situation in this area of space if playing a 4-4-2. The remaining three players will become a back three (and position themselves accordingly) until the full back returns. When possession is lost the full back returns and the back four re position in a back four shape.

So when attacking with a 4-4-2 you are in effect 3-5-2 anyway.

Formations determine where a team leaves space. 4-4-2 is the most common

3-5-2 leaves less wide options but is good to attack centrally

Do you adapt your game to stifle the opposition?

Theory

In the modern game it is clear that top teams analyse and devise strategies to deal with the opposition. Fergusson, Mourinho, Eriksson, and Rehhagel all to an extent devise defensive tactics to deal with the opposition. How much emphasis they put on stopping the opposition playing reflects the manager's personality and priorities. The Greek manager, Rehhagel, sets out to stop the opposition playing as his top priority whereas Alex Fergusson adopts a more attacking strategy. Brian Clough, one of the most successful England managers of the last thirty years, claims in his autobiography that he never considered the opposition or changed the way his team played to try and stop the opposition.

This answer to this question, therefore, depends on the manager's attitude

- The players you have available to you. Players can adapt to formations, or formations can be adapted to suit players. As a general rule it is better to adapt a formation to suit attacking players, as scoring is harder than defending.

- How confident you are that your formation and the tactics it adopts can stop the opposition scoring.

- The score at the time: if you are winning, and they are creating chances, you may adapt to stop this. If you are losing, and not creating chances, you may adapt. The key is to look at where you can exploit the space best.

- How much time is left? We have all seen the keeper pushed up for a last minute corner and the team who is behind push more players forward. You will also notice that teams who are ahead will pull players back. The reason for this is simple. The more players you have in the scoring zone the less space there is and so the less chance of the opposition having the time and space to create a chance. It is harder for anyone to score with twenty players in the penalty area than it is with ten.

- What personnel you have available. If a wide midfielder you rely on to get forward is spending too much time defending, you may adapt to release this player more. Conversely, you may move a player who is a good defender to deal with an effective opposition player.

- If they are creating numbers up situations that you are not dealing with well when defending.

- If they have key individuals: Maradona was worth adapting a formation to deal with.

- If the opposition's forwards are receiving the ball to their feet when it is played out from the back, then you may wish to play 4-3-3 and reduce the amount they play out from the back. This will make the keeper kick more often, which may suit you, or at least will not be their preferred option.

If a player uses the formation and the spaces it throws up to great effect then the answer is yes. If not, stick to what works for you.

Formations determine where a team leaves space. 4-4-2 is the most common

3-5-2 leaves less wide options but is good to attack centrally

Flat midfield or dia-mond midfield in 4-4-2

Theory

What you will learn

- The debate between a flat midfield or diamond

The debate has three aspects: attacking, defensive, best use of players in the midfield and the effect on others.

The key issue is the space and hence the time that each system uses when attacking or denies when defending. Both Flat midfield and diamond take on a zonal nature when defending. The extent to which the diamond remains in this shape when defending depends on decisions made by the players/coach as to if they can stop the switch, or deal with the switch. Porto, in the Champions League, were very good at denying space around the ball by forming their players into a tight diamond around the ball.

The success depends, to a large extent, on the decisions made by the players.

The defensive use of a diamond allows space to be compressed well. It can stop teams switching, but relies on excellent fitness. It can mean the full back does not get the usual support from the wide player to, for example, double up on the opposition's wide player or forward who comes across into the space.

The attacking use of the diamond. The current 2004 England side has this issue. Four good midfielders with the issue of who goes wide. The excellent Paul Scholes is better equipped to play in the hole. Eriksson claims he can do this by coming in to support the forwards. The space on the left needs to be covered when possession is lost and the freedom of the full back to get forward may be limited. Erickson did point out that to play wide you do not need to be a natural winger like Ryan Giggs.

A flat midfield offers good defensive cover but is not best for pressurising the ball. It allows for good width but you have to have the players to utilise this.

Eriksson – First of all you have to pick the right 11 and once you have done that you have to see what is the best organisation.
(Guardian, Saturday June 5th)

The flat midfield, without a player pushing on as in a diamond has the advantage of leaving 'the hole' for the forwards and allowing the two central midfield players to be deeper when they run, hence, they are not marked and are able to rotate who goes forward, so making it less predictable for the opposition.

Defensively the diamond can be used to pressure and win the ball high up the field. The flat shape gives good wide cover

Attacking wise the flat midfield offers good width, the diamond puts a player in the hole to support the forwards, which can block the space for a forward to drop into

167

When 4-4-2 plays 3-5-2

Theory

What you will learn

As a general rule ignore a cheat, a player should still go forward.

- • Cheating can occur all over the pitch. It is where players do not play their defensive zonal role

This has been discussed here as it is a fairly common occurrence and poses some interesting tactical responses.

The basic tactical problem for the 4-4-2 is how to deal with the opposition's numbers up situation in midfield when they are defending. The 3-5-2 has a numbers up situation and can dominate the midfield. It is questionable if a 3-5-2 has an advantage out wide as a 4-4-2 has two players - the full back and wide midfielder against 1 wing back. The 4-4-2 has four players working out wide, the 3-5-2 has two. The big advantage is usually centrally for a 3-5-2, with three players facing two.

A simple attacking solution for a 4-4-2 is to go long and wide. The forwards need to be aware of where the space is and how to use it. In simple terms, they have twenty five per cent more space to utilise (three defenders to cover the space of four).

This stretches the back three who will be reluctant to leave the central danger area and scoring zone.

It may have the effect of forcing the wingbacks into full back roles. This then allows the midfield to be dominated, especially wide where there is a two to one overload if the full back pushes forward.

> Ron Atkinson highlights the fundamental flaw of 3-5-2 defensively. **(Monday September 29, 2003 The Guardian)**
>
> *Yesterday was Tottenham's second clean sheet in a week, and for a team that was shipping goals all over the place that's no mean feat, but David Pleat has had to make some big changes for it to happen.*
>
> *Glenn Hoddle's last game as manager saw Southampton pull Spurs apart by pumping balls into the gullies for his forwards to run on to. With a back three, when the ball was played wide one of the centre-backs was pulled out of position and the attacking team had space to play with.*

We will look at the issue of the midfield in a 4-4-2, then formations in terms of their pro's and con's.

The wing backs have some difficult decisions to make

Play long and wide against a back three

168

The 4-2-3-1

Theory

What you will learn

♦ The advantages of the 4-2-3-1 formation

This was a popular system in Euro 2004. The following extract taken from an article from INSIGHT (summer 2004) by Butch Lauffer, highlights the advantages of the system.

> *Tactical flexibility is required for each positional group (defence, midfield, and attack) and also for the team as a whole. Therefore tactical flexibility is a crucial aspect of training, and using a modern 4-2-3-1 shape as a basic attacking and defending structure provides a great deal of flexibility.*
>
> *For a stronger defence, switch from 4-2-3-1 to 4-4-2 or 4-5-1. This provides broader coverage in the midfield and also allows the team to develop a defending box with the two centre backs and the two defense midfielders. This tactical innovation is based on the concept of defending the place from which most goals are scored.*
>
> *For a stronger attack, switch from 4-2-3-1 to 4-3-3. This reinforces the attackers with two extra forwards in the outside positions. A wing attack is the best way to beat a compact, ball-orientated defence formation.*
>
> *In the 4-2-3-1 shape the midfielders function as both midfielders and forwards, based on their starting positions. Of the three, the two wide players have the hardest job because of the space they have to cover. These players must be able to cope with the demands of playing midfield simultaneously. The central midfielder (and/or second forward) operates between the defending team's back and midfield line and supports the lone forward behind and in advance of the ball. The tactical problem for the opposition is how these players choose to deal with their marking responsibilities. From a defending perspective, the 4-2-3-1 shape adds another layer to the team, which helps to provide more depth, in turn covering more space and making it much harder to play through. In all cases the team playing this shape should have defending blocks of at least four to six players behind the ball to deal with the transitional aspect of the game.*

The formation defensively has four players centrally. This defends the danger and scoring zones. The other players adopt a flexible role. A lot hinges on having a forward who is able to hold the ball up without being too prescriptive big and strong.

Defensively puts plenty of players centrally

If the three players behind the front player can use the width, can be very effective

The advantages and disadvantages of various formations

	3 5 2	4 4 2	4 3 3	4 5 1
Defensive strength	Usually one central midfielder sits in front of the back 3 and the back 3 play tight and central. This gives good central cover of space.	Covers the space well. 4 players when defending.	Covers the space well. 4 players when defending. Good at stopping the opposition playing out from the back as the opposition will need 2 footballing centre halves to succeed regularly and this is rare. This can be very useful against some sides. .	On the face of it very strong defensively but like all formations it depends on the movement of the players and how many are pushed forward to attack.
Defensive weakness	The key defensive weakness of a 3 5 2 is the 25% of extra space the opposition have to work in (only 3 defenders instead of 4) whilst attacking. If someone offers you 25% extra you normally take it. This space will be wide and best exploited by the 2 forwards.	Has less concentration of players in the central area.	Less support for full backs especially on the transition.	One forward gives the opposition plenty of chance to play the ball around.
Playing out from the back	It is probably harder to play out from the back with a 3 5 2, as the wing backs dropping back for the ball mean they have fewer wide options (they cant pass to themselves). You need to work out a system to create 4 4 2 when the keeper has the ball.	The 2 full backs start in good positions to offer the option of this.	The 2 full backs start in good positions to offer the option of this. Less immediate wide support but likely that, with good delivery, wide further forward space can be found. Probably encourages a longer ball forward.	Plenty of options for this but may invite the opposition to push a full back in to midfield and so make it harder.
Effect on midfield	Dominant in the centre. In this space 3 players often meet 2.	The midfield has a shape when attacking and defending. It may be in a diamond or flat. Attacking may need a full back to push into midfield to create level umbers up against 3 5 2	The 3 will be central and probably rely on 2 of the forwards dropping back to help wide.	The midfield can be organised in many ways with two wide players and one central supporting the forward.
Effect on forwards	Good central support for a run beyond the forwards.	Depends on the mobility and willingness of midfield and full backs to get forward.	On the face of it 3 forwards to offer more up front. It could be viewed as a fairly defensive formation, due to 2 of the 3 dropping back. And leaving a lone forward	Really needs a forward who is good at holding the ball up and bringing the midfielders in to the game.
Overall	Strong centrally and in centre mid. Vulnerable to width at the back. For example in a 3 5 2 people often look at it as a wide formation because it has width. In actual fact, as the back 3 will not push up in wide areas to support, it provides less width.	Strong defensively and can be good going forward if one of the 2 full backs always plays a supporting role and you play out from back. The best formation with plenty of players in the more spacious wide areas.	Good at stopping the oppositions full backs playing. This can be very effective if they have small forwards who rely on ball to feet. Offers less width when playing out from the back but can offer more width when attacking with two good wingers e.g. Chelsea in the later part of 2005 season.	Popular today but very fluent. Some teams use it as a defensive tool others to disguise the runs from midfield and make it hard for defenders. All defenders like predictability and this formation does allow a coach and team flexibility. The team need to be able to build play well and have a forward who can hold the ball up or it can give the initiative to the opposition

What are the strengths and weaknesses of a 4 4 2 and 3 5 2?

Within a 4 4 2 there are 3 key issues explain each
The full back pushing on, what does the back 3 now do?

Diamond or Flat. What are the issues?

Ensure you cover the effect of the diamond and the flat on full backs and on the hole.

Should you adopt your formation, or the way you play, against a side with a different formation.

Is a 4 3 3 defensive or attacking? What are its strengths and weaknesses?

What are the arguments for making your formation suit your players, or your players fitting in with your formation?

Is a formation set. ?

Does a formation reflect your attacking or defending shape?

Go through a paper such as the Guardian on Saturday and look at the different formations. How many play 4 4 2. (15 out of 20 on Saturday November 1st). Of the remaining 5,2 played a slight variation with player pushing into the hole. 2 played 4 5 1.

What are the advantages and disadvantages of the 4 3 2 1 system?

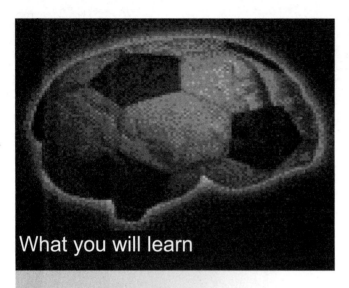

What you will learn

- Only by other players communicating to the player with the ball can spaces be identified.
- Only by people talking to the player with the ball can he know how much time he has.
- The Easy Ball- Explain

PART 12 – Communication and the Easy Ball

Communication and the Easy Ball

Theory

Only by other players communicating to the player with the ball can spaces be identified. Only by people talking to the player with the ball can he know how much time he has. When defending players need to check that the oppositions runs are picked up by others as they move between zones. They may need to be told or a player tracked until the defending player in the zone has spotted them...they can be passed on. The most common failure in communication relates to passing.

As we shall see, too often players either delay the pass so time and space are lost, or choose an incorrect pass, which means space is not best used.

Communication

- Players can only make good decisions if they are told their options by others who can see, or who are located in a better position. Good communication is essential.
- At the very least, players should use the following calls
- 'Time' - a player has time to look around
- 'Switch' - the space is on the other side of the pitch, look to pass there (this is best illustrated by looking at the playing out from the back section)
- 'Man on' - you now have no time and a player is about to challenge you
- 'Overs' (change this as it is not legal) - let the ball run
- 'Back' - play the ball back to the player who passed it to you
- 'One-two' - a wall pass around an opponent to the player who passed you the ball 'To Fozza ...' this call is made when a player sees that he can pass the ball to, for example, a midfielder who can first time pass it to a player in space. The name tells you where to play it. This first time ball is called a 'bounce' (see playing out from the back)
- 'turn' – turn
- 'Bounce' using a player to move the ball to another player with a first time pass – bounce, as bounce off a wall

A word of warning - sometimes players will communicate with the player with the ball and make a bad call. They may ask for an impossible ball or not be in the best position to receive the ball. Watch out for these players; often it is just over-enthusiasm, but they need to better inform the player with the ball.

Get offside wrong and it can cost a goal. Show players inside or outside

Forward play is about timing, and a player in space at the right time needs to inform the player with the ball

A good drill to improve communication is to put players into threes.
- 1 plays the ball to 2.

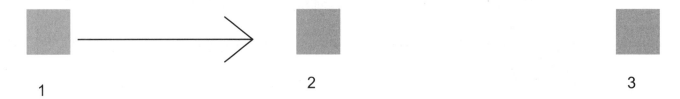

1   2   3

- If 3 stays where he is, 1 can call 'turn', 'time' or 'overs' (if 'overs' it switches to the other end).

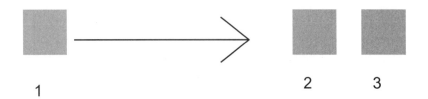

1   2   3

- If 3 comes behind, 1 can call 'back' or 'man on'.

- Good players make good decisions when they have the ball. The best decision is to pass to someone who has a better view of what's happening than you.
- Too many players (especially younger players) make the mistake of not passing to a player who has a better view than them when they are facing their own keeper.
- They also need to do this quickly Too often players hang on the ball for one second longer - this changes everything and opportunities will be lost.

It is essential that one of the first things you do with your players is to demonstrate the logic of playing a simple ball to someone with a better view.

Set this situation up (see next page)
Ask the player with the ball what he can see. Further highlight the point by asking the players behind the player with the ball to move around. Then ask the player with the ball what's happening (he doesn't know as he can't see).
Ask (x) and the other players facing forward what they can see (basically they can see the best ball).
Ask the team what the best ball is.
Ask the team if a rule can be applied.

The following drill demonstrates this
The player with the ball plays the ball shown (1) - possession is kept.

BUT, the better ball would have been to (2) who plays a first time ball for the forward (3) to run on to. The white defence has pushed up too far leaving a dangerous space in the danger zone, and the right back is playing the forwards on. The real point of the exercise is that (2) is facing forward and **can see everything**. **He should decide**. It might be he plays the same ball, but **it is an informed decision**.

Defenders and keeper need to support each other and offer an easy ball

Speed of thought to find the space and delivery to the space mean timing is essential

A final point - too often the player with the ball has many touches. Show how this one second delay can affect this potential goal scoring position by moving a defender into the space to deal with it - he has spotted the wayward right back. Show what can happen in one second if the defence works out the danger.

174

Practical Drill – communication

DRILL Set this situation up

Ask the player with the ball what he can see? Further highlight the point by asking the players behind the player with the ball to move around. Then ask the player with the ball what's happening (he doesn't know as he can't see).

- Ask the player with the ball what the best ball is (this is indicated by the arrow)
- Point out that him holding the ball, or turning, will waste the opportunity (the shaded player forward can be played in)
- Further highlight the point by asking the players behind the player with the ball to move around
- Then ask the player with the ball what's happening (he doesn't know as he can't see)

Ask 2, and the other players facing forward, what they can see (basically they can see the best ball).

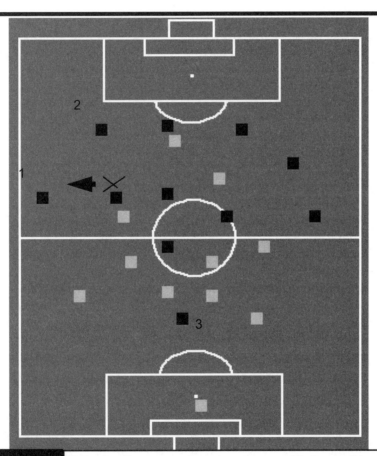

Key coaching tips– *give the ball to a player with a better view*

A final point - too often the player with the ball has many touches. Show how this 1 second delay can affect this potential goal scoring position by moving a defender into the space to deal with it- he has spotted the wayward right back. Show what can happen in 1 second if the defence works out the danger. Give the ball to a player who can see more.

Do it quickly or the situation will change.

Try to deliver a ball that makes the next ball easy.

You can come up with numerous situations on a pitch in which a similar situation occurs.

Body position

What you will learn

• The correct body position allows a player to see space. Defensively a player can also see the man in their zone and see the ball

To see space, other players and create time a player needs good body position. A good body position enables you to see what is going on and hence make better tactical decisions.

Players need to develop the technique of opening their bodies out to see space. Without developing this technique players do not receive the ball in the correct position and good tactical decisions are not possible.

A good example of working on body position is the full back. A full back when receiving the ball from the keeper needs to try and have a body position that allows the player to be looking forward as they receive the ball. A common fault a full back receiving the ball and with his/her first touch going back towards the keeper. This means s/ he is usually heading back towards the oppositions two forwards who will try to win the ball and the full back does not have a view forward to chose an immediate ball. In the second or so that this first touch takes s/he may be closed down.

Good full backs often let the ball run across their body and don't take a touch (this is of course dependent on good delivery from the keeper) to take them wide and away from the opposition players.

It is worth practicing this. The idea of letting the ball run is common to all positions. As mentioned above to often young players take a touch early this stops the ball and allows the opposition to move closer.

The example on the next page shows how important body position is. A simple drill would be to knock the ball to the keeper in a variety of positions in the area and let the full backs adjust their position to receive the ball whilst looking forward.

As a defender your body position needs to allow you to see need to see the man in your zone as well as the ball - not always easy especially if a player has *gone off the radar (see later)*.

As a centre forward your body position often needs to allow you see the goal/ opposition back four and the player with the ball. Often you will need to stay onside.

Defenders body shape need to ensure they can see the ball and any opposition player in their zone

When attacking players need to be able to see where space is and the opposition and where their own players are

Practical Drill – 'Opening your body' out'

Where you look when you have the ball is critical. You want to try and look to where the key spaces are. Opening your body out can mean 2 things 1) letting the ball run across your body to open out different space for you to see, 2) thinking about the position you are in to receive the ball.

In figure 1 the full back has received the ball from the keeper with his/her body in a position facing towards his/her own goal. The lines show what the player can see. When you consider that time is critical the opposition players will put pressure on the player and the best option may well be a ball back to the keeper. However, if the player had opened up his/her body to receive the ball from the keeper (figure 2) he/she can see the better forward options and have more time and space. Players need to practices letting the ball run across their body– too often they are too keen to take a touch which takes up time and stops the ball moving away from the opposition players.

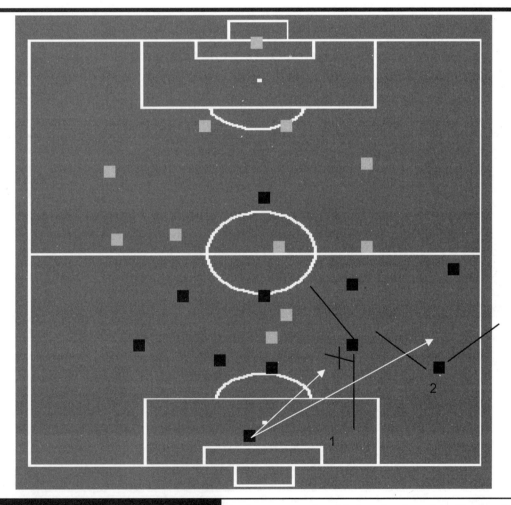

Key coaching tip
Watch the body position of players as they receive the ball. Encourage players to let the ball run to buy time.

A player opening his/her body out to the best available space means s/he can choose the correct option. It also buys more time. To open a players body out s/he may need to re-position – in this case wider and deeper to create more space and time.

Using both feet

It is an advantage to be two footed. This gives them far more options. They are not as easy to predict or deal with for defenders. If you watch many players who have a preferred foot their runs and movement is more predictable than players who are happy using both feet. . Even in the professional game there are far too many players who do not work on their weaker foot.

Whilst producing this work I taught 21 Academy players. I was amazed to discover that the majority wished to improve their left foot (or other weaker foot). The clubs they were at did no specific work to improve this nor had they consulted with them as to what they wished to improve. Of course technique can be improved. Practice can make perfect - a fact they were well aware of.

Play a game and at some point stop and ask a player who is defending which foot the opposition player with the ball or without it prefers. For defenders this is a critical factor.

If a player is 2 footed they may not know. If a player is very one footed this will have an impact on for example whether to show then out wide or inside.

There are others factors such as their pace and the position of other attackers/defenders. All this forms part their tactical response to what forwards have to offer.

The white player circled has a good left foot– show him/her inside.

The shaded player on a 1 v1 is right footed—show him on to his left foot

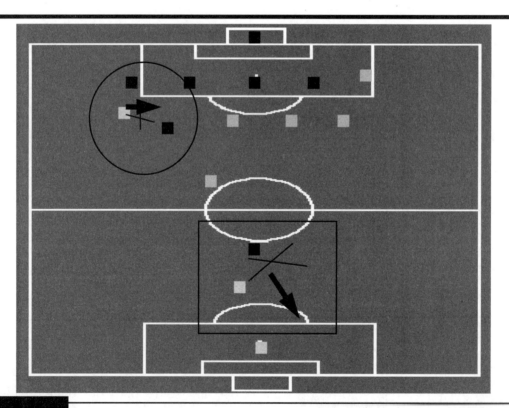

<table>
<tr><td>

Key coaching tips

</td><td>

A player opening his/her body out to the best available space means s/he can choose the correct option. Players who are heavily reliant on one foot are very predictable and don't open their body out well. Even if a player heavily favours one foot he/she need to develop the ability to open his/her body out and run into spaces on his/her weaker side.

Defenders can exploit an attackers weaker side.

</td></tr>
</table>

List as many reasons as you can why communication is essential if a team is to be successful and players are to make good decisions.

List as many calls as you can and what they mean.

'Overs' means let the ball run to a player behind you. What is one potential problem with the call of 'overs'.

What is the potential problem of listening to the instructions of a call?

Think of 10 examples for a variety of positions and scenarios in which good communication can make a big difference to the outcome.

What is the main thing that players in possession of the ball do?

What is meant by opening your body out?

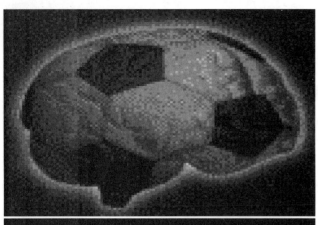

What you will learn

♦ **The skills and tactics required to play in the various positions**

There are 3 key ways to judge how good players are when attacking

- Firstly, their **movement and timing**

- Secondly, **how they bring the ball under control**

- Thirdly, **what they do with the ball once it is under control**

When defending its about understanding zonal play and ball traveling time and having the concentration and discipline to be in exactly the right place. Good defenders also stay on their feet.

What makes a good player?

What you will learn

- Good players make good decisions with the ball and have good movement, They can concentrate and are disciplined when defending.

Theory

Good players have to have

1. Technical ability
2. Tactical awareness/decision making
3. Physical fitness
4. Teamwork and communication skills
5. Psychological factors - motivation and the ability to operate under pressure - they must be mentally tough.

In an Insight interview (May 2004) technical director of Feyonord, Mark Wotte, stated

> *players are judged against TIC, this means technique, insight (tactical awareness) communication (how they deal with their opponents and their peers, whether they are a team player).*

The emphasis of this work is on good players making good decisions. Good decisions can only be made if players understand tactics and how the game is affected by time and space. Good players are in the right place at the right time. They have excellent timing.

Are good players bigger, stronger? Strength can be useful, Alex Ferguson notes of a player, Hesky that he has the strength to carry him through against challenges. However, it is the least reliable way to judge a player and as we shall see there is no evidence that bit helps. See next page.

Is pace essential? The first yard (often more) is in the head. A players decision making and tactical awareness are far more important. It is an advantage to have pace as you can use time and space more effectively, but it is not essential. Brian Clough sums up the value of pace

> *He wasn't that quick but it didn't matter that much, it never does. I've worked with players who could do 100 yards in 10 seconds (ish) ... real pace is only an asset to players who are prepared to use it when it matters most.*

How do you judge a good player? The key point to remember for all positions is that a player should be judged against two criteria.

1. How they attack. The decisions they make when they have the ball and the movement they make when colleagues have the ball.
2. How they defend. Did the player go to ground or give free kicks away? Was the player in the correct area (zone)? Did the player offer cover in the important zones?

Defensively aware of responsibilities

How to position themselves to assist in the attack

Outstanding players make outstanding decisions. It is this more than technique (although a reasonable level is essential) or physical attributes that is the key to identifying the best players. Part of this decision making is a players positional sense part of which is choosing the best passing option or if to dribble or hold the ball.

In short, decisions on how to use time and space with and without the ball. The best players understand time and space and how to use it.

Johan Cruyff places less emphasis on physical attributes like pace

> *football is a game which you play with your brain, technique , tactics and stamina are important but the main thing is tactics, insight, trust and daring.*

Cruyff backs up the point made earlier that bigger and faster players are not better players. These assumptions do more damage to football than any other. Indeed smaller players are better dribblers and passers. The two finalists in the 2004 Champions League were two of the smallest in the tournament. This does not mean smaller is better, simply that size and speed are not a legitimate measurement of a players ability.

As a general rule, the higher the level the less time players need and have and the less space there is around the ball. At a higher level teams are more likely to drop back to the edge of the penalty area and defend from the halfway line. So at top level, in your own half, players have more time. The space around the area, the scoring zone and danger zone and the thread zone are prioritised.

However, players at all levels will experience and require what is outlined in the following pages. It is always important not to give the ball away. This is more worrying from a defensive perspective than attacking and should not be viewed as the only judgment about a player. As mentioned earlier, players whose only concern is not giving the ball away don't choose or see the best passing options. Roy Keane observes of Brian Clough in his autobiography

> *Clough would spot it. A seemingly innocuous mistake that resulted in a goal conceded three or four minutes later, a tackle missed, or a failure to make the right run, or pass, would be correctly identified as the cause of the goal. It was no use pointing the finger at someone else – which is second nature to most players. He knew, you knew he knew.* Jose Mourinho wants players *who are physically, technically and tactically capable of playing in the first team (August 28th, 2004, The Guardian)*

Players in all positions need to be aware of their role defensive and attacking tactical plays. Good players will only shine if the team is a unit and they are part of this and the team plays to their strengths. Players in the team need to make unselfish movement to create space for others and it is important ,as mentioned earlier, that this is recognised. Players can create goals without ever touching the ball.

The best players as Roy Keane has observed, are not the ones with the most tricks. Four out of five actions with the ball are a pass. Players who know when to dribble can be an enormous asset to a team winning free kicks and drawing defenders towards them then releasing the ball into the space this creates. However, in reality few goals are scored as a result of a player going round a defender with skill. Just watch highlights of goals for proof. Of eighty chances analysed in a Champions League week only four were a result of a player beating (going past) a defender.

> *Football is not all about making it beautiful. It is mainly about doing the simple things. Simple is beautiful. (Champions Magazine 2004)*

We will now look at each position to highlight key tactical points.

Does size or weight matter?

Theory

In an article in the Times Premiership's tall order provides food for thought, April 2003/2004 by Daniel Finkelstein were examined on the effect of size and weight on a players ability.

Does weight matter?

Finkelstein notes *There is, however, a surprisingly large disparity in weight, with the average weight of players in the heaviest teams (Everton and Tottenham Hotspur) almost 8kg more than that of the lightest (Birmingham City). Attacks are, understandably, shorter and lighter than defences.*
Yet despite my food fears, there does not seem to be any relationship between weight and results.

Does size matter? Finkelstein observes ,

When I was watching Arsenal play recently, my wife took one look at Patrick Vieira, turned to me and said: "My goodness, they are giants." She was quite right. The tallest outfield player among Premiership regulars (or, in his case, reasonably regular) is Peter Crouch, the Aston Villa forward, at 6ft 7in. The tallest team by far is Arsenal.

Finkelstein admits that the issue is complicated, and makes the following points

- There is no relationship between having a tall defence and keeping out goals.

- There is also no relationship between having a tall attack (forwards and midfield players) and scoring more goals.

- Most surprising of all, the success of goalkeepers (measured by their ability to prevent on-target shots becoming goals) does not appear to be related to their height. At 6ft 6in, Shaka Hislop of Portsmouth, is by far the tallest goalkeeper in the Barclaycard Premiership, but also one of the least successful.

Finkelstein goes on *So height is irrelevant, right? Wrong. The taller your defenders and midfield players, the more likely your team is to prevent opponents from scoring. The reasons for this are interesting.*

- *The data shows that tall midfield players do better at preventing opponents from shooting at goal. Naturally, since the action then moves to the far end of the field, the effect on the accuracy of these shots is marginal at best.*

- *Height improves a player's ability to cross the ball successfully,*

- *However, height actually reduces their ability to pass and dribble properly. This may explain why taller attacks do not score more goals. Although our figures indicate that they convert more shots into goals, they also lose possession more easily.*

So size does affect certain aspects of the game, but not in a 'bigger is better' way; and as a yardstick by which to judge a player, it is not useful.

There is some evidence that it is an advantage defensively to be tall

There is some evidence that it is an advantage to be small as a forward

Fitness and speed for football

What you will learn

- Without a good level of fitness players cannot fully utilise time and space. They know they cannot go forward as they haven't the fitness to use ball travelling time to get back.

Theory

Speed

Whilst pace should not be overestimated as an attribute clearly players with pace can position themselves further from the person they are marking as they can cover more ground. Pace allows players who receive the ball in space to better use that space. If the defence pushes up too far then someone with space can better exploit the space (good defences don't do this). The biggest value of pace is probably latching onto a loose ball in the area.

S/he will sprint for around ten per cent of this distance. Analysis of eighty five scoring chances in the Champions league to see if pace was essential to the cross , movement before or the goal itself revealed that in only ten chances was it a factor. Useful but not essential.

Most of these sprints will last for less than five seconds and a player will sprint about every thirty seconds. The distance covered varies with position, midfield players covering the greatest distance. 'The average distance David Beckham runs in a Premiership match is 14 km. For England last week he ran 16 km'.

Fitness

Match analysis has shown us that the typical player at the top level covers around twelve kilometres.

Also worth considering is that around twenty per cent of goals are scored in the last fifteen minutes of a game.

Players use two systems to supply the energy for these efforts – aerobic and anaerobic. Aerobic (with oxygen) is used when you are generally not out of breath. Waste products, which cause fatigue, are not produced in any significant amounts.

Anaerobic (without oxygen) is when you have to sprint and are out of breath like one hundred metres (the four hundred metres race is a good example of how far you can go using your anaerobic system). Not simply one or the other extreme. If a player has high level of aerobic fitness s/he can work for longer without becoming tired. Players make a faster recovery from periods of very hard activity, such as a series of repeated sprints. The less tired a player is the less s/he is likely to make mistakes. We all make mistakes when we are tired. Tired challenges can lead to injury. You can only keep this up for a short period of time.

The higher the level of fitness the more space can be covered and the space of different levels full-time/ part-time is covered in less time. This is one of the differences between teams. A player's aerobic system can be developed by endurance training, by continuous training which involves no rests .This must not be for too long or anaerobic energy is required more often, leading to tiredness. The second method is Interval Training. Working, then resting. Again, make sure you do not work players so hard they are nearly all using anaerobic system

Defenders, especially full backs, need good fitness levels

One of the forwards needs pace. Without this the defence can push up and compress play

Goalkeeper

Theory

What you will learn

- The keeper re starts the game many times so careful consideration should go into what they do with the ball
- Keepers need to be good sweepers and good communicators

The ball will re enter play from the keeper on average around twenty to thirty times a game. This offers you the opportunity to dictate play. Simply kicking the ball up the middle with a fifty/fifty chance of getting possession is a waste and a poor tactic. The keeper can see the whole game. They should be talking to their team throughout especially when defending.

DEFENCE

The keeper needs to be a sweeper. As the defence moves forward the keeper needs to move out of goal, to be ready to come out of the area to cover the ball over the top of the defence in the space between them and the keeper (the danger zone).

Insist on your defence getting to the edge of the penalty area as soon as it is safe to do so. You are trying to create space without players in so that you can catch the ball and reduce the chances of the opposition scoring (it is harder to score from a header/shot the further out you go).

Make sure you line walls up correctly and put a tall player on the outside of the wall to make it harder for the attacking team to curl the ball over.

In the event of the opposition getting a penalty research has shown two things to improve your chances. Firstly, delay the kick as long as possible as this effects the concentration of the penalty taker. Secondly, the most reliable predictor of where the ball is going is by looking at the position of the non kicking foot just prior to striking the ball. Where it points tells where the forward will put the ball. Central means to the keepers right, more open to the left. When defending free kicks don't have a wall if it s not going to be positioned inside your area (research has shown a wall outside the area benefits the opposition as the keeper sees the ball later). Atkinson and others think that a player on the line works well at free kicks. Van De Saur talks of having a gap in the middle of the wall that allows the keeper to see the ball. If the opposition fill this it should not be done.

ATTACK

If a long ball is available into the opposition's danger zone, and you have pace up front, use it. If you are kicking long, make sure that your team is aware of where the ball is going. Players should concentrate on this area to win the 'second ball'. It is important for example the centre forward to at least challenge for the ball so not allowing the centre half to pick a pass.

Be aware of how to use the 'goal kick rule' to play the ball out from the back. Be aware of your role as offering support to full backs to switch the ball.

Ensure you communicate because you can see a lot more than most players.

Some points to consider/analyse about your game

- Distribution through kicking, ability to be keeper/sweeper, vision, awareness, general team work

- Communication, decision-making, positional play – distances with defenders.

The full back

What you will learn

- The defensive and attacking considerations for a full back. A full back who plays in a 4-4-2 formation will play 4-4-2 when the opposition have the ball however when his/her team have the ball one of the full backs will push in to midfield to create a numbers up situation

Theory

The full back is the critical link between attack and defence. They often push up to support midfield . They start the attack by receiving the ball from the keeper. They support the centre half at the same time as watching the oppositions wide player.

DEFENCE
You have two basic defensive considerations:
1) Am I offering support|/cover to the centre halves?
2) Am I stopping the winger getting a cross in? Brian Clough used to say 'if you stop the cross you stop the goal'. Ron Atkinson points out too many teams ignore that, 'I'm not sure whether enough of the ugly part of defending goes on these days, with players happy to get hit in the face'
Your position at any one time is a balance between these. The most important factor has to be offering cover in the scoring zone (see zonal).

You must:
Understand your zone (see zonal play)
Try and always **see the man in your zone and the ball.** Use body position to do this.
Move centrally when the ball is on the opposite side.

Offer cover to the centre halves in the event of a ball from the opposite side.
If the opposite side full back breaks forward into midfield the full back becomes like a centre half in a 3-5-2. A Central role as one of three. Stay like this until the other full back returns. (see next page)
Any delivery into the penalty area you must get ahead of forward and fill the space.
Get the team to the 18 yard line as soon as you can if you find yourself in the penalty area. For example corners. Be on post. Move out to the 18 yard line as soon as possible.

ATTACK
The balance between your attacking role and defensive role was well summed up by Terry Venables in a European Game between Lazio and Arsenal. He observed that a full back should not go beyond the ball as if s/he does, and the play breaks down, he is not in his defensive position. This could cost a goal.

To attack successfully you must bear the following in mind
- Use the space in your area to receive the ball from the keeper.
- Ensure you have an open body and can see forward and wide when you receive the ball.
- Ensure keeper and centre halves offer support. Ensure that one of the central midfielders offer a 'bounce'.
- Work with forwards to play a successful long ball and a ball to feet. Take what space you can quickly (move with the ball into it) and work with the wide player (see section why a winger should always get the ball in attacking strategies).
- Be aware, as space around you disappears, that you need to look to switch the ball using a bounce (see playing out from the back).
- If you can play the ball behind the defence for a forward doing a diagonal run (see attacking strategies) then do this.
- Time your runs to exploit space. Wait until the ball is about to be delivered before moving - head down of player with ball = move.
- Get the wide player to move centrally at times to create space for you. Throw in. Either take it and pretend you have a long throw to create more space or offer a ball back which can be switched.

Wide Midfielder

Theory

The stereo type wide midfielder is a player who can go wide, take players on and cross the ball. However, this need not be the case. Paul Scholes was used in this position and his role was to tuck in and attack more centrally. The wide player can move inside to create space for an overlapping full back.

DEFENCE

Understand your zone (see zonal play).

Starting position - diagonally level with full back. Number of yards in front depends on if your team is pressing.

Try and always see the man in your zone and the ball. Open body out to do this.

Needs to move centrally when the ball is on the opposite side. Can go a lot further than full back to compress area around ball. It is safe to leave the space in your zone and use ball traveling time to move across.
Offers cover to the centre midfield.

Double up on a wide player dribbling at full back (see section on ball travelling time).

Similar role to full back in terms of interaction with centre mid (slide across when the ball is on the far side).

ATTACK

should go wide to touch line and come as deep as it takes to offer for ball. If opposition follows (they shouldn't), move into space and receive the ball or stay and allow forwards to use the space.

Take what space you can quickly (move with the ball into it) and work with the wide player (see section on why a winger should always get the ball in attacking strategies).

Be aware that as space around you disappears you need to look to switch the ball using a bounce (go back or forward to do this).

If you can play the ball behind the defence for a forward doing a diagonal run (see attacking strategies), then do this.

Move centrally at times to create space for full back.

Centre midfield

Theory

It is harder to analyse midfield players. This point is recognised by the outstanding Roy Keane

Although I could dominate midfield, I didn't go on many runs, beating man after man, or carving defences apart with forty-yard passes. I read the game, intercepted passes, cut off opposing players' options, passed the ball simply myself. I worked box to box, unceasingly defending as well as I attacked. For every stunning goal I scored, and there were a few, there were a hundred little things, offensive and defensive, that went unnoticed. I worked for every second of a game with complete determination and absolute concentration. The determination was obvious, my trademark. The concentration was invisible. To catch even the most tutored eye brilliance was required.

Keane, as one of the finest midfielders in his generation, gives some further insight into the role

How to lose my marker, how to pace the game, how to time my runs into the opposition's penalty area; most of all perhaps, I learned that in every game you had to win the individual battle with the opponent in your own area of the pitch." Ron Atkinson adds to this by observing about attackers making runs out wide *'they' are runs a lot of strikers in this country don't make and I'd like to see Michael Owen doing more of that. By going wide, strikers not only disturb defences but enable their midfielders to go through in support.*

Midfielders going beyond forwards on a run is a very effective attacking strategy. It creates confusion and means that the central defenders have to concentrate not just on the forwards. It makes the game less predictable which always benefits the attackers.

As Keane matured his role changed *"...if I wanted to step up a level in the game, I would have to get more involved in the team's build up-play. I still saw myself as a goalscoring midfield player, working box to box, tackling closing people down, grafting to win the ball back. Offensively I believed that I was at my most effective running on to the ball to finish moves such as the one that produced the winning goal at Maine Road. This left Paul Ince or Robson to drop deep to receive the ball from the back four, a responsibility which, in truth I wasn't confident enough to take on. But Robson insisted this was something I had to do. Trust your own ability, was the message. He was right about me copping out of a task I wasn't sure I had the ability or vision to perform. I'd coped with the burden of my transfer fee but after six months at United, surrounded by so many gifted footballers, I still lacked confidence in possession of the ball."* It is your job to give players confidence. They cannot go into a game afraid of failing or giving the ball away.

Central midfielders need to understand the tactical game,

> *A footballing brain, able to spot the danger and nip it in the bud, and the desire to keep fighting, winning tackles, latching on to loose balls were the crucial qualities required.*

In terms of defensive responsibilities Keane observes *"Protect and support might be a fair description of my role."*

> A midfielders role is often about doing the right things and waiting for something to happen *"We desperately needed a break. If you keep doing the right things, you'll get your break in every game. It is also about* **timing** *"You need luck when timing a run into the box, but you do need to make the run. I did. Beck's cross was perfectly flighted. I just glanced it into the back of the net."*

A central midfielder, to play box to box, needs excellent **fitness. Atkinson *A midfielders commitment is probably 30% greater. In the centre of the park you have to do a lot of running to stay in the game.***

A central midfielder should be judged very much according to **how often they give the ball away. Tackling** is useful but as the game becomes better refereed and players technique improves it is becoming less important. This is especially true when you consider the need to stay on your feet and not give free kicks away. Perhaps Roy Keane would not agree with this point!

 Roy Keane still is an outstanding player. A quick look at his passing tally (below) last year 2004/5shows his value.

Category	Player/Team	Total
Top Shooter:	Thierry Henry (Arsenal)	75
Top Passer:	Roy Keane (Man Utd)	1403
Top Tackler:	Tony Hibbert (Everton)	115
Most Dribbles & Runs:	Cristiano Ronaldo (Man U)	279
Most Crosses:	Stewart Downing (Boro)	236
Most Offsides:	Paul Dickov (Blackburn)	44
Most Fouls:	Kevin Davies (Bolton)	68
Team with most fouls:	Blackburn Rovers	382
Team with most shots:	Man Utd	312

Centre half/centre forward – 'know your enemy'

Theory

You can only defeat your enemy by understanding them. For this reason both centre halves and forwards should read this. Centre forwards and centre halves need to identify how they can gain the upper hand. The defence wish to keep play predictable. For the attack, they try to cause uncertainty and test the concentration of the defenders. The following article from Ron Atkinson raises a number of issues

Arsenal are reasonably comfortable when opponents have the ball and play in front of them (defensive tactic), but this was the first time I've seen a team get behind them so much (attacking tactic), mainly because of Radzinski's movement.

As was mentioned at the very beginning of the manual (the long ball game) if a team is attacking and they have the opportunity to play the ball into the space between the defenders and keeper for a forward to run onto then this should be taken. To break down a defence not using this option is a lot harder. KEY POINT A defence should keep play in front of it. The line held should not allow the ball to be played in behind. *The striker pulled the centre-backs much wider than they would have liked with his runs into the corners, and he gave Pascal Cygan a particularly hard time.*

Attackers try to get central defenders out of the danger zone and scoring zone. This creates space for others to utilize (e.g central midfielders with a third man) Key Point– As a defender, try to stay in control as an attack to try to pull CH out wide or into the hole.

With regard to using the space out wide Atkinson observes Thierry Henry is brilliant at it and Alan Shearer went down the right and set things up in his prime. Radzinski often bent his run to get onto a ball down the right from Lee Carsley. Cygan wasn't alert or fast enough to stop him having good possession and the Canadian could cross or set things up. Cygan does have problems when he is turned. This is not unusual for a defender. Key Point– Work as a unit

To deal with Radzinski he should have shuffled across when Carsley was in possession, with Sol Campbell adjusting accordingly. That would have protected the space Radzinski wanted to run into. This highlights zonal play/advanced marking.
When the ball is wide and the full-back has been lured forward, this leaves a back 3 and hence more space out wide. The defensive response I like to see is he centre-half on that side shut off the gully. He's then got a start on anything played there and might cut out the pass. Advanced marking again.

Radzinski might then be free for a ball into feet, but that's the lesser of two problems for Arsenal. A ball to a forwards feet is preferable to one in the danger zone or scoring zone. The reason *They would have bodies behind the ball and Patrick Vieira or Gilberto Silva could sometimes deal with that. Radzinski's movement was so good he was cropping up on both flanks. Everton showed the value of taking the game to Arsenal and proved their defence can be turned. You do run a risk but there's always that risk against them, but if you defend in numbers they'll still pick you off. Arsenal have enough good players and tactical awareness to play round a deep defence with numbers according to Atkinson.*

Trying to turn defenses, getting beyond them is not easy if they play a good line. It relies on good delivery and intelligent runs

Centre half

Theory

DEFENCE
+ Essential to try not to leave the central area.
+ If a forward drops into the hole then you may have to follow. Use ball travelling time to adjust your position to still offer cover, but also be able to pressurize the person in the hole as s/he receive the ball and stop them turning. If you do move into the hole ensure the remaining three become a back three and watch central areas - become more compact.
+ Understand your zone (see zonal play).

Starting position - central slightly to left or right level with other centre half. Full backs will be a number of yards in front on either side. It is essential to move into a diamond shape to cover the danger zone in the event of a ball up the middle. One marks the player receiving the ball, the other the space behind. Space is more important than players.

As centre halves are in the critical space they should call the offside line. A full back making a mistake and playing a central player onside could lead to an opposition player scoring. The cover needs to be central so offside should be called from here.

As the ball arrives centrally one player must drop off to offer cover (see correct shape in zones section). Offside the covering player (preferably central) can drop off a couple of yards to offer cover. If discovered this player moves forward to trap the forward who is in this space using offside, then moves back when he/she can. Get team to 18 yard line as soon as you can if you find yourself in the penalty area. Any delivery into penalty area you must get ahead of the forward and fill the space (advance mark).

ATTACK
+ Go forward for set plays.
+ Don't be afraid of moving forward into space with the ball (they will usually drop off expecting a pass). You can support attacks as long as the rest of the defence goes to a back three position.
+ Offer to have the ball centrally from the keeper (understand the goal kick rule and use it).
+ Pass back if in trouble or simply step into the area before the ball arrives (you get the goal kick again).

+ Offer a switch (first time if you can) from one full back to the other.

Ron Atkison– Friday February 28th 2003 sums up what is required to be a centre half
> *In the centre of the park you have to do a lot of running to stay in the game but at centre half its more about concentration, awareness and reading situations early. You can get away without being the quickest. Bobby Moore is still rated as the best defender we've produced but he was lightening slow. What gave Bobby a head start was he was three yards quicker in the head than anybody else.*

Centre forwards

Theory

It's nice to have a big person/someone good in the air. The big person offers a heading option. Without that you are more predictable, with the defence knowing you are going to play to feet, or into the space behind them. One of the two needs pace or the defence can push up more easily and predict the tactics - ball to feet. Understand zonal play. (You need to know your enemy and how they defend)

DEFENCE

Do as much as you can but beware of overtiring and not being able to offer an attacking option. Where the team decides to press should be decided beforehand, or should be done at an appropriate time (you have a chance of winning the ball without them passing around you). Football is to an extent a numbers game. If you look around, and there are two of you and four of them, then you don't need to help out your defence. Be aware that as the ball changes hands in your area there will be occasions when you will need to chase back and slow the opposition down whilst your team gets its shape back.

ATTACK

Be aware of straight run diagonal ball and straight ball/diagonal run. Use 'the hole' to find space. Your role in holding up the ball to allow support or being used first time for a switch. Shoot when you get the chance.
Use the wide areas to find space.
Try and find if a full back is weak on a particular side and exploit it.
Work with centre mid to release them into space beyond you (centre halves don't like this). Understand their formation. If they play three at the back go wide to find space.

Some key points for centre forwards are emphasised by Atkinson in an article on how Chelsea's lack of pace gave West Ham the edge (Monday, May 5th, 2003,

West Ham were excellent and got their tactics spot on by raining in crosses and giving Chelsea no time to play. Chelsea had a team which had no pace to counter-attack. Everything had to go to feet, so West Ham could squeeze the game.

West Ham's centre-backs played high up the park knowing Chelsea couldn't turn them round by hitting balls over the top. And Glen Johnson could support attacks with little danger of passes being played in behind him. Zola and Gudjohnsen can hurt you given space, but Chelsea had no quick outlet ball over the top to use. West Ham ensured they were kept deep and if a pass went to Zola's feet, Tomas Repka closed him down, forcing it out to midfield. Chelsea had no one getting beyond the strikers. Graeme Le Saux can do it but was pushed back by Johnson. Frank Lampard likes to get between the strikers in the last 30 yards, not 80 yards from goal. I think Chelsea could have started with Jimmy Floyd Hasselbaink or Carlton Cole to add pace. Hasselbaink's not had a great season but he would have made things harder by stretching the game. Repka and Christian Dailly would have worried about losing a sprint for balls over the top. And once centre-backs are turned and running towards their own goal, the rest of the team has to get back. Emmanuel Petit's best pass is over the top from left to right. And once the centre-halves have slackened, Chelsea could feed their other striker - Zola or Gudjohnsen - in more space, buying time for the support to get up.

This emphasises that going long with the option of pace will force the oppositions defence back so creating space for others in the hole, in this example, Zola.

Summarise the key factors that affect each position. For each position give 5 examples of good players

Goalkeeper

Centre forwards

Centre half

Wide Midfield

Central Midfield

The full back

Pick your best 11 from players playing in the world today. Justify your choices. Describe your tactics.

Explain the inverted U theory

Explain tunnel Vision

Explain the concept of a 90 minute head.

Describe how far players have to run.

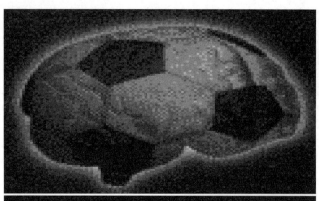

What you will learn

♦ Some tips on analysing your team and players

The key point to remember for all positions is that a player should be judged against two criteria

1. How they attack. The decisions they make when they have the ball and the movement they make when colleagues have the ball.

2. How they defend. Did the player go to ground or give free kicks away? Was the player in the correct area (zone)? Did the player offer cover in the important zones?

Therefore if a player asks, how well did I play? A good response would be something like this

'You defended well. Your concentration was excellent. You did not give free kicks away, stayed on your feet and were in the correct zonal position throughout the game. On one occasion on the transition you did not react as quickly as you should when defending and so were a couple of yards off the player in your zone. Luckily the ball did not arrive there.

You did not do so well when we had the ball. You should have moved the ball more quickly when you made two interceptions in the second half (during the transition). Whilst you did not give the ball away you did not make good decisions on three occasions when a forward ball was available. Once to the centre forwards feet and twice when a forward was making a diagonal run behind the full back and wanted a ball into space.

How do you analyse your team attack

Theory

It is often claimed that most goals are scored using under five passes. This measurement is however not subtle enough. The key point is not the number of passes, but the length of **time** between having possession and an attempt on goal. In other words, it's speed of attack, not number of passes, which more accurately reflects soccer.

It is often the case that the faster the attack the more space available. This especially applies when possession is regained from the opposition in a team's own half. They will be spread out.

There is plenty of analysis available of goals scored but one thing that is never measured is how many players a team commits to an attack and how fast a team gets a shot in after re-gaining possession.

The ball changes hands every fifteen seconds, if we take off stoppages and time for throw-ins, etc, then if your team have half the possession you will have around forty opportunities to attack per half.

A useful analysis may be to look at a ten minute spell to see how well fast you react to the transition, how many players were committed forward, and did the move succeed in a shot on goal or cross? Look at the tally chart below. What does this tally chart tell us?

The team do not commit enough players forward (never more than 4). They are very effective at creating chances/crosses (only lost the ball 3 times).

Possession re-gained – 10 minutes 25-35					
	Where? Def, Mid, Attack	Time to shot on goal/cross (seconds)	Number of players committed	Was there a switch? Did this gain ground? Did it involve bounce?	Possession lost
1	Mid				x
2	Mid	9	4	Yes, Yes, Yes	
3	Def	15	4	Yes, Yes	
4	Def				x
5	Attack	2	4	No	
6	Def	12	3	Yes, No	
7	Def	14	4	Yes, Yes, Yes	
8	Def	8	3	No	
9	Mid				x
10	Def	9	4	No	
11	Def				x

How do you analyse your team defence?

Theory

Defensively a team can be looked at in terms of its shape.

- The number of times the team loses its shape
- Does the back four have a good offside line so the opposition cannot deliver a ball into the danger zone?
- Were players close enough together?
- Was there cover available?

More specific analysis like looking at the current leaders of the Premiership (Jan 2005) Chelsea have the highest clean sheets 13 (Man U 9), least shots on target conceded 38 (Man U 49) Least conceded within the box 18 (Man U 27). The table below looks at shape, cover and players going to ground. With a good defence....

if we score one goal in our minds we think the game is finished Chelsea Keeper

Defensive Team Shape and player decisions				
	Did anyone go to ground or out of position?	Was the offside line correct?	Did we have good cover?	Did the midfield work with the defence?
Attack 1	Yes, centre mid	Yes	Yes	Wide right was slow on transition
Attack 2	No	Yes	Yes	Yes
Attack 3	No	No left too much space in danger zone for easy ball	No, centre halves too flat.	Yes
Attack 4	No	No, keeper not on edge of area	Yes	No, right mid did not support right back when winger approached area to cross
Attack 5	Yes, left back not close enough to centre halves	Yes	Yes	Yes
Attack 6	No	Yes	Yes	Yes
Attack 7	No	Right back slow coming to edge of area	Yes	Yes
Attack 8	Yes, right back gave away free kick	Yes	Yes	Yes
Attack 9	No	Yes	Yes	Yes
Attack 10	No	Yes	Yes	Yes

Analysing individuals in your team

Theory

Another analysis used much more often is if players keep possession when they have the ball. This analysis is useful but players must not be encouraged to just keep the ball for keeping its sake. They must have a purpose. This is usually to get the ball to a player from the same team who is further forward. This tally chart therefore adds in the criteria of 'was the correct pass chosen?

Keeping possession is not enough. Some conclusions from the above are on the next page.

What would they be? All players made more mistakes late on in second half. Why is this?

Name of player 1 = correct pass chosen 2 = ball not lost but bad choice x = possession lost	First half	Second half
Bob Gray	1112xxx11221112	11111xxxx2xx
Mark Denton	1111211211x	111122111111x1
Steve Abdulla	1212111x111111	11111111x12
Daz Croxton	1111112111x	111112111x
Mark Curry	111222211xx	111121121212
Phil Wymer	1111111111111112	11111111211122
James Foster	111111111212111x	111111122111xxx
John Linnell	1111111222121212	11221122111x1x2
Wes Johnston	11111212121xx12xx	11112212112212x
Mike Cherry	11111111112111x	11111x1122x
Alan Crofts	111112122211111	1111x

What the analysis tells us

Theory

Some conclusions from the analysis on the previous page.
- ❖ Crofts did not get the ball enough in the second half.
- ❖ Johnston had a poor game.
- ❖ Gray was better in the second half.
- ❖ Curry made bad decisions throughout.
- ❖ Wymer was most consistent.
- ❖ The team made more mistakes later in the game. This is down to fitness, with concentration always suffering late on.

Just doing this analysis has a good effect on players. Try it and see: they are always interested and become very focussed and competitive.

Get someone who understands the game to do the analysis. Some decisions are good but just don't come off. For example
- ♦ A good ball in the final third that the defence only just clear should not count against a player
- ♦ A player plays a ball into space but the forward was slow making the run, or made the wrong run
- ♦ Any ball into space relies on timing and decisions by the person receiving the ball: it may be the receivers fault.

Here are some areas you could analyse.
Success playing out from back to halfway.
Entries in the attacking third - only if the team retain possession, even if only for one touch. This should include when the attacking team gain a set play in the attacking third.
Regaining possession of the ball in the attacking third - when the attacking team regains possession of the ball in the attacking third of play.
Achieving effective crosses - creating the opportunity for an attempt at goal.
Dribbling / Turning Attempts - in the attacking and middle thirds should be recorded. It is often successful **dribbling and turning in the middle third** that leads to strikes at goal, etc.
Strikes at goal but off target - shots and headers but not blocked shots within one metre of the striking player. **Strikes on target** - strikes on target whenever a goal is scored or the goalkeeper (or defender) has to make a save; this does not include strikes that hit the post or the crossbar.

Let us now look at the conclusions from a match analysis on TV. (see next page)
- ♦ Arsenal switched the ball twelve times in the first half and four in the second. Sixteen times in all. All of the tactics in this work were in evident.
- ♦ How a player or team defends, where they hold their line, how the midfield and forwards support defence or where they close play down. Successful teams can compress play and win back possession.
- ♦ How a player or team attacks, who supports who, how many players a team commits forward. How the team goes wide and long. Successful teams switch the ball frequently.
- ♦ A good shape is essential.
- ♦ Don't give the ball away.
- ♦ Do things quickly.
- ♦ Good technique means players can operate in less space.
- ♦ **Defenders try to compress play.**
- ♦ **Attackers try to go wide and long to use as much space as possible.**
- ♦ **For defenders it is always about concentration.**

Analyse a TV game – Inter Milan V Arsenal 25th November 2003

It is often very hard to analyse games on TV. The camera does not allow you to see the movement away from the ball. The exceptions to this are often European as the stadiums are large and so the cameras are high and allow a good view. It is important to look away from where the ball is because when the ball is played things change very quickly.

Time in Game		Tactic to watch for
0.14	SWITCH	Switch – note the opposition trying to stop them
1.50	SWITCH	Switch
2.19	THE HOLE	The hole
2.55	DOUBLE UP	Defend near post – ball goes to Henry they double up
5.28	ROAMING DIAMOND	Compact play
6.01	PROTECT SCORING ZONE	Defenders move to edge of box
7.26	PROTECT SCORING ZONE	Get to edge of area
9.00		Kanu confidence
9.17		Loads Arsenal player around ball
9.40	COMPRESS PLAY	Milan players around the ball
9.53	SWITCH	Switch
10.20		Wide player gets ball
11.15		Defence closes up
11.53	SWITCH	Switch
12.08		Note they have twenty three at the back
12.30		Arsenal have four forward
13.01		Milan have four forward
1329		Watch Campbell drop off how compact its defensive goal kick
14.18		Good shape off kick
16.30		Parlour poor first touch
19.44	SWITCH/BOUNCE	Switch/bounce
21.00	SWITCH	Switch
21.34		Player should chest it
23.02		Good wide position Cole
23.30		Kanu - leave wide player two up
24.00	SWITCH	Switch
24.36	SWITCH	Switch
		GOAL
25.50		Look how deep defence gone to deal with long ball

Analyse a game on TV – Inter Milan v Arsenal 25th November 2003

Analysis

Time in Game		Tactic to watch for
27.50		Faked offside Campbell drops
28.20	SWITCH	Switch
30.33		Compact back four
31.33	SWITCH	Switch
32.00		Gave possession away
33.37	SWITCH	Switch
34.14		Defence goes eighteen yard line
35.18		Defence marks space to deal with crosses
35.36	SWITCH	Switch
36.30		Look off the goal kick two centre mid in front of back four two wide slightly further forward.
37.22		Parlour goes to ground
38.00		No space for Vieri
38.45	SWITCH	Switch
Half time	twelve switches	
47.07		Look at pressure around ball
49.35		Watch how they fill space plus Milan won the header but look how far out
52.00		Long ball look at the three
53.00		**look at the defence mid formation**
59.47	SWITCH	Switch
60.37		Campbell does not offer to the keeper
61.18		Going to ground
64.30		Arsenal players around ball
65.51		Look players round ball
66.28		Players round ball pressure
73.22		Central defence and mid
79.00	SWITCH	Switch
80.36		Three round ball
82.14		Third man run
86.00	SWITCH	Switch
89.47		Look at the zones defenders

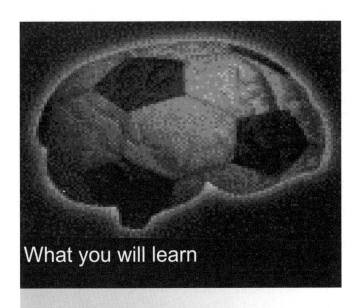

What you will learn

◆ Some tactics that can help gain advantage in a game

18 tactical tips

Bobby Davidson's 'kind whisper'	I was marking Bobby Davidson (an ex professional centre forward). The winger was going down the left. He said 'near post Kev' right next to my ear. He started to move there. I followed. He had said this loud enough for me to hear but not the winger and the ball was played to the back post . He scored .
Get the opposition to mark the corner taker	If you always place 2 people at the corner when taking it, the opposition will bring out 2 defenders so the corner taker, who is in an ineffective positioning will be marked. This benefits the attack leaves more space in the area,
Do a near post corner quick - the stats say it works	Statistics show that a near post corner is most effective if taken within 10 seconds of getting it.
Dave Morris shout	To a forward player, who was watching the ball and couldn't see the offside line. Dave 'ref he's off' the forward stepped back. He wasn't offside. This tactic keeps the attackers on their toes. Make sure the rest of the team know or they could be confused.
Mark the person on the back post	By doing this you may find that the opposition regard you as marked as there is a defender next to you and you can move into space elsewhere as the ball is played.
Never fear offering to have the keeper pass you the ball off a goal kick	If its not a good time to have the ball (you are being closed down) just step in to the area. The ref blows the keeper takes the kick again. The keeper also can change sides, and the chances are the other side, away from the ball, has space for someone to receive the ball as the opposition will have been drawn to you
Leave 3 up from a corner	A manager I know had a keeper who was excellent at catching the ball off corners. This would be helped by having fewer players in the area to get in the way. He always left 3 players up at the half way line and the keeper would quickly deliver to them. It is very true that you are vulnerable defensively when you have a corner, as your defence will be at the halfway line leaving lots of space in the danger zone.
The old saying of its still 0 0 (Insight)	A player and team are at their most effective when the score is 0 0, This has been proven in research. So after taking the lead try and get your team to be in the 0 0 mentality.

Huddle to cause muddle

If a team have 2/3 players together all aiming for the same space then they are difficult to mark and offer a good target area with allowance for inaccuracy off a set play such as a corner.

The ball to the back post

England played Croatia and Strachan in the Guardian warned (Monday June 21st 2004) Beware the long cross from the left that targets Cole's lack of height-Exploiting Zonal defence. He was concerned that the Croatians would adopt the tactic of playing balls over the centre halves to the back post defended by a weaker in the air full back. Strachan noted that *crosses into the penalty area to exploit Ashley Cole's size. At over 6ft Rosso's quite a bit taller than Cole. Although his main job will be to look after Paul Scholes, he's also capable of getting on the end of the balls that Rapaic sends over from the left. As Rapiac is about to cross, the strikers head towards the front post. England's centre-halves go with them and then Rapiac sends the ball to the back post, beyond John Terry and Sol Campbell, where Rosso is trying to get ahead of Cole.*

If England minimise Croatia's aerial threat I don't think there will be much to trouble them. Their defenders will be able to handle themselves one against one when the ball's on the deck. Although Prso will probably come deep, that won't be a big threat because England's narrow midfield will make it hard for Croatia to thread balls through to him.

Play long for the first 10.

If you play a long ball game for the first 10 minutes it makes their defence drop back and gives you more space to play in. This tactic should be adopted whenever they are squeezing on and playing a high offside line. Too often teams like to play the ball around and but don't adapt their game to create the space to play it.

Hide your formation

At kick off or at other stoppages get a full back to push up and pretend to be a midfielder (in a 4 4 2 for example). The opposition will probably work it out after a while but it does cause confusion

Don't underestimate a new face

Someone who has often in a game come up against a particular player will always be concerned and unsure when a sub is made. Wesley had one trick, it always meant he could get a cross in. the next time the defender read it. That one cross may make the difference.

Chess Pieces

Use them in the dressing room. They are good for differentiating between players (players will have a laugh when you first do it) but it works.

Follow the ball

Get your forward players to follow the side the ball is on when the opposition are attacking. If your full back gets the ball and plays a ball up the line they are then in a better position to receive early. How often do you see possession given away as a full back plays a ball up the line and it goes straight to the opposition. I watched German side do this.

Its harder to adapt tactics after half time

A sneaky tactical ploy often works better in the second half as the other team can come in at half time and make changes. If you have played a certain way in the first they may adapt if it is working. So change it again.

The 2nd ball

Get your keeper to do a drop kick before every game. Judge where he/she can reach. Place your big centre forward there to challenge for a flick on. The centre half may win the ball but as long as there is a challenge the ball will drop in to an area which you can predict and put your midfield players in. They should use ball travelling time to choose when they arrive so as not to make it obvious.

Big man
Little man with pace

It is true that it is useful to have at least one player of the 2 forwards who is good in the air as he can flick the ball on for the other forward who is quick or an advancing in midfielder, Not to have these option makes you r attacking options less and so the defence has less to worry about.

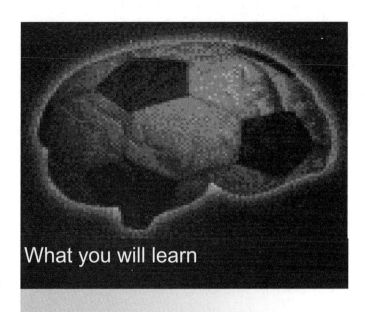

What you will learn

- How to organise you match day

Good players are mentally tough

Theory

What you will learn

Being mentally tough requires three things
- Endurance
- Staying calm under pressure
- Concentration

Insight (May 2004) had an article by Steve Bull, a Sports Psychologist who works with cricket teams. He identified three types of mental toughness.

Endurance – if players will push themselves physically, will this hurt? A good example is a player who pushes him/her self when doing the bleep test. Transferred to a game situation it is a player who runs for ninety minutes who doesn't stop. Roy Keane is the obvious example.

Final Put – this term refers to the pressure a golfer is under when putting to win a game or tournament. In soccer the obvious example is a penalty. Can a player handle the pressure?

Concentration – Bull talks of cricketers attempting to intimidate players, put them off their game. Good players stay focused and don't let it affect their performance.

These three types of mental toughness can all apply or just some. The best players will display all three. There is, however, a fourth.

The ninety minute head, even when bored! Although the three types of mental toughness above are a

useful guide to the mental side of the game it is worth noting a fourth type of mental toughness. The fourth is a players ability to concentrate for ninety minutes. To do their defensive role, react to the transition and their attacking role. The need to be in the correct position even if the ball doesn't arrive. The need to make good decisions. Switching the ball is an attempt to test a teams defensive shape. It probes looking for gaps. Defenders only have to switch off and be out of position for a second and a good opposition will find the space and exploit it. One goal is often enough to win a game. If we look at a brief analysis of goals from the Premiership we see around half came from errors. The majority of these errors are players slightly out of position.

Top coaches - Sir Clive Woodward and Arsene Wenger-frequently talk in percentages and how to extract that extra one or two per cent from players, physically and mentally. They are the margins at the highest level. It may not be all in the mind but a fraction can be.

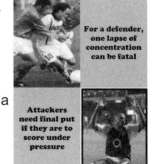

For a defender, one lapse of concentration can be fatal

Attackers need final put if they are to score under pressure

How a player's mental state can affect what he/she can see and take in during a game - (Tunnel Vision)

Theory

There are 2 factors that influence the extent that a player can be tactically aware when receiving the ball. Firstly, Players with **poorer technique** or less experience will, when the ball is travelling toward them, have to focus on the ball and so be less aware of what is going on around, and tactical considerations.

Secondly, a player's **mental state** can change what s/he takes in and, negatively or positively affect performance. The mental state can influence physically what players can see.

It can make a player have narrow 'tunnel vision' where they only take in a limited amount of information and miss key points that would help them towards the correct decision.

There are many variables which players could take in during a game. The crowd, the oppositions coach shouting, they could be concentrating on non relevant players, they could have negative thoughts about their own ability, they could be concentrating on tactical objectives, their own technique, players around them. To make the best decision a player needs to listen for information as well as observe movement.

The lines below indicate the width of a player's focus.
*   At point 1 a players is affected by all these things, both positive and negative. (under aroused)
*   At point 2 a player is aroused and is taking in all the positive messages required whilst ignoring the negative. Negative messages are not affecting players focus/concentration.
*   At point 3 a player is over aroused. At this point a player is not taking in all the positive messages. S/he may concentrate on the players round him/her and so technique fails . May disregard tactical considerations , not listen to messages from their own players

Awareness of how over arousing or under arousing a player effects their game should help you get the best from your players.

1

Negative The crowd
Negative Their coach shouting
Negative none relevant players
Negative thoughts
Positive concentration on tactical objectives
Positive concentration on technique
Positive concentration on players around me
Negative The crowd
Negative Their coach shouting
Negative none relevant players
Negative thoughts

2

Negative The crowd
Negative Their coach shouting
Negative none relevant players
Negative thoughts
Positive concentration on tactical objectives
Positive concentration on technique
Positive concentration on players around me
Negative The crowd
Negative Their coach shouting
Negative none relevant players
Negative thoughts

3

Negative The crowd
Negative Their coach shouting
Negative none relevant players
Negative thoughts
Positive concentration on tactical objectives
Positive concentration on technique
Positive concentration on players around me
Negative The crowd
Negative Their coach shouting
Negative none relevant players
Negative thoughts

The Team Talk

Theory– team talk
Thanks to Shane Kent (MSc) for help with this section

- Players are all different. Arousal effects performance. If players are over aroused they will under perform.

The first thing to consider is are there any tactics changes needing to be made depending on which way your team is kicking. If the decision as to which end you are playing Is made on the pitch you may effectively have to have two tactical team talks along the line of if we kick uphill we play 4-4-2 and prioritise playing the ball out from the back, if we play downhill we play 4-3-3 and play a slightly longer game. It is also important as mentioned earlier that your tactics deal with eventualities with being a goal down or a goal up. Much of this discussion may have been done earlier because the final team talk before a game should be short (around 5 minutes) and not complicated (don't throw lots of last minute tactical points at players). The most important thing about this team talk is getting your players mentally ready for the game. Every football player is different and will react in their own way to stressful situations.

Gordan Strachan observes 'Most managers have always recognised that players have different personalities and temperaments and that it is asking for trouble to try and motivate them all in the same way '.

How aroused players are significantly affects their performance, the mental state affects the physical state. Football is about decisions; decisions are based on information and what people see. If players are over aroused they may have 'tunnel vision', they will make mistakes and ultimately, as we shall see, may have to be substituted. It is important that you know your players and are aware that before a game you may need to 'hype up' some players, others you may need to calm down.

In simple psychological terms the optimum level of performance can be explained via the inverted U hypothesis:

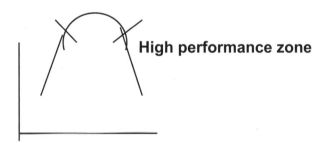

Performance

High performance zone

Arousal

The inverted 'U' hypothesis suggests that performance will be poor if under aroused and poor if over aroused. Performance should be best if a player is at a 'mid' point in their arousal. This explanation is OK in general terms, but the high performance point may be different for different individuals. For example I know that I perform best about ¾ of the way up the upward curve of the inverted U. Other players may perform best ¾ of the way down the downward curve. Therefore most players will not necessarily perform best at the top of the inverted U, but for the majority of players the optimum arousal level will 'normally' be somewhere within the high performance zone.

As a general rule of thumb - do not relax your players too much or over arouse them too much.

What to look for and how to overcome arousal problems

You may well be thinking now, so OK, I know that I need to keep my players arousal to a 'mid' level, but how do I know if they are under or over aroused. One suggestion is to look at their body language. If player is under aroused they generally do not seem interested, for example their shoulders may slump. To help increase their arousal you may give them clear goals to aim for - get five shots on target before the end of this half. Another method can be to give a player responsibility - make him the corner taker, or even captain.

The more common arousal problems (normally stated as anxiety) are related to being over aroused. The symptoms of this can come in two types: Cognitive anxiety is usually mental - thoughts of negative performance, worry, tunnel vision. The second type is Somatic anxiety which is usually physical - sweaty palms, wanting to go to the toilet, dry mouth.

One strategy to overcome Cognitive anxiety is to be positive - tell your players their good points - make them feel they are great players. In general get them to think positively about themselves and their oncoming performance.

One strategy to overcome Somatic anxiety is deep breathing - get the players to concentrate on their breathing - slow deep breaths (counting can often be used - 5 seconds in 5 seconds out). This strategy often gets players to focus on their breathing rather than the feeling of having sweaty palms or wanting to go to the toilet.

As well as Somatic and Cognitive anxiety problems there is a phenomenon known as the Catastrophe theory. This is when a player becomes so over aroused s/he, for want of a better word, 'blows up'.

Gordon Strachan again observes 'Hence the fact that, when a manager lets rip at a player, the danger of 'losing' him – of the player allowing it to have an adverse effect on his performances – is probably more pronounced than ever'

If over aroused footballers may lose all clarity of thought, and their decision making is non-existent, in general their brains cannot function in a clear and rational manner. An example of this from another sport (tennis) was from Jana Novotna in the 1993 Wimbledon final. Jana was about to go two breaks up in the final set when she missed a second serve, and consequently lost that game. Her whole world fell apart and she barely won another point. This can happen in football, for example a player may miss a penalty and feel that it may be his/her fault that a game may be lost.

If 'catastrophe' occurs you have two choices: If their performance becomes so poor and detrimental to the team you may have to substitute them. Alternatively,
 act positively, as coach tell them that that moment in the game has gone. They can still contribute and help win.

Winning is, by many players, coaches, and spectators, seen as everything. It is important to recognise the performance. You may have been beaten due to:

- A moment of balance
- A mistake by a player
- Over aroused / tunnel vision

Players may have given their all, the team played as well as they could...... is this a failure. If you have a team where development of the team or players is a priority then if both performed well, but you lost, did you fail? No.

Get the players to concentrate on how they can affect the game through a positive contribution from now on. Give them clear and simple guidance, as they may not be thinking clearly. Too much information may well overwhelm them

***The above strategies are simple suggestions to overcome anxiety (or over arousal). There are other techniques such as progressive relaxation, cue words, focusing techniques, but be careful you should really be a qualified sport psychologist to perform such practices**

'Leaving thought' - Get to know your players and how they react in certain situations. If one method of optimising psychological performance does not work try a different one. There is no magic formula, but the better you get to know your players the more you can get out of them.

Strachan makes some other interesting observations.

> *'West Ham United's Glenn Roeder will have prompted nods of agreement from most managers with his recent comments on the problems of giving footballers what one could call a 'good old-fashioned rollicking' these days. ......as Roeder pointed out, this is not the only reason why the occasionally abrasive, confrontational approach of men such as Alex Ferguson has become more difficult to sustain. Fergie referring to those verbal blasts at players, which earned him the nickname of 'Hairdryer', once said: 'Footballers respond to anger.' Unfortunately, because managers have to deal with players from so many different cultures now, and because of the changes that have taken place in British Society, many top-level players no longer respond to it in a positive way'.*

> *It can take time for a manager to really get to know his players and mistakes are inevitable. I have certainly made mistakes in this department – there have been a couple of occasions when my approach to a player has been too abrasive for a player to handle and, minded, I have apologised to him for this a day or two later.*

> *One of my most embarrassing memories concerns my time at Coventry, and a verbal rocket I gave to a 17-year-old who had been invited to spend a morning working with the senior professionals. I overreacted to a mistake he made in a training game and, even worse, hauled him over the coals about it in front of the other players. I had no compunction about making sure all those players were present when I apologised to the youngster the following day.*

> *When it comes to managers fully expressing their anger or disappointment with their players the most 'dangerous' periods, of course, are at half-time or immediately after a match. In my own case, my reaction to performances that have displeased me has become considerably more calculated than it was in my early days as a manager. One thing you quickly learn as a manager, is the value of saving any stick you might wish to dish out until a day or two after a match when all concerned can look at things more rationally.*

> *Indeed while I might give the impression that I struggle to control my emotions during a match, I like to think that my players would readily confirm that I am much less excitable in my dealings with them than many might imagine.*

Henri commented in a recent article that they are laughing and joking until 5 minutes before the game.

The problems Strachan faces are the same for all clubs at all levels. Strachan tries to be rational and calm. This is the only way to be successful as a manager. The days of the ranter are gone.

Match day food

Theory

It has been recommended that carbohydrate should be taken on board every 15 minutes during prolonged bouts of exercise! This may be not very practical for soccer but it is worth considering.

The best recommendation that can be made is that players attempt to take on board fluids containing carbohydrate, like lucozade sport, as much as possible during a game.

With this in mind the nutritional approach to half time is of vital importance. Players must avoid taking on board too much food as it can result in an uncomfortable "full" feeling in the stomach. Players should drink a sports drink and maybe attempt to incorporate 1 or 2 pieces of fruit into their half time routine.

Sports drinks are recommended as they are formulated to be digested and available for use quickly. Other drinks may be very high in sugar content and the body has a harder time digesting these and therefore they should be avoided.

So what should a soccer player attempt to consume after a game? Immediately after the game the soccer player should attempt to take on board a significant quantity of carbohydrate, with sports drinks again being good idea at this point.

Various researchers have suggested that around 100 grams should be consumed at this point. Then around 2 hours after a game carbohydrate should be consumed again. The dose this time should be slightly lower than before.

Jack Charlton insisting his team eat fish and chips before a game is not the best nutritional advice.

Warming Up

Theory

The warm up has 2 key benefits: Physical- in that it warms the body up, and Mental, - in that it gets players focusing on the game, pitch etc.

Many teams do whole team warm ups to ensure everyone follows good practice to generate a collective spirit. Some argue that individuals are different and need their own time and space to practice what they want, and mentally prepare how they want (Nigel Clough believes this). The best warm up should therefore involve a group session and then time for individuals to prepare.

Aim to start your warm up at least 40 minutes before kick off. If it lasts for 20 minutes this allows around 5 minutes of individual time before going in for the final team talk (5 minutes). Players will still be warmed up at kick off.

Warming up was introduced in England after it was clear that opposing teams were doing it up to an hour before a game. Today most teams in England have a warm up before the match and also before undertaking the more strenuous parts of their training sessions.

The main reasons for warming up are to:

•   Increase body temperature and muscle temperature to increase performance
•   Reduce the risk of injury and muscle tightness
•   Stimulate the nervous system
•   Practice game skills
•   Raise arousal level
•   Familiarise with the pitch etc (environment)

Stretching the main thigh muscles is especially important in cold weather conditions. Players should concentrate on calf, hamstrings and hip muscles as they are often tight in these areas.

It is best to include the movements typical of a game situation such as running backwards, sideways, sharp turns and jumping.

It is important that the warm up should not be too long or too strenuous. If it is, then the effort begins to draw on the body's energy stores rather than get it ready for action. All the requirements of a good warm up can be incorporated into 20-25 minutes without being hurried.

Theory – substitutions

Today's game is about 14 players. Often the mere fact there is a sub will affect the game . A sub can create change and people don't like change. If you are behind don't take off goal scorers. Substitutions can be used late on just to waste time or slow the tempo of the game down.

Warming down

Theory

Why Warm Down? Whilst most teams warm up many do not warm down. A 90 minute match can put great stress on the body. Warming down helps the recovery process as the body begins to recover more quickly. Gentle exercise helps get rid of waste products more quickly. It also helps to clear blood lactate from the circulation (this is what makes you ache in the morning).

Other benefits include
- There is a smoother drop in body temperature as the heat load induced from exercising muscles is reduced gradually
- Often the nervous system is so aroused that it is difficult to sleep. A warm down can result in improved quality of sleep in subsequent nights
- A reduction in the depression of the immune system which reduces the risk of minor infections

What to do in a Warm Down

- After a game it is important to take in fluid in order to start the re-hydration process as soon as possible. Having done this, and any match analysis, do a 25 minute warm down.
- Jogging is the best form of warm down, with 10-15 minutes or longer. The intensity of the warm down should not exceed half that of match play.
- Gentle stretching exercises for calves, hamstrings and adductors can be built into the warm down.
- 'Shaking down' the legs from a lying position can also be used.
Low intensity drills in small groups may also be used as warm down practices at the end of normal training

Key Questions/Activity Sheet

Chalkboard/ Classroom

Explain the inverted U theory

Explain tunnel Vision

Explain the concept of a 90 minute head.

Explain why we warm up and warm down

Complete a table of timings for a match day allow at least 70 minutes.

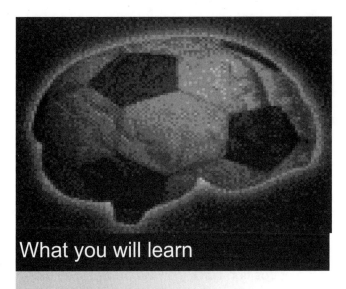

What you will learn

- A look at top sides
- The limitations of the long ball game
- How to analyse your team

Defeats such as those of Real Madrid and Arsenal show the difference between football and formula One. If the best driver has the best car, as in the case with Michael Schumacker, there can be no sensations. In football you can lose with the best team in the world against an underdog.
Rudi Voller, German coach

Tactics in the cham-
pions League

Chelsea's failure in the semi final of the Champions League 2004 was due to a failure to adapt tactics during a game. Chelsea, who needed to score two goals, played an open attacking style which led to chances at both ends, Chelsea took theirs and were in a winning position. At that point they should have changed to a more defensive approach defending deeper, denying space, and hitting the opposition quickly on the break. They didn't ,but continued with an open high tempo style perhaps waiting for half time to change tactics. The opposition got a goal back, and Chelsea's chance was lost. Tactical Strengths– Play high tempo. Have the ability to pack defence but their failure to change to this cost them. One of the best defensive records in the Champions League but, as stated above, poor tactics in semi cost them. Formation– changes formation constantly often at half time.

Monaco with coach Didier Deschamps have more defensive full backs than for example Porto and are happier to play longer and give away possession. They are happy with a counter attacking game. They used this counter attacking tactic well to defeat Chelsea. Morientes drops deep to find space and times his run to beat the offside line.

Coaching lesson– Built success on defence. Did not adapt tactical game to deal with change in circumstances. Don't wait until half time to bring in a tactical change. This can be too late. Changing tactics at half time can catch the opposition out– they may have made changes based on first half

Coaching lesson– Using a player in the hole can be very effective in breaking an offside trap. Beware playing a trap as you may catch a player in an offside position but another player may be onside and the goal will stand.

Champions League- February/March 2005

Arsenal V Bayern Munich GAME 1
Arsenal lost a stupid goal to Bayern. Khan the keeper played a long ball up the middle the 2 centre halves did not adopt the correct shape a goal was score. The game was characterised by the keepers kicking long in the first half (all I saw) this led to a disjointed game with little good possession.

Manchester United V Milan GAME 1
Milan dominated Man United although part of this is a tactical decision by Man United to move the ball quickly. Milan defended deep and compressed the area around United's wingers. Man U failed to get in effective crosses and this is Man United's main attacking tactic. Teams that cross more, like United, are no more likely to be successful than teams who like for example Arsenal adopt a more centrally attacking game. It is a matter of style.
Milan played a probing game building often slowly up from the keeper throwing the ball virtually every time.

Barcelona V Chelsea GAME 1
Barcelona were playing a high defensive line and left Chelsea with the easy long ball in to the space between defence and keeper- you wont see this space in other games at this level. Chelsea could have scored 2. The attacking ability of Barcelona won through with constant probing resulting in a defender centrally over committing and space being created for an equalising goal. The second was a converted cross but the lesson for a defender, who could have cut out the cross, was always block a cross unless you are sure there is no-one behind you.

Chelsea v Barcelona GAME 2

A fantastic game and a tactical battle between the best attacking side in the competition and the side with one of the best defences and a manger, Jose Mourinho, with a flexible approach to the tactical side of the game. Anyone who has watched Chelsea this season knows they can keep the ball and play a possession based build up game as well as fast break. In addition, especially early on in the season, they are superb at set plays. Chelsea's Tactics in this game relied on defending deep and allowing Barcelona possession in Chelsea's half.

One of the statistical characteristics of a successful side is the ability to maintain possession in the opposition half. Barcelona were excellent at this. I analysed 75 minutes of play using the criteria – *did a team string together 3 or more passes to their own players in the oppositions half?* In the first 25 minutes Barcelona did this 5 times, Chelsea not once. Chelsea were 3-0 up. The tactic they adopted was to steal the ball and attack at speed.

Barcelona played a high line giving Chelsea the chance to attack wide space and cross score if they took the time on the transition quickly which they did.

The second goal was a shot, deflection and Lampard, who I mention earlier , demonstrated his world class timing to beat the offside trap and score.

The third once again the ball was stolen from a Barcelona side in a spread out attacking shape and the space between full back and centre half exploited quickly, before the full back reacted and closed it, for a goal.

Barcelona were so preoccupied with attacking they failed on 2 counts. Firstly, as in the first leg, they played a high offside line. At this level indeed any level this is a mistake.

Secondly, the preoccupation with their full backs to attack meant they had a poor shape to deal with a fast attack when the ball was stolen centrally, which it was.

Chelsea's winning goal came from a set play-corner, another attacking option they excel at. Barcelona scored twice and the brilliance of Chelsea's keeper kept them out for a third.

The tactics Mourinho adopted was to suck Barcelona in but deny then space in the around the area. He went for a fast attack on the break. It worked. The second half saw the ball passed 3 times or more 18 times in the oppositions half, Barcelona 17, Chelsea 1, possession on minute 53 was 60/40 Barcelona. Chelsea lost out in terms of having good possession in the opposition half or possession itself but by adopting a suck in defend deep, attack quick tactic they won.

TACTICAL CONCLUSION- Defence wins Championships. Arsenal and Barcelona belief in outscoring the opposition falls down against a team with superior defensive organization and a range of attacking options.

Rafael Benitez- Champions Magazine Feb/ March 2005

In the past Liverpool teams hunted like a pack. They were a true team , the team was the star. I believe in is the mentality that all great teams have possessed. Benitez took a gap year to study football. His ideas and Theory… The most important thing is tactics, the movement of your players once the ball starts roiling. You can start with on formation but it will change

> The coaches I like to take as my reference points are Cruyff, Arrigo Sacchi and John Toshack at Real Madrid. Sacchi stands as the greatest coach of the modern era and his model is still prevailing at the moment.

> Milan had extremely good footballers and they worked as a team- I've heard about Jose Mourinho and myself reinventing football b……..this is over exaggerated Mourinho and I simply recovered the values of the collective, Football has been marketed as the 'starr name' concept. Valencia and Porto each proved that the work of a team as a whole sometimes is better route to follow.

What was the idea behind TOTAL FOOTBALL The 1970's Ajax revolution- Tactics that enthralled the World Champions Mag Feb/March Rinus Michels

I wanted to put Ajax on their planet their positional sense and ways of using space. To build that sort of side you need to stay with them for years, repeating the same instructions and training routines. The other thing I have always insisted on is the use of the long pass. The best long pass is when a defender wins the ball and knows immediately where to play it. You have to work on the right movements and the right co-ordination.. If you succeed in making people believe it's easy you have attained perfection. It doesn't happen in every game. Develop a team with a strong sense of positioning and capacity for creating and using space. We looked for long passes, through balls and opportunist attacking play and aimed to dominate midfield. My goal was to mix a direct approach into our combination play because more recently we have seen Ajax sides concentrating almost exclusively on retaining possession and passing the ball around until any chance of surprising the opposition is lost. What I developed at Ajax was baptized total football but I don't think they had any idea what it meant…I certainly didn't. Whatever it was it wasn't easy to develop. It was based on perfecting team play without restricting individual ability we had in the squad.

TACTICAL CONCLUSION= Tactics matter, total football played long as well as short.

Champions League- April 2005 Week 6th 7th April

Game 1
Liverpool V Juventus 5th April- No one in the press stated it but overall in this game Juventus were the superior team. However, the best team does not always win in football. Juventus maintained possession in Liverpool's half twice as often as Liverpool although there was not much in it in the first half and created more and better chances.

From the start Liverpool tried to press the Juventus team and force errors by a high tempo game. Liverpool also should be complimented on the clear tactic of not giving away free kicks the usual Premiership tackles were abandoned and replaced by more calculated stealing of the ball when the defending players was sure it was there to be won. Players rarely if ever went to ground and were conscious of raising studs. Why? Well the clearest answer was demonstrated by the fact that Juventus scored as a result of a cleared free kick, In the Milan Derby both goals were scored from set plays, in the Chelsea game of the six goals one came from a corner, one from a free kick and one from a penalty.

Even though Liverpool had a good first half Juventus had a disallowed goal (offside) that should have stood and hit the post as well as drawing the young Liverpool Keeper in to an excellent save.

Liverpool's 2 goals are worth looking at.

GOAL 1
The first was a set play, Juventus adopted a mixture of man for man and zonal and Hyypia lost his marker and found space at the back post. The finish was superb a left footed volley that any forward would have been proud of. A full back on the post would have stopped it but many keepers and teams don't do this all the time. Petr Cech for Chelsea often has no-one on the posts. (He did in the recent Champions League game V Bayern).

GOAL 2
- The second goal started with a ball inside to Gerard in the position he received the ball he should have perhaps turned and switched the ball but his body shape did not allow for this.
- He played a chest high ball to La Tallec who controlled it superbly.
- Baros (the centre forward) had made a run towards him pulling one of the centre halves out of the back line (this didn't look intentional to create space as he was disappointed not to get the ball and the space it created for Garcia was a by product of this run).
- La Tallec played the ball over Baros and in to space for Luis Garcia to run in to,
- The Centre half for Juventus had already reacted and moved back in to the back four.
- Garcia was 25 yards out with plenty of defenders in from of him and a midfield player closing him down. Not a particularly dangerous situation.
- Garcia, first time, struck the perfect half volley with pace and direction that beat one of the best keepers in the world from distance. An unstoppable goal.

218

Juventus movement was excellent and the way Nedved came inside to the hole and threaded balls through was impressive.

CHELSEA v BAYERN

When Chelsea played Barcelona, as was mentioned in the last edition, Barcelona were so preoccupied with attacking they failed on 2 counts. Firstly, as in the first leg, they played a high offside line. At this level indeed any level this is a mistake.

Bayern played a deeper line but Mourinho had the ideal tactics to exploit this. His centre forward, Drogba, is superb at heading easily defeating Bayerns Centre halves and directing the ball to Lampard to score of for Duff to run on to.

This Tactic needs further explanation. Bayerns, and many other centre forwards, hold the ball up well allowing midfielders and others to join in and receive the ball. However, holding a ball up requires often 2 touches this gives defences the chance to react and whilst not always winning the ball be defensively compact and comfortable.

Drogbas abilities are fully exploited by Chelsea in a number of ways. At times he will drop back off centre halves to head the ball and flick it on, not to the traditional 1 man but 3 men who advance in a co-ordinated line so being available no matter where the flick goes. I observed this in previous games.

Drogba is the best in the world at the lone striker role which is why last year he got to the final not a possession based game but longer fast break, knock down game.

Chelsea used Drogba's abilities to stretch the game length ways and as Bayern defended deep, as most teams do, this put them on the opposition area. It wouldn't have worked against Barcelona who play a high line. Mourinho also realised that Glenn Johnston was a liability and replaced him with the reliable Huth. This also stops the opposition Forwards exploiting a lack of height at full back by playing a diagonal ball to the far post and beating the player in the air there who is a full back and not as good as a centre half. Juventas Goal cam from a header from a wider position where a forward also has the advantage of running on to the ball and so is better able to win a header,

Chelsea faced the same issue that Holland did in the Euro Championships. A well organised team that defends deep sometimes cannot be broken down.

Holland responded to this problem during a game by putting on a bog man (Van Hoydonk) and going long. They got a goal.

Chelsea went longer and this shows an amazing flexibility of tactics as this was not what they did against Barcelona. They started with the intent of going long often (flexible tactics mean you haver a few options but in any given game you do what works) Bayern defended deep like Barcelona so not allowing the ball in to the space behind them. Chelsea tried to pass through but in Drogba they had the best player in the world to go long and hold it up, or flick it on. He had the ability to direct his headers to players in dangerous positions as well as doing enough to make for an unpredictable second ball. Hargreaves has conveniently failed to mention that Bayerns opening goal was scored by a long ball up the middle and flick on (passed direct from the keeper Khahn). Stopping delivery of the long ball- one tactical solution is to cut off supply- is nearly impossible as it requires pushing players up to stop delivery from the back four. This leaves space in midfield for the opposition to exploit and many attacks may start from a long kicking keeper- impossible to stop. The offside line is critical and Bayern could push up then Chelsea would have to try and exploit the space.

> Owen Hargreaves- Times 8th April- Hargreaves gave some interesting tactical insight into the Chelsea game. *When Arsenal were 2 goals down against us in the previous round they were still trying to pass it through the middle. Chelsea are the exact opposite. They couldn't hurt us passing the ball, I don't think they once created a chance. Only once they started to bang it forward with Drogba flicking it on did they cause a lot of problems. It reminded me of Celtic with Hartson and Sutton and Larsen running onto the second ball. Its tough to defend because the ball can go anywhere and Drogba is good at attacking balls in the air. So we are going to have to find a way to defend a bit better against that.*

Tactics in the champions League

Jose Mourinho Chelsea and former Porto coach. The value of tactical strategies are demonstrated by the success of teams in the Champions League (2004) and more recently wining the Premiership with Chelsea. **At top level football he is Manager and Coach.**

The value of Mourinho's tactical strategies are demonstrated by the success of his Porto against Manchester United in the Champions League (2004) Porto had less experience and were away from home when they qualified. The game against Manchester United at Old Trafford was characterised by United being forced in to playing a predictable long ball game. *Porto stopped the opposition playing.*

In the semi final 2004 against Deportivo la Coruna (Friday May 7th). Mourinho spoke to his players for five consecutive days on what the tactics would be if Deporto played Walter Pandiani up front; how they would change if Diego Tristan started instead; how they would react if they fell a goal behind; what they would do if they took the lead etc. He has a tactical solution to deal with all eventualities in a game.

The best sides switch the ball frequently to find space. One of Mourinho's main tactical strengths has been his ability to stop the opposition switching the ball. His teams minimise space all over the pitch and concentrate on denying the switch.

Attacking wise his teams are excellent at switching. The Full backs were important going forward but he has amended this as he has acquired better more attacking players in midfield at Chelsea.
His teams play a short passing game that favours possession. They play out from the back a great deal. The best organised unit defensively of any team with superb cover and shape at the back. Play high tempo but also like to suck teams in by playing along the back line. If possible Mourinho will to press high up the field even when ahead.

Formations have varied at Porto he played a 4 4 2 often with a diamond in midfield with many attacks through player at front of diamond. He doesn't like to be categorised as playing a particular formations talking of playing between the lines in a 4 4 2. Recently at Chelsea he has played 4 3 3 as an attacking formation having in Robben and Duff two wide players who can deliver in this system. The formation 4 3 3 can be defensive the 3 players stopping the full backs playing out from the back- is can be used defensively. Another example of an attacking 4 3 3 was the Danish team in Euro 2004 (see Danish way.)

His team Chelsea have a collective defensive mentality to hold on to a 1-0 (they are clear of their roles and cover the correct spaces). Early on in the season (2005) they won numerous games 1-0 often by a well worked set play. This efficiency allows Chelsea (unlike Arsenal) to add more set plays to their attacking armoury (up to 60% goals come from set plays).

The confidence that the team has in its defensive ability is summed up by keeper Czech has talked of their confidence the side have when 1-0 ahead *that they can hold on to the lead*. Mourinho's tactical abilities were also demonstrated by his choice of keeper for a big game against Manchester United (League Cup 2005). He palyed Czech instead of his other keeper who had played in the previous rounds. His reason he is better at dealing with crosses and Manchester United rely heavily on crossing for their attacks (it is a myth that all good sides cross a lot it is a matter of style).

Mourinho's sides have been accused of lacking flair and being efficient (comments made by Arsen Wenger). Mourinho responded- *what is flair in football? To me 5-4 is not flair it is a hockey score not football. To me flair is a team who defend fantastically well because defence is always an important part of a game, and we score goals too* (Sun Sat 29th Jan). In response to the allegation of his side playing average football- *we have only failed to score in three games- Chelsea always play with three forwards two attacking wide men and a central midfielder who is there to create and not destroy*

Mourinho claims *for some reason people confuse out ability to organise well in defence with a lack of desire to attack.* This attention to detail and very specific planning of roles for his players sets him apart from Wenger.

Wenger's Arsenal Team play a fantastic mixed passing game, they have the ability to play through a packed defence which is very difficult and rare. However, Wenger's team are not so effective in scoring or defending set plays.

Arsenal have the potential to win the Champions League but so far have failed. Maybe it is part to do with the reliance on the individual and free spirited attacking football that Arsenal play instead of the meticulous defend first collective approach of the more calculated Mourinho Chelsea.
Success can also be part down to luck. Mourinho admitted last week in the game against Liverpool (Jan 05) that luck is a factor. In a game of so few goals where one mistake or incorrect decision by a referee can make the difference between winning and losing, luck is a factor.
Mourinho's tactics reduce the reliance on luck to a minimum and he will win the Premiership with this strategy.
Juventus coach Fabio Capello believes Chelsea are the leading side in Europe this season. Capello has also hailed the impact of Blues boss Jose Mourinho, labelling him "the number one coach at the moment".
Tottenham Manager Martin Jol predicts Chelsea boss Jose Mourinho will change the shape of English football as the clubs chasing the Premiership leaders copy his ideas. Jol admitted he is was tempted to switch to the 4-3-3 formation which has seen big-spending Chelsea take the Premiership by storm this season. Mourinho plays this with the winders Duff and Robben. These players use the wide space but are happy attacking centrally.

What does Mourinho look for in a player Mourinho can be part summed up by this quote-

> *He is due to play in tonight's friendly with Roma- I think it surprised quite a few people he is in our squad but he is a team player, he is tactically intelligent and he covers different positions.* Another insight was Mourinho's reaction to a defensive situation summed up by a player who talked of *Mourinho's tantrum when a forward had been left one on one with a defender*

Chelsea played Manchester United (Premier League 2004/5). They scored first and then kept United out to win 1-0. If Man United had scored first Chelsea would have had a hard time scoring and it would have tested Mourinho's offensive attacking credentials. However he has plenty of attacking options.

Drogba for height to offer 'flick on's', hold the ball up and bring in midfield or get on the end of crosses. Lampard in Midfield to push on and time attacking runs (always difficult to defend against). Lampard's timing was demonstrated by his goal against Manchester United (26th Jan League cup) when he arrived in the penalty area at exactly the moment the ball was passed and scored. This was un-defendable. It was a good goal not due to a defensive mistake.

Duff and Robben two players who offer dribbling centrally to distort a defence, win free kicks as well as offering width.

Set plays are an integral part of Chelsea's attacking armoury at one point 9 out of 11 goals had come from them when he did not have all of the other attacking options available.
Chelsea had plenty to offer.

Finally what does Mourinho have to say on the English Game-

> *football here is played with passion , love and instinct but we have to think a bit more. We have to stop solely backing out instincts because when English teams meet teams which reflect and can adapt their game to the situation during a match it comes unstuck.*

> *Sometimes football is beautiful because of competitiveness, effort, organisation and enthusiasm.* On his sides chance of winning a trophy *if we keep our mental, physical and tactical strength nobody can stop us.*

The high pressure game of Leeds United/The French way

Leeds United reached the semi final of the Champions League 3 years ago. David O Leary now at Aston Villa, recently outlined the reason for their success. **(Guardian Saturday April 17th 2004)** *I Believe in teams defending high up the pitch and operating at a high tempo. It's a style that takes time to bring in properly. It's very effective but very demanding and players have got to be very fit to make it work. I think our training came as quite a shock to Nolberto Solano when he joined from Newcastle.* O Leary talks of the demise of Leeds as linked to the strategic decision to abandon the tactic of deploying a high defensive line, thereby effectively squeezing opponents into submission before blitzing them with high energy attacks.

A new coach (Brain Kidd) was appointed with a brief to slow things down and develop a more patient European style possession team. It did not work and O Leary admitted
I'm a high tempo coach, just before I was sacked by Leeds, I'd made the decision to go back to playing that way. The article quotes a fellow manager who explained *'Davids problem was that if you buy Rio Ferdinand and Robbie Fowler, you quickly find they are not over keen on playing relentless high tempo.* Regarding Villas current style Solano (one of their players) observes: *we work very hard in training and play the high tempo game which is very well suited to the premiership but we also have quality and when we attack the manager gives us freedom to try things.* Aston Villa have achieved the best that any coach can achieve in O'Leary's words: *we've over achieved and could easily become a one season wonder...we've got the maximum out of this squad*

Coaching lesson– Had successful tactics and players to follow then through. Changed them and had less success. Always try the new but don't be afraid of admitting something hasn't worked and change again. High pressure game means your team have to be very fit.

France one of the most successful teams of the last 10 years are identified as
⇒   Coping with changing circumstances and anticipating the unexpected
     ⇒   Defending as a team
     ⇒   Attacking as a team
     ⇒   Being creative but with a collective spirit
These were all identified as key to France's success (*Insight winter 1998*).

The keeper Bartez's expertise at saving penalties is a major factor in their success and perhaps why Manchester United bought him.

Coaching lesson– Managed to have the best of both worlds. Great match winning players such as Henri and Zidane and a hard working organised team ethic that defends well and gets the best from these players.

Arsenal had an outstanding away victory against Inter Milan (the gane is analysed in more depth later). Wenger's team stopped the opposition playing by successfully compressing the area around the ball.

When in possession their play was characterised by switching the point of attack to create space. Arsenal's game revolves around passing the ball at speed and moving the point of attack. They are very good at maintaining possession centrally where there is little space.

Tactical Strenghts
     •   Can play high tempo or more slowly,
•   The finest passing side in the Champions League,

Coaching lesson– Arsenal are one of the finest passing sides around. They move the ball quickly and using 1 touch will attack down the middle as well as switching and using the width. Arsenals narrow pitch may assist in their tight passing game.

Mourinho—how long before a game does Mourinho start tactical planning?

Does he have a specific game plan?

What was his defensive strength?

What are the attacking strengths?

Chelsea were beaten in the semi-final - What is the reason given?

Morientes plays in hole between attack and defence. How did he use this to defeat Chelsea?

Leeds's tactics changed. Describe them and the change?

What are 2 reasons for France's success?

Arsenal's attacking game is characterised by what?

Manchester United's (Alex Ferguson's) tactics

It would be inappropriate for this work not to look at the tactics of the most successful team of the last 2 decades. Manchester United's Alex Ferguson has, unlike Arsenals Wenger, succeeded on the European stage winning the Champions League.

The quote on page 4 highlights his recognition of tactics as the biggest difference between British Teams and those in Europe. He comments about a crucial game against Porto some years ago *Tactics were bound to be important.* He played 3 up front with one dropping into a deeper position to feed them. His instructions ' get the ball to Cantona (the dropping player) and let Giggs find the spaces left by out 2 strikers. Giggs came in from wide and deep to search for the space the forwards created. The tactic worked.

Ferguson shows his excellent analysis of this side of the game in his autobiography when talking of how Barcelona play. He identified that they had the objective of creating a numbers up situation in midfield. This was done by either one of the forwards dropping back or a player from the back 4 stepping into midfield. He worked with his side to negate these tactics. The defence played high to squeeze space (Pallister offered the covering pace and Schmeichel the sweeping keeper). He instructed forward player to drop into the hole and stop the back 4 player who was stepping into midfield with the ball from having room to operate and pick a pass. He made his defenders aware of the need not to be pulled into midfield so leaving space, and instructed his midfield to pick up the dropping forward. The importance here is in the fact that he identified the problem and had specific tactics to deal with it. The tactics worked.

Fergusson points out the importance of concentration and the fact that lack of it can be costly. British players need to develop this and the need to curtail what they feel is their game to fit in with the team. An example he identifies Paul Ince who as a player who would not always follow instructions. In a crucial European game he was told to stay in front of the back 4 in a defensive role. Ince played his own game. Ferguson saw this as one main reason Man United were defeated in a European game. This emphasizes his point above about the need to play as a team.

Ferguson was also happy to plan his defensive tactics around stopping one of the oppositions star players (Romario) from playing. He implemented a man marking strategy with a player able to be focused enough to do this. He laments the fact that he had worked on this throughout the week and how it would interact with the normal zonal system. He was disappointed when for one instance in the game the defence ignored this and Romario scored. At top level teams will use a mixture of zonal and man for man if the opposition have a player of significant ability (Zidane for example).

He also talks about his early European experience when stating of Montpellier

> *The tactical and technical superiority of our opponents,* this was in the early years before technically players caught up. He also talks of the ' *suddenness with which opponents can change their pace.*

His recurring team talk theme is *'don't give the ball away"* he goes on 'even I am fed up with listening to this edict but players cannot be reminded often enough of its importance.

Ferguson on defence– *it is important they play together a lot and have good understanding.* Whilst not stating it directly he recognises that whilst pace is an attribute it is not essential here.

The difference between defence and attack is

> *'Forwards too need to be on the same wavelength but failure to do so usually leads to no more than a wasted opportunity' in defence it can lead to a goal and cost you the game.*

Regarding fitness - when he took over after Brian Kidd left he did stamina work after Christmas 'stamina was one of their most effective weapons on the \way to the treble'.

Some interesting other tactical points:

The opposition were forcing us to play in to Yorke (his forward) while deploying plenty of bodies to smother his threat. We had to spread our play forget our strikers until the penalty box

When talking of tactics he points out –

> *its about flesh and blood not some abstract thing. The best teams stand out because they are teams, because the individuals members have been so truly integrated that the team functions as a single spirit. Feeding of strengths and compensate for weaknesses.* Talent and team spirit lead to success.

In response to a team who '*were clever in midfield'* Ferguson played with one forward and more in the centre of midfield to counter this.

On another occasion he considered matching the oppositions formation '*to ensure they didn't have an advantage in possession on such a tiring pitch* he discussed this\ with players, a sign of a more democratic style than he is credited with….In a previous game Liverpool had had a lot of possession but they had not troubled them much. He was concerned that the *midfield would not become too spread out so Liverpool could find their forwards.* Cantona suggested a player (Roy Keane) should sit in frot of back four to stop their forward using the hole. This was used and worked. He also talks of keeping the tempo high as slower play benefited the oppositions midfield.

Versus Inter Milan *Tactically , there were 2 points Ferguson identified:*
DEFENSIVELY They were vulnerable to crosses

> *ATTACKING Their game plan was counter attack down the middle. That meant our full backs had to go and play in front of our central defenders where the Italians operated with 2 attackers withdrawn into positions behind their main striker. Their withdrawn players had plenty of ability and could not be given room to create openings. When our attacks broke down we need to re-group, we surrendered the wide areas and closed off the central midfield. This is consistent with the theory section on time and space.*

Against Chelsea a player was included (Neville) to man mark who Ferguson considered their playmaker Zola

When playing Milan with 'Ronaldo' one of the best forwards in the world, Fergussons two central midfield players chocked the space he liked. In terms of attacking as neither Ronaldo nor Baggio pressure full backs the team used the full backs who were urged to use the ball well and to stretch play. It is often a neglected part of the game to use an opposition's strength to an advantage when you have the ball.

Against Juventus of Manchester United's two wide players only one should push up. They ignored this and had to be told at half time. The United full backs were instructed to force their wingers to retreat—this failed so in the 2nd half David Beckham in tight Giggs push on– for the *2nd leg Zidane had seen the last of wide open spaces he found early at Old Trafford.*

With regard to one of his players who is an excellent dribbler but lacking in other areas (Ryan Giggs) Ferguson tried to improve his overall game and appreciation of space etc and passing but emphasised that he needed to do what he did best, run at defenses.

Ferguson philosophy, *all my life I have based my creed on passing the ball, rhythm and tempo.* His sides play a pacey mixed passing game but can also play a slower tempo.

With regard to pitches he observes that in the Champions League final the Nou Camp for final was narrowed at Bayern's request to stop Giggs.

Manchester United's tactics vary from the Premiership where they play a high tempo pressure based game, to a slower game in European games. This is based around the fact that in the Premiership teams will give you the ball back before long, in Europe they will not.

Tactical Strengths:

- high tempo when required
- good winners of the second ball for example off a drop kick from the keeper,
- have the ability to press teams high up the field in the Premiership.
- the best defence in the Champions league (conceded the least goals)

Does Ferguson change his tactics against teams?

Give 2 examples.

How do Ferguson's comments relate to time and space?

Why is concentration critical when playing top teams - the same could be said for any level of football where there is not much between teams. Relate your answer to 2 facts - 1.) The percentage of goals scored from free kicks, 2.) The statistics of 'first goal usually wins'.

What is his recurring team talk based around?

Why is it important for a defence to play together as opposed to attack?

Ferguson was faced with a team with a strong midfield - what was he worried about and how did he counter it?

Tactics in the 2004 European Championships

Roy Hodgson comments: -

> *The world of football is now becoming much smaller and teams are much better organised. The big five-Italy, Spain, England, Germany, and France have the best leagues and the biggest names but this does not guarantee success.*

In the Observer 11 July 2004 a Letter from Chris Paitent noted

> *what is probably happening in world football is that increasingly defensive strategies are holding the upper hand and teams do not seem to have sufficient attacking strategies to break down organised defences.*

This point is echoed by another letter Glenn Forbes pointed out The Greeks Trianos Dellas after the final said

> *we shut all their avenues and their strong points. Sometimes we were freezing their game and that's why we did it. Its not very lovable, but who cares. Antony Stam added to this simplicity grace and beauty in the finest expression of teamwork.*

Good organisation of the mediocre is often more effective than the artistry and spontaneity of the gifted. It was Tactics that won the European Championships for Greece as well as the Champions League for Porto. The importance of the team is emphasised by this comment by the Greek manager Rehhagel

> *they were always great individualists, but now they have come to understand that success only comes through the team. It is always about the team*

The final was contested by two sides which were both technically able with some excellent players but both beat teams with better players. Regarding the coaches as *Amy Laurence* in The Observer notes

> *This tournament is proving a triumph for demanding, inspiring, charismatic coaching. These are smart, strong-willed coaches who have a vision of how to run their team and have carte blanche to put it into practice. As far as their players are concerned, the coach is, unequivocally , number one. Greece did not muscle their way to victory . The statistics from the semi against the Czechs show fouls committed Greece 15, Czech 24 Free kicks Greece 20, Czech 29.*

A Greek players commented regarding their coach Rehhagel: *'He has given us confidence. We try to take whatever he says on board. We love him very much'.* Rehhagel noted the used to play how they wanted to play, he went on *they now play how I want them to play.* Rehhagel also has the advantage of not having the egos of big players to deal with. In soccer no one can be bigger than the team. This point is echoed by the Czech coach Bruckner who says *'I don't have stars, I have human beings,'* he said, adding that Pavel Nedved, the team's number one *superstar 'does not hesitate to put his ability at the service of the team'.* The team ethic of the Greeks and the way they kept the ball when they won it were excellent. They had a high degree of success on set plays, excellent delivery and timing. They defended deep and suffocated teams of space. When the midfield ventured forward the speed they returned to defend was incredible. Having lost out in the world cup qualifiers to England when Teddy Sherringham dived to win a free kick that Beckam scored the Greeks gave away few free kicks unlike the at times cavalier attitude of England who continually gave away free kicks in dangerous areas. England conceded 22 fouls against Portugal.

Greece's secret according to the Observer

Rehhagel chose a 4-2-3-1 formation that the French struggled to combat. The midfield and defence denied France and especially Zinedine Zidane space. The German's meticulous organisation has proved too much for European football royalty; Luis Figo, Raul, Zinedine Zidane and Pavel Nedved have each been summarily overthrown. Under Dellas' impeccable leadership, the Greeks hunted the ball in packs with devastating effect, seemingly invulnerable to lapses of concentration. With every player on the field dedicated to destruction, there was little room for invention and rarely did Rehhagel offer the most rudimentary entertainment. But, contrary to popular belief, sport is not part of the entertainment industry. Great sport and great sportsmen can, for all the pundits' efforts, never be distilled into one convenient sound bite; it's a welcome change for a great team and a great coach to break from the tiresome status quo.

The tournament had 2 sides who went all out to attack. The first one, Denmark a very attacking minded side who used the width of the pitch playing 4 3 3 or 4 2 3 1 and going out with the intention of outscoring the opposition. Secondly, the Czech republic, playing 4 4 2 who outscored Holland in the best game of the tournament. The Czech's had plenty of attacking options with a big man up front ,Koller, who was dangerous at crosses and could flick the ball on or hold it up, and the more mobile Baros.

Holland talk attacking but played with one lone forward and were poor against Germany who dealt with their wide players. Holland responded by mainly long ball against Germany from the start and ended up with this single tactic. Against Portugal four four two comments

Coach Dick Advocaat again gets his tactics wrong. Holland sleepwalk to 2-0 down and finish the game with three centre forwards but no wingers. Not so much total Football as total shambles in the first half, route one (long ball) in the second.

Sweden were a very underestimated team. Like Greece they worked extremely hard as a unit to defend. They also showed good counter attacking and set play work and created plenty of chances. Interestingly the joint coaches were slated in the national press for their deliberation on a substitute. In response to bringing on a sub one coach is heard to comment *does he know what to do at set plays* the other coach stated *well he had the notes*. This shows the depth of planning that goes on. When substitutions went on in the tournament on a number of occasions players looked at notes. This makes the use of this resource seem more relevant to today's game. A lot of tactical information is hard to take in so writing it down for players can only help.

Portugal were the tournaments best team at switching the ball. Switching the ball well, as has been mentioned earlier, is a reliable indicator of a good team. Against Spain they switched the ball successfully 17 times in the first half, Spain only managed 4.
Four Four Two talks of Scholari

When you have won a world cup you can make big decisions without fear.

He did dropping 5 older players. Portugal reached the final.

Italy's attitude was very conservative defensively minded. They are one of a few teams who could have won the competition if they got out of their group. Many argued that their tactic of simply defending a lead was bound to fail. The modern game has many more free kicks so part of the Italian spoiling game could not come in to play.

The tactic of sitting back and defending a one goal lead, as England found out, is much harder in today's game. Referees give more free kicks, pitches are in better condition, teams are better able to keep the ball (more technically able).

Playing the Danish way

by Patrick Wymer

What you will learn

- Attacking tactics can suceed

Denmarks attempt to recapture the title they won in fairytale fashion in 1992 came to an abrupt end at the quarter-final stage, when the Czech Republic scored three goals in the space of fifteen second half minutes. The main tactical criticism aimed at the coach, Morten Olsen, concerned his not using his substitutes until after the Danes were three goals down, when the livewire Bochum striker Peter Madsen was brought on for the ineffective Charlton player (now Fulham) Claus Jensen. Generally, however, the Danish and international media were impressed with the way the Danes approached the tournament, and their style of play won them many plaudits and this has much to do with Morten Olsens' football philosophy.

Olsen inherited a group of players in 2000 devoid of 'star players' such as the Laudrup brothers Michael and Brian and of course their gigantuan goalkeeper Peter Schmeichel. In his four years at the helm he has moulded the players into a strong collective team built around the midfield dynamo Thomas Gravesen of Everton. Olsens philosophy is definitively to win games. This may sound like an obvious tactic to have in football, but Olsens approach has never wavered and he is consistent when asked how he intends to handle opponents with high profile individuals, saying that Denmark will play their own game and not change their system on account of their opponents. A case in point was the first group game of the championships, against Italy.

Denmark play a 4-3-3 system and unlike other teams, the Greeks for example, that play this formation they have 'real' wingers, who are quick, mobile and positioned in attacking roles, and not as 'extra' midfielders who attack when they have the chance. Gordon Strachan is a fan of the way the Danes play 4-3-3 for this very reason:

> but the 4-3-3 I enjoy most is the one used by Denmark. At times you could even call it 4-4-2 because they're playing with a second striker, Jon Dahl Tomasson, who drops back to give a hand in the middle. Tomasson helps there when he needs to and gets up to play as a second striker when he can. For that you need two wide men who can take people on and Denmark have a few to choose from with Dennis Rommedahl, Martin Jorgensen and Jesper Gronkjaer. [Strachan 2004]

Against Italy, Denmark attacked from the whistle and had the Italians on the back foot for much of the game. Gravesen was suspended for the game so Olsen decided to use Schalke 04's Christian Poulsen as part of his defensive midfield duo, a decision that ultimately led to the suspension of one of the pre-tournament stars, Francesco Totti, for spitting in Poulsens face - presumably out of frustration. Poulsen had performed a similar role in the 2002 World Cup, when he put the shackles on Frances' **Zinedin Zidane.** The Danes performance in this first game surprised many, but it can be seen as a prime example of the 'The Danish Way' under Morten Olsen at its best. Quick passing combinations, high mobility from the players and especially the challenging and direct style of the wingers were only kept at bay by the routine of the Italian defence and the lack of a cutting edge from the Danish forwards. A towering performance by the goalkeeper Thomas Sorensen (including a fantastic double save at the end of the first half) and a commanding display by Aston Villa's new centre half, Martin Laursen, contributed to a great start for Denmark. The usually very critical TV-commentator, Günter Netzer was suitably impressed:

'The tactics could not have been better, and I have only praise for Morten Olsen and the way he has communicated his tactics to the team, that has really impressed me with their application. The mobility of the Danes made a big impression. It was a fantastic presentation by the Danes, who played with great assurance and confidence. From the very start they utilised their resources and dominated the game. I cannot praise them enough' [Netzer 2004; ARD homepage]

This attacking mentality was evident in all of Denmarks games at the championships, and especially in the first half of each game the team dominated proceedings. With Schalke 04's Ebbe Sand leading the line with his hard running and competitiveness, space was created for Jon Dahl Tomassons intelligent forward runs which resulted in him being their leading scorer with three goals. But as is often the case in 4-3-3 formations it was often the final ball that was lacking quality. Despite overwhelming possession in all of their games (against the Czechs the statistics read 62/38 in their favour) they failed to translate this dominance into the goals that could have brought them another fairytale ending.

Ultimately it was personal failures and an apparent collective loss of concentration against the Czechs that led to their downfall. Martin Laursens failure to pick up the giant Jan Koller gifted the Czech striker the first goal in the quarter final. Two goals in as many minutes by Liverpools Milan Baros sealed their fate, and although both were executed clinically after great through balls from Poborsky and Nedved respectively, the Danes seemed to fall apart somewhat after they went behind - perhaps this is the reason Olsen is so uncompromising in his attacking approach to the beautiful game. He has little time for more defensive minded teams such as the eventual winners Greece who he believes adjust their game to negate the opposition instead of playing their own game and attacking. Appropriately then we give the last words to Morten Olsen and his reflections on the Greeks as championship finalists:

the Greeks have many good football players, but we are back in Flintstone times with their playing style. But okay, they were the underdogs in all of their games and we shouldn't hold it against them. But from a subjective standpoint we can discuss whether they are worthy finalists, and I don't think they are (...) They play a form of 5-3-2, that to a high degree is designed to cope with the opposition. Luckily for football most teams have shown a willingness to be positive and attack at the championships. I can see no future for the type of football where two or three men are man-marking and we must hope that it is the exception that the Greeks have come so far in the tournament. [Olsen 2004, own translation]

The Danish way is attacking orientated and it is difficult not to share some of Olsen's sentiments.

Why is the world of football becoming smaller?

What, according to their managers, was the reason for Greece's success?

What view of 'star players' do the Greek manager and Czech manager hold?

List 4 reasons (tactical) for Greece's success?

What criticism can be made of Holland?

What did Portugal do well?

Why were Italy's defensive tactics (defend a lead) harder to get away with in the modern game?

Did the media in Denmark like the approach adopted? How does this compare with England?

What is Olsens philosophy? Does he change when playing teams?

Is 4 3 3 Danish style attacking? What is the difference between this and how other teams play this system?

What cost Denmark in the end?

2004 European– England's failure

England's performance can be best judged against the following criteria
•   Defensive tactics
•   Attacking tactics
•   Technically
•   Physical and mental– if players are tired they make mistakes hence these have been put together

Defensive performance

We had to defend a lot when maybe we should be going forward' said Michael Owen. *We were forced to defend deep and you can't keep doing that and getting away with it.* said David James. *Sooner of later one of the opposition's possessions or power plays is going to come off*, Sol Campbell agreed.

There is a difference between constantly defending and having to defend deep. The BBC's commentary on numerous occasions made the allegation that England were defending 'too deep'. Strachan is the only commentator to note

People might say that the back four played too deep but they can't hold a line 30 yards from goal unless there's good pressure on Portugal further up the park to stop them picking up a pass. Otherwise Portugal will end up with players running in behind. This danger has been discussed earlier in this work.

Attacking performance

As has been mentioned elsewhere in this work it is a disadvantage to have similar forwards. There are clear advantages in having a big forward who can hold the ball up and flick the ball on as well as a forward with pace to get beyond the defence into the danger zone. England were defeated by Portugal on penalties but more significantly failed to hold onto the ball or mount attacks when they had the ball. The forwards , once Rooney had gone off, were too similar and not good enough at flicking on, holding up or playing in the hole. The much praised midfield failed to hold on to the ball or slow play down. Gordon Strachan - Saturday June 26th 2004

England played with strikers who were too similar after Wayne Rooney went off. Michael Owen and Darius Vassell both look to run in behind defenders and be the furthest man up the field, and without someone like Rooney dropping deep to get the ball off the midfield it was much harder for England to retain possession.

When England's midfielders won the ball under pressure they would have wanted to see someone 15 yards away to prod it. But the problem was that Owen and Vassell were playing flat with each other 30 yards up the field. They were running away from the game so the midfielders were looking at their backs.

England had to hit long balls to try to get behind Portugal's defence but they were mopped up or intercepted and Portugal came straight back. England's back four and midfield didn't have the time to get up the park and were under pressure again.

Eriksson brought on a 'ball winning midfielder Phil Neville. This didn't work. Neville neither won balls nor is he/she not the type of player to run with the ball from deep. He was off the pace. A better option may have been Dyer could have come on the left. As a manager Strachen observes you are considering 'If it goes into extra-time is it better having a ball-winner or a game-winner?' If Portugal hadn't equalised it wouldn't be an issue. For Portugal's first goal the central defence were deeper than the crosser and when he made contact a goal was likely. As we have seen earlier to push up as far as is possible makes it harder for the forward to score.

Technical ability
Clearly England need to work on technique and team play, individuals on improving touch, passing and movement so that the team retain the ball for longer periods, assembling moves that endure rather than slinging it forward to relieve pressure and hoping a front man can hold it to enable the midfield players to join in. Ian Ridley 27th June 2004 noted of England

> *Of course, the quality of technique and appreciation of team play will always be the most significant constituents of any winning side. In those departments too, England were found wanting again.*
> *Though Eriksson pointed out that matches are not always won by superior technique-no, but it helps. Good technique*

allows players to have more tactical options. They are more able to switch play and can play in more central areas where space is limited.

> *Henry Winter writing in four four two declares of England's attacking...England gave the ball away far too easily //if first touch and distribution had been superior then Eriksson's men would not have been so lax in possession against France. ...Against Portugal England kept ceding the ball and inviting Christine Ronaldo and Deco on to them.*

Whilst England's defence and Cole in particular dealt with this threat the sentiment of Winter that England gave the ball away too easily is true. Winter also points out England's players are forever handicapped by the style of the premiership football. If the domestic game had a mission statement it would declare: Players must rush from end to end, keeping their tempos as high as the fans fervour and not worrying about losing the ball because the opposition will soon give it back. The four semi finalists in Euro 2004 kept possession and on the whole (the Dutch were disappointingly route 1) varied their attacks.

Physical and mental
England got tired then made mistakes. It is a fact that you work harder chasing the ball, defending , than when attacking. Hence England's failure , unlike the Greeks, to keep the ball meant they got tired. This inevitably leaves more space for the opposition. The cross for the goal should not have been allowed in. Beckham was too far off and Neville might have got closer. They were tired.

England had clear tactics. The problem was that going ahead so early on they gave themselves a near impossible task of defending for 87 minutes. Going back to the point made about Mourinho who covers all eventualities, Eriksson did not deal tactically with Rooney going off. As Rooney was clearly a major factor in determining the teams tactics it needed a plan to deal with his absence. England defended magnificently in particular Ashley Cole but as we are aware successful teams also attack well. Sol Campbell's disallowed goal was a foul by John Terry and so should not have stood, the English way of tackling and physical contact always gives away fouls in Europe. The bottom line is they are fouls. They may be not given in England but that is our problem with the Premier League. At the end of the day Portugal's possession and better attacking meant they deserved the win.

The Premiership
A further disadvantage that the England players and manager face is the domestic league. The style of play in the Premiership, fast and furious, alongside the fact that referees do not give fouls that are given in the European League conspire to hinder players. The interpretation of the rules stifle creativity and in particular, skilful players that dribble. In short our league is technically and tactically inferior to Spain, Italy and if you factor in the fact that we 'buy in' the best from other leagues they also are superior. We need to change our domestic game.

What is wrong with the comment 'England defend too deep'?

What was the problem with England's forwards, and the midfields that meant England were disappointing in attack?

The four semi finalists in Euro 2004 all kept possession TRUE / FALSE

Why is the physical linked to mental in the analysis?

Why is it hard to defend a lead for a long time? What is required if this tactic is to work?

The Premiership does not help the England team. Discuss this?

Football in the 1990's - The Gladiatorial game

Football in the early 90s, the following article from David Lacey in the Guardian, highlights the physical nature of football during the early 90s. It is worth reading what I consider the finest football article I have ever read. It highlights the worst side of football.

After Wimbledon had won 2-1 at Bramall Lane on Saturday, prolonging the agony of Sheffield United's uncomfortable return to the First Division, it was generally agreed that this had been the game of the century. But opinions differed on which century. Maybe the Goths and Visigoths, had football been invented then, would have produced a match like this-but they were, after all, quite civilised. Ghengis Khan against Ghengis Khan's Reserves then, but he was a methodical man whose conquests retained a sense of order and direction. No, Saturday's events really belonged to pre-history. It was a game between an Iguanodon's Invitation XI and Tyrannosaurus Rex Select, slow moving, befuddled herbivores against quicker, hungrier carnivores. TRS won despite the fact that for all but two minutes of the second half one of their dinosaurs went missing.

The peculiar appeal of the fixture lay in the fact that both sides were creations of Dave Bassett, now manager of Sheffield United or, as they might be called, Quatermass II. Bassett's methods do not vary. His teams remain faithful to the long high ball-route one to the uninitiated –and when they confronted each other on a wet afternoon with a gale-force wind blowing straight down the pitch, motorway madness soon set in. There were several shunts on a Saturday, the worst involving Vinny Jones, the Sheffield United captain and a former Wimbledon player, and Wimbledon's John Gayle. In the first half Jones had been cautioned for piling into Blackwell from behind, elbow raised.

After two minutes of the second half Gayle went over the top and left Jones in a painful heap. For this he was shown the yellow card. Another two minutes and Gayle had caught Jones off the ball. Now he faced the red. After the match Gayle, who earlier in the week was reported to have been involved in a training incident with his own captain, Keith Curle, stalked the corridors at Bramall Lane looking like the man who loaded 16 tons and what did he get, another day older and deeper in debt. Jones's proffered handshake was scored in a way that you assured if the right one did not get Gayle the left one would. At this point, Bassett broke off a conversation with reporters to remind Gayle and Jones that "you're professional footballers, so be professional footballers". Everything calmed down. "Don't try to make more of it than there is," was Jones's parting shot to the press.

Presumably he meant the corridor confrontation with Gayle. But they could have been talking about the match which on more than one occasion found a body lying in the goal-mouth while play moved down the other end. It was a wonder police did not appeal for witnesses. "You're always going to get that sort of game in those conditions", said Ray Harford, the Wimbledon manager. Correction: with these teams you will always get that sort of game in any conditions. The referee, poor man, became so confused that when Cork, a Wimbledon striker, fouled Barnes, a Sheffield defender, in the United area he awarded a penalty to the attacking team.He immediately realised his error and gave Sheffield United a free-kick, but you could understand the mistake because it was easy to forget which way the teams were supposed to be playing.

Terry Lunt, from Ashton-in-Makerfield, is a day-centre officer for the mentally handicapped. Who said the football League did not have a sense of humour? Saturday's game was largely lacking in imagination, subtlety and an acceptable level of First Division skills, yet the crowd enjoyed the football on it's own knockabout terms until it became obvious that the home side were going to lose. Not that the match was totally devoid of individual qualities. The goalkeepers, Segers and the aptly-named Kite, made several fine saves; the speed with which the Wimbledon centrebacks Blackwell and Curle dealt with Deane and Agana was commenable; Barton and Marwood had a sense of time and space; and the way Fashanu, on for the injured Sanchez, held the front line for Wimbledon after Gayle had departed proved crucial to their victory.

Each of the goals, moreover, carried a mark of quality. Barnes's left-footed shot, following one of Jone's long throws, gave United an early lead, but Fairweather's over-head kick, after Kite had turned a shot from Kruszynski against the bar, brought the scores level before the half time. Fashanu's winner was a well-struck shot into the far corner of the net which caught Kite unsighted. Sheffield United were left to rue missed chances and near misses: the shot from Deane that rebounded from the inside of the far post and a late header from Beesley against the bar. They have yet to win a League match this season because they have yet to readjust to the increased pace of the First Division. Until they do life is going to be a struggle.

A store near Bramall Lane offers all kinds of safety equipment: "Boots, respirators, ear muffs, goggles, helmets, rainsuits, and visors". Perhaps this is what Bassett's teams, past and present, ought to wear. Somehow football kit did not seem entirely appropriate on Saturday.

Why does Lacey question which century the game was played in?

What is the tactic of Dave Bassetts team?

Why is there so much physical contact/tackling if you adopt this tactic?

What does Lacey say with regard to the comment by the Wimbledon manager -"You're always going to get that sort of game in those conditions?"

In what position do you think Barton and Marwood play (who had a sense of time and space) ?

Was the game devoid of 'good football' ?

Does the team with the best players always win?

Describe if you can the tactics of the following - Manchester United, Arsenal, Porto, Monaco, the Leeds team that reached the semi final of the Champions League

The long Ball game of Ireland. If you can, get hold of a video of Ireland at that time. It highlights the limitations of the long ball, but also, perhaps, the advantage of having a team that was clear in its tactical purpose.

Name a team which has won a major competition while playing Charlton's long ball game.
Why is it better to play longer on a bad pitch?
If the opposition's defensive line is high (there is a lot of space between the back 4 and keeper) should your team play the ball long into this space?
What kind of runs should your forwards make?
Is it important to have pace up front? Why?

Plan a team talk which explains how to deal with a team who play an exclusively long ball game. Explain when it is a good idea to play long.

List as many factors as you can that make a successful team.

Glossary

Advanced Marking	A better term for zonal defence as it describes how a player can anticipate where an opponent wishes to be and go there in advance.
Attack	The whole team needs to be aware of their position when their team have the ball in any particular position.
Ball in the Channel	Between the full back and central defender will be a space. If the ball is played down the line of this space it is said to be played in the channel. This tactic fits in with straight ball to diagonal run, or diagonal ball to straight run, if the ball is played through diagonally. If the opposition play a back 3 there is often more opportunity to play this ball.
Ball travelling time	How long it takes the ball to be moved between two points. It is important to understand how this time can be used over long and short distances.
Behind the Ball	How many players a team has behind the ball.
Blind side	A defender, will be watching the ball and men in their field of vision. They cannot see what is happening behind them all the time. This is a defenders blind side.
Bounce	Playing a ball to a player who first time plays it to someone else in your team. This is a ball that is unavailable to the player who passes the ball due to opposition players blocking the way. A bounce is an excellent way to switch the ball. Central midfield players are key bouncers.
Box to Box	A description of an attacking central or wide midfielder who pushes up to support the attack then quickly gets back to help the defence.
Chalkboard	A term used to describe the tactical discussion of football on a blackboard, whiteboard or any other medium.
Cheating	A term used to describe a player, usually in midfield, who does not defend his/her zone. Such players seek to exploit the space left as the opposition attack and get the ball in the transition.
Compress play	As press the ball (see below)
Concentration	A game lasts over 90 minutes. It is constantly changing between attack and defence . Teams try different things to catch the defence not concentrating, in the wrong position. T
Covering Defender	The defender, often one of the centre halves, who is in the danger zone and drops off a couple of yards to offer cover.
Crossover	A player with the ball runs past a player from the same team this means any player who is following the player with the ball has to go round this player so creating space and time.
Danger Zone	The central area, roughly the width of the penalty area, between the halfway line and the penalty are. Where the defence pushes up to determines how much space is in this area.
Decision Making	A term used to describe how good a player is at choosing the best option, for example the best pass from a range of options.
Defence	The positions of the team when the opposition have the ball.
Diagonal Ball to Straight Run	An attacker can break into the space between the defence and keeper using this. They can see the ball and the space, as well as getting on the blind side of a defender.

Diamond of support	The diamond will not necessarily be of equal proportions but it is a good description of the passing options that a player with the ball should have.
Double up	When, for example, a wide midfielder and full back both try to get the ball off an opposition's wide player. This tactic is essential near the scoring zone.
Four Four two	The most favoured formation. Remember often 4 4 2 is only in this position when the opposition has the ball. When your team has the ball you may try to create a numbers up situation by a full back moving in to midfield so a 4 4 2 is a 3 5 2 when you have the ball.
Get a players head down	If a player is under pressure S/he will look down at the ball to protect it and so cannot look around.
Get sucked in	A team moves too far into the space around the ball, leaving too much space elsewhere, which the opposition then uses to gain advantage. It is acceptable that a side may switch and gain ground if they do it quickly. However, getting sucked in could describe a team getting ball travelling time wrong and the defence not being able to get across or back to stop the progress of the opposition forward.
Going to Ground	Slide tackling.
Good Angle	When a winger for example offers an easy ball for a full back to pass to them. The opposition's defending player in that area will not follow as they fear leaving the space they leave for another opposition player to use, or the player offering the angle to run into. They would be able to initially get into this space first because of reaction time.
Inverted U theory	A player may be so motivated, over aroused they under perform or become a liability. They may get tunnel vision.
Long Ball Game	A simple tactic of trying to play the ball into the space between the opposition's defence and keeper. Has been used to describe Wimbledon, and Ireland under Jack Charlton.
Man for Man	Following a particular man when defending. An ineffective defensive tactic in open play.
Mental toughness	Used to describe a variety of mental states. Is probably best used to describe a player's ability to concentrate and do their job even when behind , playing away from home, or against good opposition.
Numbers Up	When a team has more players in an area than the opposition.

overs	An expression used to describe a player leaving the ball, not making contact, and letting it run to a player on the same side.
Passing line	The imaginary line that runs between the player with the ball and a team mate.
Second Ball	The ball is played forward to a centre forward who is challenged by the oppositions centre half. The ball will land in an area near to them. A good tactical ploy is to have players in this area to pick up to this 2nd ball. If you know how far your keeper can kick and where he/she is aiming for you can put players in position to challenge for the second ball.
Shift him/her	An expression used to let a player on the same team know you want them to move and take a defender away from a space.
Short Short Long	An expression used to describe how 2 short passes usually draw players from the opposition towards the player with the ball. This means there is space elsewhere. By using a longer ball this space can be found.
Show inside/Show outside	A teams defence needs to work as a unit and communicate. They will 'double up' and cover each other. These expressions are used to tell a team mate to direct a player in a certain direction. This may be to direct them into an area where there is cover., it may be they have pace and it is stopping them using space, it may be the opposition player has a weak left foot (very common) in which case you will make them run right. It may be a delaying tactic to allow players to get back.
Square defence	A myth. Defences are only ever square for a brief period to catch an attacker who has spotted a covering defender drop off and is trying to use the space.
Slow, slow, quick	A description of the tactic of 'sucking' the opposition into an area then moving the ball to space. The same as short , short long but related to specifically to time
Straight Ball to Diagonal Run	An attacker can break into the space between the defence and keeper using this. They can see the ball and the space as well as getting on the blind side of a defender.
Switch	Moving the ball from one side of the pitch where space is congested to the other where there is space. If this is done quickly enough then the team in possession will have the ball nearer to the oppositions goal, they will have gained ground.
Tactic	Players positions when attacking, defending or in transition. Understanding time and space theory and applying this to game situations.
Takeover	A player with the ball runs towards a team mate and as they cross the team mate takes the ball. The aim is to cause confusion and create space.
Technical Ability	How good a player is in terms of first touch, how they initially deal with the ball, their shooting, right foot, left foot, heading.
The Hole	The space between defence and midfield and midfield and attack where players can move to receive the ball.
The Mixer	An expression to describe the penalty area. Lots of players lots of movement. Get the ball in the mixer to score. Late on in a game with little time to build play teams will simply try to get the ball forward into the mixer.
Theory	A way of looking at a game or situation that allows you to understand it.
Third man run	Two players interchange passes at the same time a third player makes a movement. The advantage is that the opposition will be concentrating on the ball. The third man is up to speed and if timing is right can beat the offside trap as the defence reacts.
Too deep	An expression to describe a team that has a deep offside line. This term is usually misused as a team can't safely push up unless they move the ball into the oppositions half. Too deep is the fault of the midfield or attack not usually the defence.
Transition	The brief time when a team loses possession and adapts from attack to defence or when a team gains possession and adapts from defence to attack.
Tunnel Vision	A term used to describe how a player may make decisions that are not good as they are being influenced by things that are not helping them, the crowd, are not taking in to consideration good things such as a call from their own side , or not noticing one of their own players. He/she is not choosing the best option, for example the best pass from a range of options.
Zone	An area in which a player is responsible for any opposition player who moves into it.
Formation	Where a team positions its players. As the ball goes forward or the team defends the formation will adapt. A 4 4 2 when attacking may become 3 5 2. A 3 5 2 when defending may look more like a 4 4 2. Within formations like 4 4 2 there are variations as to the shape the midfield is in.

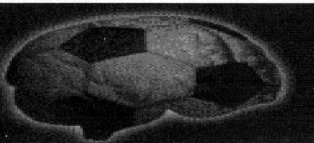

Football Tactics.com

Soccer Tactics.com

Thanks!

The following people have all helped in the production of this manual and I would like to thank them all

John Purkiss who I have had numerous conversations with about tactics and who understands the game more than anyone I know. Dave Ridley and Shane Kent for their ideas and advice. Thanks to my team of the last 10 years Georgia Pacific. I have been manager, coach and player. The team have put up with my ideas (which were sometimes completely wrong) and have enabled me to learn more about the game.

Our current home pitch is really well maintained with a great surface that allows our team to play the 'mixed passing game'. It also has a grass bank next to it at the halfway line from which to view the game from an elevated position. I would argue it is impossible to have a true grasp of the tactical side of the game from the touchline.

In my early years I was coached by John Warnock (Neil's brother) who first showed me that a long ball from full back over the oppositions full back for a forward to run on to could be very effective. (He also annoyed me by making all 22 of us stand around while he demonstrated this pattern of play). This, I now realise, is essential to developing the tactical side of the game. My advice would be to do as much as you can in the summer and avoid people standing around in the wind and rain.

Thanks to Kevin Fogg who has more enthusiasm than any other coach I've come across and Ron Reid both who inspired me on the UEFA B licence. To the Sheffield Wednesday and United Academy U19 teams who I could run ideas by.

To John Ryan for creating the website and Sharon Bell for her support.

To Cath and my Dad and Mum for putting up with me and helping me find the time to finish this work. Emma Pitfield for all her work correcting changes, and to Nikki Phillips and Sarah-Jane Walker for the same.